German
Political Parties

German
Political Parties

A Documentary Guide

G. E. EDWARDS

UNIVERSITY OF WALES PRESS

CARDIFF

1998

British Library Cataloguing-in-Publication Data
A catalogue record for this book is available from
the British Library.

ISBN 0-7083-1417-1

Typeset by Action Typesetting Ltd., Gloucester
Printed in Great Britain by Dinefwr Press, Llandybïe

Contents

Preface

The unification of Germany in 1990 has placed the country in a key position in Europe, both economically and politically. Germany's role in the integration of Western Europe has already been considerable and this will increase, but her traditional interest in Central and Eastern Europe will also make her into a potent force in that part of the continent in the longer term. It is also to be expected that Germany will play a more important role on the world stage in the coming years. Thus, what happens to Germany and the decisions her politicians make are of considerable importance and interest to her neighbours and allies.

The collapse of the communist bloc as a whole, and particularly the collapse of the East German state, the German Democratic Republic (GDR), has had a considerable impact on the Federal Republic of Germany. Since unification there have been many problems in integrating the economically weak East Germany into the West German economy. There are social and cultural divisions between the fifteen million East Germans and their more affluent brothers and sisters in the West, particularly since the collapse of the GDR has led to a complete change of life-styles and often to much personal insecurity. The political landscape of the GDR has disappeared almost completely and a new structure built on democracy, personal freedom and the rule of law has replaced it. The impact of twelve million East German voters on the political scene in united Germany is bringing about changes, the outcome of which is, as yet, unforeseeable. It is for this reason that the GDR constitutions, the SED and its successor, the PDS, are included in this study.

The new role that Germany will play in Europe will be moulded politically by her reactions to the increasing integration of Western Europe, the broadening of the European Union through the accession of an increasing number of states in Central Europe, by the development of the security framework in Europe, the remaining problems of unification between the two parts of Germany and the stance and platforms of the political parties in Germany herself. The new Federal Republic, now free of the constraints imposed by the Cold

War and the division of her territory, can develop further her political system, in accord with the democratic principles of her constitution, the Basic Law. The manner in which she does this and establishes her role in Europe will provide an absorbing field of study for many years to come.

The book is divided into two sections. In Part I the constitutional and political system of the Federal Republic is examined in the light of key sections of the Basic Law. In somewhat less detail the GDR constitution is also examined, for failure to comply with some of its basic principles was part of the reason for the collapse of that system and for some of the ensuing political problems. Certain sections of the treaties between the West and East German governments on unification are also touched upon since they form the basis for some of the political and economic changes that have taken place. Questions on the excerpts taken from the constitutional texts are included.

In Part II, after a general introduction, each of the major parties is examined individually – that is, the CDU (Christian Democratic Union) and its sister party, the CSU (Christian Social Union) in Bavaria, the SPD (Social Democratic Party), the FDP (Free Democrat Party), the Greens (together with Bündnis 90), the East German SED (Socialist Unity Party) and its successor party, the PDS (Party of Democratic Socialism). A number of representative texts is given in the original German for each party, and in some cases extracts from speeches made by leading politicians of that party, together with a brief portrait of the person, are included. A short vocabulary is appended of words and terms that the average reader will not have encountered. This is intended to save the reader time in consulting dictionaries, but it should be noted that it gives only translations within that given context. Questions relating to the extracts are posed to facilitate their understanding and analysis. The introductory section on the given party should be read and understood before answering the questions. At the end of the book a number of cross-party questions will be found. The texts can be used as a basis for discussions on how the parties differ in their policies from their counterparts in, for instance, Britain or the United States. They can also be used for linguistic exercises such as paraphrasing, comprehension, summary writing, précis work or translation.

The texts have been selected to cover the basic ideologies of the parties and their policies towards issues such as unemployment, women's equality, the environment, the continuing process of integration of East and West Germany, European integration and security issues. They have been chosen partly to cover, for each party, the same major areas of domestic, security and foreign policy so that a cross-party comparison can be made, and partly to show where a party has different or more pronounced views on a particular area than the rest, as, for example, the emphasis of the CSU on the rights of the unborn baby, of the Greens on the distribution of work in a society where the work-force is being displaced by new technology, or of the PDS with its suggestion of a new third chamber in Parliament. In one or two instances a recent short extract from a book or article on the party by an academic or journalist is given. The far right is examined only briefly since it is not represented by a major party and texts are not included.

The book concludes with a summary of the present situation reached by the parties and an outline of the questions that the parties need to address in a period of rapid political, economic and social transition.

The Author

Gwyneth Edwards has specialized since the mid-1960s in twentieth-century German studies – history, politics, society and culture – and in European studies. She has lectured at the University of Ulster, Coleraine, Northern Ireland, Loughborough University and at the Humboldt University, Berlin (as a guest lecturer appointed by the European Commission to help in the reconstruction of the university after the end of communism). She has broadcast on radio and television and given guest lectures in many parts of Europe. She has published widely, particularly on East Germany, including *GDR Society and Social Institutions* (London and New York, Macmillan, St Martin's Press, 1985). She is also an expert on national minorities and on the Conference (now Organization) for Security and Co-operation in Europe.

Acknowledgements

The author and the publishers wish to thank the following for providing material and giving permission to publish extracts in this volume from party programmes, the works or speeches of prominent politicians or analyses:

CDU Bundesgeschäftsstelle, Bonn
CSU in Bayern, Munich
SPD Bundesgeschäftsstelle, Bonn
FDP Bundesgeschäftsstelle, Bonn
Bündnis 90/Die Grünen, Bundesgeschäftsstelle, Bonn
PDS Bundesgeschäftsstelle, Bonn
Bundeszentrale für Politische Bildung, Bonn, for extracts from *Aus Politik und Zeitgeschichte, Die Beilage zur Wochenzeitung Das Parlament*
Max Planck Institute, Arbeitsgruppe Transformationsprozesse in den neuen Bundesländern, Berlin
Sozialwissenschaftliches Forschungszentrum, Berlin
Atwerb-Verlag, Grünwald
Bund-Verlag, Cologne
Dietz Verlag, Berlin
edition-ost, Berlin
Rowohlt Taschenbuch Verlag, Reinbek

Abbreviations

APO	Außerparlamentarische Opposition
AUD	Aktionsgemeinschaft Unabhängiger Deutscher
BFD	Bund Freier Demokraten
BHE	Bund Heimatvertriebener und Entrechteten
BP	Bayernpartei
BRD	Bundesrepublik Deutschland
CDU	Christlich Demokratische Union
CSCE	Conference on Security and Co-operation in Europe
CSU	Christlich-Soziale Union
DA	Demokratischer Aufbruch
DBD	Demokratische Bauernpartei Deutschlands
DDP	Deutsche Demokratische Partei
DDR	Deutsche Demokratische Republik
DFD	Demokratischer Frauenbund Deutschlands
DFU	Deutsche Friedens-Union
DGB	Deutscher Gewerkschaftsbund
DJ	Demokratie Jetzt
DKP	Deutsche Kommunistische Partei
DRP	Deutsche Rechtspartei (up to 1950)
DRP	Deutsche Reichspartei (after 1950)
DSU	Deutsche Soziale Union
DVP	Deutsche Volkspartei
DVU	Deutsche Volksunion
EU	European Union, Europäische Union
FDGB	Freier Deutscher Gewerkschaftsbund
FDJ	Freie Deutsche Jugend
FDP	Freie Demokratische Partei
GATT	General Agreement on Tariffs and Trade
GAZ	Grüne Aktion Zukunft
GDR	German Democratic Republic
GLU	Grüne Liste Umweltschutz
HO	Handelsorganisation
KB	Kulturbund

KJVD	Kommunistischer Jugendverband Deutschlands
KPD	Kommunistische Partei Deutschlands
KPdSU	Kommunistische Partei der Sowjetunion
KSZE	Konferenz für Sicherheit und Zusammenarbeit in Europa
LDPD	Liberal-Demokratische Partei Deutschlands
LPG	Landwirtschaftliche Produktionsgenossenschaft
NDPD	National-Demokratische Partei Deutschlands
NF	Neues Forum
NKFD	Nationalkomitee "Freies Deutschland"
NPD	Nationaldemokratische Partei Deutschlands
NATO	North Atlantic Treaty Organization
NSDAP	National-Sozialistische Partei Deutschlands (Nazi)
OSCE (OSZE)	Organization for Security and Co-operation in Europe (Organization für Sicherheit und Zusammenarbeit in Europa)
PDS	Partei des Demokratischen Sozialismus
RAF	Rote Armee Faktion
REP	Republikaner
RGW	Rat für Gegenseitige Wirtschaftshilfe
SED	Sozialistische Einheitspartei Deutschlands
SMAD	Sowjetische Militäradministration in Deutschland
SPD	Sozialdemokratische Partei Deutschlands
SPV	Sonstige Politische Vereinigung
UdSSR	Union der Sozialistischen Sowjetischen Republiken
USPD	Unabhängige Sozialistische Partei Deutschlands
VdgB	Verein der gegenseitigen Bauernhilfe
VEG	Volkseigenes Gut
WEU	Western European Union, West Europäische Union

Part I:

The German Constitutions

Germany has had a number of constitutions since 1849 – the liberal constitution of that year (which failed to be implemented), the Bismarck constitution of the Second German Reich (16 April 1871), the Weimar constitution of 11 August 1919, the Basic Law of the Federal Republic of Germany (23 May 1949 and subsequent amendments) and the constitutions of the German Democratic Republic (7 October 1949 and 6 April 1968, with amendments in 1974). The Weimar constitution, born as it was out of the chaos of defeat in the First World War, had liberal and democratic elements, but was bitterly opposed by many factions, had few supporters who were prepared to fight to defend it and had within it the seeds of its own destruction. These were used by Adolf Hitler and the national socialists to smash democracy with the *Ermächtigungsgesetz* ('Enabling Act') of 24 March 1933, which led Germany into the nazi dictatorship.

The Weimar constitution set down that the Reich president should be elected by the people once every seven years and gave him considerable powers. He was the supreme commander of the *Reichswehr* (the armed forces) which, in practice, allowed president and army to intrigue against Parliament and government. The president could declare a state of emergency (*Ausrufung des Ausnahmezustandes*), which led to laws being overturned or modified by decree; could intervene in any *Land* (regional) government if it failed to fulfil its obligations under the constitution, and this presidential right was increasingly used; could dissolve Parliament (Article 25), and up to 1933 this led to a number of dissolutions and to the weakening of government. The president appointed and could dismiss the chancellor (Article 53) – this could lead to arbitrary dismissal and disarray in Parliament. There was no mention of the parties in the constitution, and this contributed symbolically to a weakening of the position of the parties in public opinion. No-confidence votes could be taken against both the chancellor and ministers, and the frequent use of votes of no confidence led to instability. It was possible for laws to be introduced as a result of plebiscites, and this could be used by extremists – for instance, the plebiscite on the Young Plan in 1929.[1] The constitution was also weak in that it could easily be amended (the most extreme case of this being the *Ermächtigungsgesetz*), even on basic principles such as the distribution of powers or the relationship between central government and the *Länder*. The constitution was neutral with respect to values and legally permitted the creation of parties or organizations that were anti-democratic. There was no means of banning them. Civil servants and judges were not required to give their allegiance to the constitution, and in fact these two groups showed deep-rooted hostility to it.[2]

The introduction of proportional representation, although an expression of democracy, resulted in a large number of parties being elected to the Reichstag and to weak coalition government. Between 1919 and 1933 more than thirteen parties were represented in Parliament, and in just fourteen years there were eight Reichstag elections. Clear policies and perspectives were lacking in most of the parties during this period – it was the political extremes of communists and nazis who knew what they wanted, and their uncompromising positions helped to make them electable by a population that was longing for economic stability and clear leadership. The system of proportional representation used also created problems. The electorate voted for parties rather than individual candidates, since parties contested in multi-member constituencies and gained one seat for approximately every 60,000 votes cast. The number of seats in the Reichstag itself fluctuated according to the number of people who turned out to vote – a low turn-out meant a smaller Reichstag.

1. The Basic Law of the Federal Republic of Germany

In 1945 Germany surrendered unconditionally to the Allies (Britain, USA, Soviet Union, France) and was occupied by them. Under the Potsdam Agreement of August 1945 (which will be discussed later) the Allies took over responsibility for governing Germany and were committed to creating there an anti-fascist, democratic order that would eventually lead to a united Germany regaining her sovereignty and position among the nations of the world. A legal system was to be created on the principles of democracy and justice, the rule of law and equality for all citizens before the law. The administration of Germany was to be decentralized, parties were to be formed and local elections were to take place.

The constitution that emerged after the Second World War in West Germany was a reaction to the shortcomings of the Weimar constitution and showed clearly that much had been learnt from the earlier mistakes. Naturally, the conditions were very different from those after 1919: the population had just experienced twelve years of dictatorship and were ready to support a new, democratic beginning; the German state had collapsed; the power of the army had been destroyed; within a few years the economy was successful. But even with all these favourable factors, it is surprising how quickly a modern democracy could be developed – and one which has won the overwhelming support and loyalty of the people.

The development of a constitution could take place only with the permission of the four Allies. With the increasing division of Germany, this meant that distinct constitutions developed in West and East Germany, respectively, and they were to remain separate until reunification in 1990.

On 1 September 1948 the *Parlamentsrat* (Parliamentary Council) was created in Bonn, in which representatives from the parties in West Germany met to decide on a constitution.[3] Since the Soviet Zone was not represented, the West Germans were intent on producing a Basic Law (*Grundgesetz*) to operate until a reunited Germany could decide on its own constitution. They were adamant that the *Grundgesetz* would not be a barrier to unification. The Basic Law, in its 1949 version, will be examined later, together with the amendments made after unification.

The structural principles on which the Federal Republic is founded are democracy, the *Rechtsstaat* (a German form of constitutionalism that is a slightly broader concept than that of the rule of law), the *Sozialstaat* (social state) and the *Bundesstaat* (federal state). The political system covers Parliament, government, courts of law, elections, parties, interest groups and administration.

The *Rechtsstaat* has a tradition in Germany that stretches back in some aspects to the 'enlightened despotism' of Friedrich II of Prussia (although the term was not used until 1809, when it was introduced by Adam Müller). In the nineteenth century German liberals placed the focus on replacing government by the king with government by the people, and on ensuring the rights of the individual *vis-à-vis* the state through a written constitution. The *Rechtsstaat* imposes limitations on the intervention of the state into the areas of freedom and property. As Hans Kremendahl explains, 'Rechtsstaat meint vor allem den rechtlich gebundenen, in seiner Macht begrenzte, der Willkür entsagenden Staat.'[4] The *Rechtsstaat* aspect of the *Grundgesetz* covers basic rights in Articles 1–19, emphasizing that they cannot be limited, but can be asserted through the courts of law. Equally the individual knows his or her personal limitations within the law. The law is impartial and applies equally to all. The division of powers between the executive, legislature and judiciary ensures a system of checks and balances. Here, too, the contribution of the *Länder* by means of the Bundesrat (Article 20.2 and Section VII) is important. The rights enshrined in the *Grundgesetz* come under the jurisdiction of the *Bundesverfassungsgericht* (the Federal Constitutional Court – Articles 93–4), which has its seat in Karlsruhe. The higher courts of law, that is, the Federal Supreme Court, Federal Administrative Court, Federal Finance Court, Federal Labour Court and Federal Social Welfare Court (*Bundesgerichtshof, Bundesverwaltungsgericht, Bundesfinanzhof, Bundesarbeitsgericht, Bundessozialgericht*) ensure review at the highest level in the specific area of jurisdiction (Article 95). The independence of the judiciary is guaranteed (Articles 97–8). In the case of prosecution and arrest guarantees are also given (Articles 101–4): for instance, everyone has the right to be heard before a court of law; no one can be punished more than once for the same deed.

The *Sozialstaat* is laid down in Articles 20.1 and 28.1 but it is not worked out there as a concrete model. References are made only indirectly in Articles 3, 9, 12, 14 and 15. The *Sozialstaat* has evolved, however, to cover, firstly, social policy (*Sozialpolitik*) and, secondly, societal policy (*Gesellschaftspolitik*). Social policy encompasses social security (pensions and benefits for sickness, accident, invalidity, unemployment), social welfare, training and retraining programmes. Societal policy ranges over social participation (*Teilhabe*), autonomy of wage-bargaining, right of association, labour and social matters, co-determination at the place of work (*Mitbestimmung*), redistribution of wealth, progressive taxation and control of cartels.

Federalism is a very important aspect of German politics. There has been a long tradition of regional states in Germany. Up to 1815, for instance, there were 314 'states' or independent territories within Germany. It was not until 1871 that a united nation state was finally achieved, and even then regional differences and aspirations remained. The Weimar Republic weakened the power of the individual states and renamed them *Länder*. Their power, as expressed in the institution of the Reichsrat, was strictly limited. The nazis completely removed the powers of the *Länder* through a series of laws: *Erstes Gleichschaltungsgesetz* (31 March 1933), *Zweites Gleichschaltungsgesetz* (7 April 1933) and *Gesetz über den Neuaufbau des Reichs* (30 January 1934). The Reichsrat was dissolved in February 1934.

After 1945 the *Länder* were anxious to gain devolved powers after twelve years of nazi centralization. Equally, the Western Allies were determined to limit the power of central German government by creating a strong *Länder* system. In fact the Allies returned the proposals of the Parliamentary Council for further discussion on three occasions because they felt that the powers to be given to the *Länder* were not strong enough. It was the Allies who decided on how the territories should be allocated across the *Länder* and, in that sense, the *Länder* are artificial creations in many cases – only Bavaria, Hamburg and Bremen kept borders that had existed earlier. The Western Allies disagreed on the nature of federalism in the new Germany. The French favoured a loose confederation of states, but the Americans, with British support, preferred a federal state. With the increasing division of Germany during the Cold War the Americans won the argument and were supported by most West German politicians.

Since the creation of the Federal Republic in 1949 the relationship between *Bund* and *Länder* has changed considerably. Within the period 1949–84 there had already been twenty-four amendments to the constitution that had implications for the federal system. There has been a marked transfer of powers from the *Länder* to central government, and the *Länder* themselves have become increasingly dependent financially on Bonn.[5] The principle on which the relationship between *Bund* and *Länder* functions is that of 'subsidiarity'. State powers are delegated downwards as long as the lower level of government can fulfil the tasks. If it cannot, then the task is dealt with higher up the hierarchy. The *Länder* are responsible for legislative powers except for those reserved to central government. They have wide-ranging responsibilities for the administration of federal and *Land* laws. The *Länder*, in their turn, pass down responsibilities to the next tier, namely to local government. Constitutional disputes between *Bund* and *Länder* are settled by the Constitutional Court. The *Bund* is responsible for foreign affairs, defence, citizenship, passports, immigration, currency and customs.

In contrast to the Weimar constitution, the federal president is to a great extent purely representative, with greatly reduced powers. The chancellor is elected by the Bundestag and is directly responsible to it. The chancellor and his (or her) government can be removed from power only by a constructive vote of no confidence by Parliament electing a successor. This reduces the possibility of a government crisis and ensures the continuance of government even in times of emergency. The creation of the *Bundesverfassungsgericht* ensures that the actions of government can be scrutinized (particularly by the opposition or by the minority) for adherence to the *Grundgesetz*. Political parties not standing on the basis of democracy and the rule of law can be banned, and individual laws can be scrutinized to see how far they lie within the constitution.

In common with other democracies the government is responsible to an elected Parliament. The Bundestag is elected by citizens over the age of eighteen for a period of four years, and is the key body in the democratic process. The Bundesrat is the second house in Parliament and represents the interests of the *Länder*. The main activities of Parliament are legislation and the scrutiny of government policies. It is not a debating forum to the same degree as is the British Parliament and, in many cases, is much less confrontational. Strict party discipline is enforced in the Bundestag (*Fraktionszwang*).

The federal government (*Bundesregierung*) is made up of the chancellor and the federal ministers, and works on the basis that the chancellor decides on the direction that policies should take (*Kanzlerprinzip*), the federal government decides in disputes between ministers (*Kollegialprinzip*), and each minister is responsible for the area assigned to him (*Ressortprinzip*).

The federal president is the head of state and represents it both within Germany and abroad. He or she (there has not been a female president up to now) undertakes state visits, represents Germany internationally and signs state treaties.

Sources

Text A: Das Grundgesetz für die Bundesrepublik Deutschland. Vom 23. Mai 1949. Bundesgesetz Blatt, 1ff. (key clauses and inclusive of major modifications prior to unification)

Präambel

Im Bewußtsein seiner Verantwortung vor Gott und den Menschen, von dem Willen beseelt, seine nationale und staatliche Einheit zu wahren und als gleichberechtigtes Glied in einem vereinten Europa, dem Frieden der Welt zu dienen, hat das Deutsche Volk in den Ländern Baden, Bayern, Bremen, Hamburg, Hessen, Niedersachsen, Nordrhein-Westfalen, Rheinland-Pfalz, Schleswig-Holstein, Württemberg-Baden und Württemberg-Hohenzollern,* um dem staatlichen Leben für eine Übergangszeit, eine neue Ordnung zu geben, kraft seiner verfassungsgebenden Gewalt dieses Grundgesetz der Bundesrepublik Deutschland beschlossen. Es hat auch für jene Deutsche gehandelt, denen mitzuwirken versagt war. Das gesamte deutsche Volk bleibt aufgefordert, in freier Selbstbestimmung die Einheit und Freiheit Deutschlands zu vollenden.

I. Die Grundrechte (Artikel 1–19)

Artikel 1
(1) Die Würde des Menschen ist unantastbar. Sie zu achten und zu schützen ist Verpflichtung aller staatlichen Gewalt.
(2) Das deutsche Volk bekennt sich darum zu unverletzlichen und unveräußerlichen Menschenrechten als Grundlage jeder menschlichen Gemeinschaft, des Friedens und der Gerechtigkeit in der Welt.

Artikel 2
Jeder hat das Recht auf die freie Entfaltung seiner Persönlichkeit, soweit er nicht die Rechte anderer verletzt und nicht gegen die verfassungsmäßige Ordnung oder das Sittengesetz verstößt.

---

*Later to become the single *Land* of Baden-Württemberg.

Artikel 3

(1) Alle Menschen sind vor dem Gesetz gleich.

(2) Männer und Frauen sind gleichberechtigt.

(3) Niemand darf wegen seines Geschlechtes, seiner Abstammung, seiner Rasse, seiner Sprache, seiner Heimat und Herkunft, seines Glaubens, seiner religiösen oder politischen Anschauungen benachteiligt oder bevorzugt werden.

Artikel 4

(1) Die Freiheit des Glaubens, des Gewissens und die Freiheit des religiösen und weltanschaulichen Bekenntnisses sind unverletzlich.

(2) Die ungestörte Religionsausübung wird gewährleistet.

(3) Niemand darf gegen sein Gewissen zum Kriegsdienst mit der Waffe gezwungen werden. Das Nähere regelt ein Bundesgesetz.

Artikel 5

(1) Jeder hat das Recht, seine Meinung in Wort, Schrift und Bild frei zu äußern und zu verbreiten und sich aus allgemein zugänglichen Quellen ungehindert zu unterrichten. Die Pressefreiheit und die Freiheit der Berichterstattung durch Rundfunk und Film werden gewährleistet. Eine Zensur findet nicht statt.

(2) Diese Rechte finden ihre Schranken in den Vorschriften der allgemeinen Gesetze, den gesetzlichen Bestimmungen zum Schutze der Jugend und in dem Recht der persönlichen Ehre.

(3) Kunst und Wissenschaft, Forschung und Lehre sind frei. Die Freiheit der Lehre entbindet nicht von der Treue zur Verfassung.

Artikel 7

(1) Das gesamte Schulwesen steht unter der Aufsicht des Staates.

(2) Die Erziehungsberechtigten haben das Recht, über die Teilnahme des Kindes an Religionsunterricht zu bestimmen.

(3) Der Religionsunterricht ist in den öffentlichen Schulen mit Ausnahme der bekenntnisfreien Schulen ordentliches Lehrfach ...

Artikel 8

(1) Alle Deutschen haben das Recht, sich ohne Anmeldung oder Erlaubnis friedlich und ohne Waffen zu versammeln.

(2) Für Versammlungen unter freiem Himmel kann dieses Recht durch Gesetz beschränkt werden.

Artikel 9

(1) Alle Deutschen haben das Recht, Vereine und Gesellschaften zu bilden.

(2) Vereinigungen, deren Zwecke oder deren Tätigkeit den Strafgesetzen zuwiderlaufen oder die sich gegen die verfassungsmäßige Ordnung oder gegen den Gedanken der Völkerverständigung richten, sind verboten.

Artikel 12a

(1) Männer können vom vollendeten achtzehnten Lebensjahr an zum Dienst in den Streitkräften, im Bundesgrenzschutz oder in einem Zivilschutzverband verpflichtet werden.

(2) Wer aus Gewissensgründen den Kriegsdienst mit der Waffe verweigert, kann zu einem Ersatzdienst verpflichtet werden.[6] Die Dauer des Ersatzdienstes darf die Dauer des Wehrdienstes nicht übersteigen.

Artikel 14

(1) Das Eigentum und das Erbrecht werden gewährleistet.

(2) Eigentum verpflichtet. Sein Gebrauch soll zugleich dem Wohle der Allgemeinheit dienen.

II. Der Bund und die Länder (Artikel 20–37)

Artikel 20

(1) Die Bundesrepublik Deutschland ist ein demokratischer und sozialer Bundesstaat.

(2) Alle Staatsgewalt geht vom Volke aus. Sie wird vom Volke in Wahlen und Abstimmungen und durch besondere Organe der Gesetzgebung, der vollziehenden Gewalt und der Rechtsprechung ausgeübt.

(3) Die Gesetzgebung ist an die verfassungsmäßige Ordnung, die vollziehende Gewalt und die Rechtssprechung sind an Gesetz und Recht gebunden.

(4) Gegen jeden, der es unternimmt, diese Ordnung zu beseitigen, haben alle Deutsche das Recht auf Widerstand, wenn andere Abhilfe nicht möglich ist.

Artikel 21

(1) Die Parteien wirken bei der politischen Willensbildung des Volkes mit. Ihre Gründung ist frei. Ihre innere Ordnung muß demokratischen Grundsätzen entsprechen. Sie müssen über die

Herkunft und Verwendung ihrer Mittel sowie über ihr Vermögen öffentlich Rechenschaft geben.

(2) Parteien, die nach ihren Zielen oder nach dem Verhalten ihrer Anhänger darauf ausgehen, die freiheitliche demokratische Grundordnung zu beeinträchtigen oder zu beseitigen oder den Bestand der Bundesrepublik Deutschland zu gefährden, sind verfassungswidrig. Über die Verfassungswidrigkeit entscheidet das Bundesverfassungsgericht.

(3) Das Nähere regeln Bundesgesetze.

Artikel 22
Die Bundesflagge ist schwarz-rot-gold.

Artikel 23
Dieses Gesetz gilt zunächst im Gebiet der Länder Baden, Bayern, Bremen, Groß-Berlin, Hamburg, Hessen, Niedersachsen, Nordrhein-Westfalen, Rheinland-Pfalz, Schleswig-Holstein, Württemberg-Baden und Württemberg-Hohenzollern. In anderen Teilen Deutschlands ist es nach deren Beitritt in Kraft zu setzen.

Artikel 28
(1) Die verfassungsmäßige Ordnung in den Ländern muß den Grundsätzen des republikanischen, demokratischen und sozialen Rechsstaates im Sinne dieses Grundgesetzes entsprechen.

Artikel 30
Die Ausübung der staatlichen Befügnisse und die Erfüllung der staatlichen Aufgaben ist Sache der Länder, soweit dieses Grundgesetz keine andere Regelung trifft oder zuläßt.

Artikel 31
Bundesrecht bricht Landesrecht.

Artikel 32
(1) Die Pflege der Beziehungen zu auswärtigen Staaten ist Sache des Bundes.
(2) Vor dem Abschluß eines Vertrages, der die besonderen Verhältnisse eines Landes berührt, ist das Land rechtzeitig zu hören.
(3) Soweit die Länder für die Gesetzgebung zuständig sind, können sie mit Zustimmung der Bundesregierung mit auswärtigen Staaten Verträge abschließen.

III. Der Bundestag (Artikel 38–49)

Artikel 38

(1) Die Abgeordneten des Deutschen Bundestages werden in allgemeiner, unmittelbarer, freier, gleicher und geheimer Wahl gewählt. Sie sind Vertreter des ganzen Volkes, an Aufträge und Weisungen nicht gebunden und nur ihrem Gewissen unterworfen.

(2) Wahlberechtigt ist, wer das achtzehnte Lebensjahr vollendet hat; wählbar ist, wer das Alter erreicht, mit dem die Volljährigkeit eintritt.

Artikel 39

(1) Der Bundestag wird auf vier Jahre gewählt. Seine Wahlperiode endet mit dem Zusammentritt eines neuen Bundestages. Die Neuwahl findet frühestens fünfundvierzig, spätestens siebenundvierzig Monate nach Beginn der Wahlperiode statt. Im Falle einer Auflösung des Bundestages findet die Neuwahl innerhalb von sechzig Tagen statt . . .

IV. Der Bundesrat (Artikel 50–3)

Artikel 50

Durch den Bundesrat wirken die Länder bei der Gesetzgebung und Verwaltung des Bundes mit.

Artikel 51

(1) Der Bundesrat besteht aus Mitgliedern der Regierungen der Länder, die sie bestellen und abberufen. Sie können durch andere Mitglieder ihrer Regierung vertreten werden.

(2) Jedes Land hat mindestens drei Stimmen, Länder mit mehr als zwei Millionen Einwohnern haben vier, Länder mit mehr als sechs Millionen Einwohnern fünf Stimmen.

(3) Jedes Land kann so viele Mitglieder entsenden, wie es Stimmen hat. Die Stimmen eines Landes können nur einheitlich und nur durch anwesende Mitglieder oder deren Vertreter abgegeben werden.

V. Der Bundespräsident (Artikel 54–61)

Artikel 54

(1) Der Bundespräsident wird ohne Aussprache von der Bundesversammlung gewählt. Wählbar ist jeder Deutsche, der das Wahlrecht zum Bundestage besitzt und das vierzigste Lebensjahr vollendet hat.

(2) Das Amt des Bundespräsidenten dauert fünf Jahre. Anschlie-
ßende Wiederwahl ist nur einmal zulässig.
(3) Die Bundesversammlung besteht aus den Mitgliedern des
Bundestages und einer gleichen Anzahl von Mitgliedern, die von den
Volksvertretungen der Länder nach den Grundsätzen der Verhält-
niswahl gewählt werden.

Artikel 56
Der Bundespräsident leistet bei seinem Amtsantritt vor den versam-
melten Mitgliedern des Bundestages und des Bundesrates folgenden
Eid: 'Ich schwöre, daß ich meine Kraft dem Wohle des deutschen
Volkes widmen, seinen Nutzen mehren, Schaden von ihm wenden,
das Grundgesetz und die Gesetze des Bundes wahren und verteidigen, meine Pflichten gewissenhaft erfüllen und Gerechtigkeit gegen
jedermann üben werde.'

Artikel 58
Anordnungen und Verfügungen des Bundespräsidenten bedürfen zu
ihrer Gültigkeit der Gegenzeichnung durch den Bundeskanzler oder
durch den zuständigen Bundesminister.

Artikel 59
(1) Der Bundespräsident vertritt den Bund völkerrechtlich. Er
schließt im Namen des Bundes Verträge mit auswärtigen Staaten. Er
beglaubigt und empfängt die Gesandten.

Artikel 60
(1) Der Bundespräsident ernennt und entläßt die Bundesrichter, die
Bundesbeamten, die Offiziere und Unteroffiziere, soweit gesetzlich
nichts anderes bestimmt wird.

VI. Die Bundesregierung (Artikel 62–9)

Artikel 62
Die Bundesregierung besteht aus dem Bundeskanzler und den
Bundesministern.

Artikel 63
(1) Der Bundeskanzler wird auf Vorschlag des Bundespräsidenten
vom Bundestage ohne Aussprache gewählt.
(2) Gewählt ist, wer die Stimmen der Mehrheit der Mitglieder des

Bundestages auf sich vereint. Der Gewählte ist vom Bundespräsidenten zu ernennen.

(3) Wird der Vorgeschlagene nicht gewählt, so kann der Bundestag binnen vierzehn Tagen nach dem Wahlgange mit mehr als die Hälfte seiner Mitglieder einen Bundeskanzler wählen.

Artikel 64

(1) Die Bundesminister werden auf Vorschlag des Bundeskanzlers vom Bundespräsidenten ernannt und entlassen.

(2) Der Bundeskanzler und die Bundesminister leisten bei der Amtsübernahme vor dem Bundestage den in Artikel 56 vorgesehenen Eid.

Artikel 65

Der Bundeskanzler bestimmt die Richtlinien der Politik und trägt dafür die Verantwortung. Innerhalb dieser Richtlinien leitet jeder Bundesminister seinen Geschäftsbereich selbständig und unter eigener Verantwortung. Über Meinungsverschiedenheiten zwischen den Bundesministern entscheidet die Bundesregierung.

Artikel 67

(1) Der Bundestag kann dem Bundeskanzler das Mißtrauen nur dadurch aussprechen, daß er mit der Mehrheit seiner Mitglieder einen Nachfolger wählt und den Bundespräsidenten ersucht, den Bundeskanzler zu entlassen. Der Bundespräsident muß dem Ersuchen entsprechen und den Gewählten ernennen.

VII. Die Gesetzgebung des Bundes (Artikel 70–82)

Artikel 73

Der Bund hat die ausschließliche Gesetzgebung über:

1. die auswärtigen Angelegenheiten sowie die Verteidigung einschließlich des Schutzes der Zivilbevölkerung;
2. die Staatsangehörigkeit im Bunde;
3. die Freizügigkeit, das Paßwesen, die Ein- und Auswanderung und die Auslieferung;
4. das Währungs-, Geld- und Münzwesen, Maße und Gewichte sowie die Zeitbestimmung;
5. die Einheit des Zoll- und Handelsgebietes . . .

Vocabulary

wahren	to maintain
unantastbar	inviolate
verfassungsmäßig	constitutional, in accordance with the constitution
das Sittengesetz	moral law or code
gleichberechtigt	equal before the law
die Abstammung	origin
die Anschauung	view
das Gewissen	conscience
weltanschaulich	ideological
zugänglich	open to
die Berichterstattung	reporting
bekenntnisfrei	non-denominational
gewährleisten	guarantee, ensure
zuwiderlaufen	to run counter to, go directly against
der Widerstand	resistance
der Anhänger	supporter
gefährden	to endanger
verfassungswidrig	unconstitutional
die Befügnisse	competences
auswärtig	foreign
die Gesetzgebung	legislation
die Staatsangehörigkeit	citizenship

2. The constitutions of the GDR

In 1949 the SED (Sozialistische Einheitspartei Deutschlands) in East Germany also created a constitution for the newly founded German Democratic Republic. In its formulation in some respects it resembled the Basic Law in the Federal Republic and was liberal and democratic. This was seen as politically essential so as not to frighten away West Germans from the idea of a unified state (albeit, a state with a clear left-wing bias). The very first article stated that Germany was an indivisible republic based on the principles of democracy and was made up of the *Länder* – in other words there was to be a distribution of powers between central and regional government. (This did not happen in practice. Power was increasingly centralized and the *Länder* were replaced by *Bezirke* in 1952.) Only one German nationality was recognized by the constitution – that is, the division of Germany into two separate states was not recognized or wished for by the GDR at that time. (The GDR national anthem also expressed the wish for unity – 'Auferstanden aus Ruinen und der Zukunft zugewandt, laß uns dir zum Guten dienen, Deutschland einig Vaterland'). The national colours were the same as those of West Germany. The capital of Germany was to remain Berlin. In other words a reunified Germany would be governed not from Bonn but from Berlin, and in the interim East Berlin would be the capital of the GDR. The power of the state was to be founded in the people, yet in reality the people had no control over the state and were granted little room for political participation. Article 3.6 guaranteed the independence of civil servants from any party or interest, yet, in practice, they were totally dependent on the SED and had to carry out its will if they wished to remain in office. Under Stalinist and Soviet influence the system of the *Nomenklatura* was introduced increasingly after 1946. Most staff in the civil service, the universities, the management of the state-owned industries, the officer corps of the army, the state security apparatus and police officers had to be members of the SED. As members they were then subject to party discipline (see text A, p.194–5). Expulsion from the party for deviant views or behaviour would mean loss of job; as a result, little resistance to the SED developed.

A section of the constitution (Articles 6–18) was devoted to basic rights. A number of these provisions were put into practice, others were not. For instance, the sections of the Civil Code (*Bürgerliches Gesetzbuch*) of 1903 which formed the basis of East German law up to 1956 and which discriminated against women were rescinded.[7] These sections were felt to be completely alien to a society which aimed for equal opportunities for both sexes. In fact, from the 1950s onwards to the end of the 1980s, the GDR introduced progressive legislation – well ahead of that in most other countries, including West Germany – which discriminated positively in favour of women in the areas of child care, education and training, pension rights, holidays, support for women to move into middle-management functions and into the professions. Other individual rights, however, were not observed. For example, there was widespread interception of post and telephone calls where dissident or oppositional activities were suspected. Freedom of opinion was limited since the SED feared the development of opposition to its system and control.

Spontaneous demonstrations were not permitted, particularly after the uprising of 1953, as the SED was afraid they could get out of hand. East Germans could not emigrate freely, despite the guarantee in the constitution, and in 1961 the Wall was built to seal off West Berlin from the east of the city and from the surrounding territories of East Germany in order to prevent emigration. From 1971 onwards, one year before graduation students had to sign a contract with an employer and stay for three years in the same job even though it may not have been their wish. Article 11 on the rights of the Sorbs (the only minority in the GDR) was put into effect, and Sorb language and culture were protected and subsidized. Yet, even here there were problems, since opencast mining for lignite (brown coal), particularly in the 1980s, led to the destruction of many Sorb villages, and once the population was dispersed to other towns and villages it tended to become assimilated and lose both language and culture.

The right to work (Article 15.2) was a fundamental tenet of the communist system, and it was coupled with the duty to work. The state did provide work for virtually everyone (including many people with physical disabilities or learning difficulties). By 1956 everyone who wanted a job had one. Unemployment benefit was phased out since it was expected that everyone who was fit enough to work would do so. Virtually all men worked, and by the 1980s 93 per cent of women were also in employment, education or training (the highest percentage in the world). Providing work for all, however, led to the creation of some jobs for social rather than economic reasons and to low productivity. The constitution guaranteed and implemented social security benefits to those not in work through illness, disability or old age.

The right to strike existed in the 1949 constitution, and there were occasional strikes up to June 1953, but after the uprising, which escalated from a strike in East Berlin, no further strikes were tolerated and the article was removed from the 1968 constitution.

The articles that dealt with the economic system in effect confirmed nationalization, sequestration and land reforms that had already taken place. The right to own private property was upheld as long as it could not be used to 'exploit' other people. The right to inherit was maintained.

Freedom of the arts, science and teaching was guaranteed (Article 34.1) but was not implemented, as will be explained later. On the other hand there were considerable subsidies from government to the cultural sphere, so that going to concerts and the theatre, art exhibitions and museums was either very cheap or free. Books were also heavily subsidized and cheap to buy. Culture became easily accessible to the whole population.

The Volkskammer did not resemble a Western-style Parliament. It only met a few times each year, there was little meaningful discussion or debate, it was not able to scrutinize the government or the actions of the SED. Its composition could not be altered from one election to the next, since each party or mass organization was granted a specific number of seats. Its politicians were not paid a salary but only expenses, remaining formally employees at their previous place of work. When the Volkskammer became a democratically elected body in March 1990, the members were clearly unused to the parliamentary system that increasingly was being taken over from the West Germans.

Sources

Text B: Verfassung der Deutschen Demokratischen Republik (1949) (Gesetz Blatt, I, pp.5ff.)

Grundlagen der Staatsgewalt

Artikel 1 (Republik und Länder)
(1) Deutschland ist eine unteilbare demokratische Republik; sie baut sich auf den deutschen Ländern auf.
(2) Die Republik entscheidet alle Angelegenheiten, die für den Bestand und die Entwicklung des deutschen Volkes in seiner Gesamtheit wesentlich sind; alle übrigen Angelegenheiten werden von den Ländern selbständig entschieden.
(4) Es gibt nur eine deutsche Staatsangehörigkeit.

Artikel 2
Die Farben der Deutschen Demokratischen Republik sind Schwarz-Rot-Gold.
(2) Die Hauptstadt der Republik ist Berlin.

Artikel 3
(1) Alle Staatsgewalt geht vom Volke aus.
(2) Jeder Bürger hat das Recht und die Pflicht zur Mitgestaltung in

seiner Gemeinde, seinem Kreise, seinem Lande und in der Deutschen Demokratischen Republik.

(3) Das Mitbestimmungsrecht der Bürger wird wahrgenommen durch:
Teilnahme an Volksbegehren und Volksentscheiden;
Ausübung des aktiven und des passiven Wahlrechts;
Übernahme öffentlicher Ämter in Verwaltung und Rechtsprechung;

(4) Jeder Bürger hat das Recht, Eingaben an die Volksvertretung zu richten.

(5) Die Staatsgewalt muß dem Wohl des Volkes, der Freiheit, dem Frieden und dem demokratischen Fortschritt dienen.

(6) Die im öffentlichen Dienst Tätigen sind Diener der Gesamtheit und nicht einer Partei. Ihre Tätigkeit wird von der Volksvertretung überwacht.

Artikel 5
Kein Bürger darf an kriegerischen Handlungen teilnehmen, die zur Unterdruckung eines Volkes dienen.

Rechte des Bürgers

Artikel 7
(1) Mann und Frau sind gleichberechtigt.
(2) Alle Gesetze und Bestimmungen, die der Gleichberechtigung der Frau entgegenstehen, sind aufgehoben.

Artikel 3
(1) Persönliche Freiheit, Unverletzlichkeit der Wohnung, Postgeheimnis und das Recht, sich an einem beliebigen Ort niederzulassen, sind gewährleistet.

Artikel 9
(1) Alle Bürger haben das Recht, innerhalb der Schranken der für alle geltende Gesetze ihre Meinung frei und öffentlich zu äußern und sich zu diesem Zweck friedlich und unbewaffnet zu versammeln . . . niemand darf benachteiligt werden, wenn er von diesem Recht Gebrauch macht.
(2) Eine Pressezensur findet nicht statt.

Artikel 10
(3) Jeder Bürger ist berechtigt, auszuwandern.

Artikel 11
Die fremdsprachigen Völkerteile in der Republik sind durch Gesetzgebung und Verwaltung in ihrer volkstümlichen Entwicklung zu fördern; sie dürfen insbesondere am Gebrauch ihrer Muttersprache im Unterricht, in der inneren Verwaltung und in der Rechtspflege nicht gehindert werden.

Artikel 14
(2) Das Streikrecht der Gewerkschaften ist gewährleistet.

Artikel 15
(1) Die Arbeitskraft wird vom Staat geschützt.
(2) Der Staat sichert durch Wirtschaftslenkung jedem Bürger Arbeit und Lebensunterhalt. Soweit dem Bürger angemessene Arbeitsgelegenheit nicht nachgewiesen werden kann, wird für seinen notwendigen Unterhalt gesorgt.

Artikel 18
(2) Mann und Frau, Erwachsener und Jugendlicher haben bei gleicher Arbeit das Recht auf gleichen Lohn.
(3) Die Frau genießt besonderen Schutz im Arbeitsverhältnis. (Einrichtungen) werden geschaffen, die es gewährleisten, daß die Frau ihre Aufgabe als Bürgerin und Schaffende mit ihren Pflichten als Mutter und Frau vereinbaren kann.

Wirtschaftsordnung

Artikel 19
Die Ordnung des Wirtschaftslebens muß den Grundsätzen sozialer Gerechtigkeit entsprechen.

Artikel 20
Die genossenschaftliche Selbsthilfe ist auszubauen.

Artikel 22
(1) Das Eigentum wird von der Verfassung gewährleistet
(2) Das Erbrecht wird gewährleistet.

Artikel 24
(3) Die Betriebe der Kriegsverbrecher und aktiven Nationalsozialisten sind enteignet und gehen in Volkseigentum über. Das gleiche gilt

für Privatunternehmungen, die sich in den Dienst einer Kriegspolitik stellen.

(4) Alle privaten Monopolorganisationen, wie Kartelle, Syndikate, Trusts ... sind verboten.

(5) Der private Grundbesitz, der mehr als 100 Hektar umfaßt, ist aufgelöst und wird ohne Entschädigung aufgeteilt.

Artikel 34

(1) Die Kunst, die Wissenschaft und ihre Lehre sind frei.

(2) Der Staat nimmt an ihrer Pflege teil und gewährt ihnen Schutz, insbesondere gegen den Mißbrauch für Zwecke, die den Bestimmungen und dem Geist der Verfassung widersprechen.

Aufbau der Staatsgewalt

Artikel 50

(1) Höchstes Organ der Republik ist die Volkskammer.

Artikel 51

(2) Die Abgeordneten werden in allgemeiner, gleicher, unmittelbarer und geheimer Wahl nach den Grundsätzen des Verhältniswahlrechtes auf die Dauer von vier Jahren gewählt.

(3) Die Abgeordneten sind Vertreter des ganzen Volkes. Sie sind nur ihrem Gewissen unterworfen und an Aufträge nicht gebunden.

Artikel 63

Zur Zuständigkeit der Volkskammer gehören:

    die Bestimmung der Grundsätze der Regierungspolitik und ihrer Durchführung;

    die Bestätigung, Überwachung und Abberufung der Regierung;

    die Bestimmung der Grundsätze der Verwaltung und die Überwachung der gesamten Tätigkeit des Staates;

    die Beschlußfassung über den Staatshaushalt, den Wirtschaftsplan, Anleihen und Staatskredite der Republik;

    die Wahl des Präsidenten der Republik gemeinsam mit der Länderkammer;

    die Wahl der Mitglieder des Obersten Gerichtshofes der Republik und des Obersten Staatsanwaltes sowie deren Abberufung.

Vertretung der Länder

Artikel 71
Zur Vertretung der deutschen Länder wird eine Länderkammer gebildet. In der Länderkammer hat jedes Land für je 500 000 Einwohner einen Abgeordneten. Jedes Land hat mindestens einen Abgeordneten.

Regierung der Republik

Artikel 91
Die Regierung der Republik besteht aus dem Ministerpräsidenten und den Ministern.

Artikel 92
Die stärkste Fraktion der Volkskammer benennt den Ministerpräsidenten; er bildet die Regierung. Alle Fraktionen, soweit sie mindestens 40 Mitglieder haben, sind im Verhältnis ihrer Stärke durch Minister oder Staatssekretäre vertreten. Staatssekretäre nehmen mit beratender Stimme an den Sitzungen der Regierung teil.

Vocabulary

die Angelegenheiten	affairs, matters
die Unverletzlichkeit	inviolability
benachteiligt	disadvantaged
berechtigt	entitled to
genossenschaftlich	co-operative
unmittelbar	direct

The GDR Constitution of 1968

The constitution of 1968 differed significantly in a number of ways from that of 1949. The building of the Berlin Wall in 1961 marked a deepening – and permanence – of the division of Germany. It was no longer necessary to maintain liberal elements in the constitution in order to be attractive to West Germans since unification was no longer on the cards. Other guarantees such as the right to strike could not be implemented so they were removed. The distinctly socialist or communist aspects were strengthened.

The GDR is described as a socialist state but is still part of the German nation, and indeed is to act as a model for a future, reunified German state. The leading role of the SED is now enshrined in the constitution (Article 1). The SED broke a number of the Articles of the 1968 constitution, for instance, after the eighth Party Congress of the SED in June 1971 the period for which the Volkskammer was elected was increased from four years (Article 54) to five, and in the same year the powers of the *Staatsrat* began to be cut back, while those of the *Ministerrat* were increased in 1972. The Volkskammer also took over increased powers from the *Staatsrat* after 1971 without the authority of the constitution.

In 1974 a number of revisions to the 1968 constitution were made in the *Gesetz zur Ergänzung und Änderung der Verfassung*. The new preamble defined the ultimate aim of the GDR as communism. It no longer spoke of the German people, of a single German nation or of the GDR leading that reunified nation to communism. This change in direction marked the rejection of a special relationship with the Federal Republic and further strengthened the close ties with the Soviet Union. The national colours remained the same as those of the Federal Republic, but the emblems of the working class (hammer and compasses) and of agriculture (the ears of corn) were added to the flag and other official symbols. Relations with the Soviet Union received an article to themselves. The environment was mentioned for the first time in the constitution but little was in fact done to protect it, and the level of air and water pollution became high. This led to widespread discontent among people in the areas affected. Nor was there any longer any pretence that judges were independent – 'Richter kann nur sein, wer dem Volk und seinem sozialistischen Staat treu ergeben ist' (Article 94).

Text C

Die Verfassung der Deutschen Demokratischen Republik (1968)

Artikel 1

Die Deutsche Demokratische Republik ist ein sozialistischer Staat deutscher Nation. Sie ist die politische Organisation der Werktätigen in Stadt und Land, die gemeinsam unter Führung der Arbeiterklasse und ihrer marxistisch-leninistischen Partei den Sozialismus verwirklichen.

Artikel 6

(2) Die Deutsche Demokratische Republik pflegt und entwickelt entsprechend den Prinzipien des sozialistischen Internationalismus die allseitige Zusammenarbeit und Freundschaft mit der Union der Sozialistischen Sowjetrepubliken und den anderen sozialistischen Staaten.

Artikel 8

(2) Die Herstellung und Pflege normaler Beziehungen und die Zusammenarbeit der beiden deustchen Staaten auf der Grundlage der Gleichberechtigung sind nationales Anliegen der Deutschen Demokratischen Republik. Die Deutsche Demokratische Republik und ihre Bürger erstreben darüber hinaus die Überwindung der vom Imperialismus der deutschen Nation aufgezwungenen Spaltung Deutschlands, die schrittweise Annäherung der beiden deutschen Staaten bis zu ihrer Vereinigung auf der Grundlage der Demokratie und des Sozialismus.

Artikel 24

(1) Jeder Bürger der Deutschen Demokratischen Republik hat das Recht auf Arbeit. Er hat das Recht auf einen Arbeitsplatz und dessen freie Wahl entsprechend den gesellschaftlichen Erfordernissen und der persönlichen Qualifikation. Er hat das Recht auf Lohn nach Qualität und Quantität der Arbeit. Mann und Frau, Erwachsene und Jugendliche haben das Recht auf gleichen Lohn bei gleicher Arbeitsleistung.

(2) Gesellschaftlich nützliche Tätigkeit ist eine ehrenvolle Pflicht für jeden arbeitsfähigen Bürger. Das Recht auf Arbeit und die Pflicht zur Arbeit bilden ene Einheit.

Artikel 66

(1) Der Staatsrat erfüllt als Organ der Volkskammer zwischen den Tagungen der Volkskammer alle grundsätzlichen Aufgaben, die sich aus den Gesetzen und Beschlüssen der Volkskammer ergeben.

(2) Der Vorsitzende des Staatsrates vertritt die Deutsche Demokratische Republik völkerrechtlich.

Artikel 78

(1) Der Ministerat organisiert im Auftrage der Volkskammer die Erfüllung der politischen, ökonomischen, kulturellen und sozialen sowie die ihm übertragenen Verteidigungsaufgaben des sozialistischen Staates.

(2) Der Ministerrat arbeitet wissenschaftlich begründete Prognosen aus, organisiert die Gestaltung des ökonomischen Systems des Sozialismus und leitet die planmäßige Entwicklung der Volkswirtschaft.

The following amendments were made, among others, to the constitution in 1974:

Artikel 1
Die Deutsche Demokratische Republik ist ein sozialistischer Staat der Arbeiter und Bauern . . .
Das Staatswappen der Deutschen Demokratischen Republik besteht aus Hammer und Zirkel, umgeben von einem Ährenkranz, der im unteren Teil von einem schwarzrotgoldenen Band umschlungen ist.

Artikel 6
(2) Die Deutsche Demokratische Republik ist für immer und unwiderruflich mit der Union der Sozialistischen Sowjetrepubliken verbündet. Das enge und brüderliche Bündnis mit ihr garantiert dem Volk der Deutschen Demokratischen Republik das weitere Voranschreiten auf dem Wege des Sozialismus und des Friedens,
Die Deutsche Demokratische Republik ist untrennbarer Bestandteil der sozialistischen Staatengemeinschaft.

3. Changes due to unification

The unification of Germany was sealed by both German states ratifying the *Einigungsvertrag* on 20 September 1990. The GDR ceased to exist on 3 October by its *Länder* joining the Federal Republic under Article 23 of the Basic Law. Article 3 of the *Einigungsvertrag* applied the Basic Law to the East German *Länder*, and Article 8 stipulated that all the laws of the Federal Republic would be introduced there. The GDR had a completely different system of social security (pensions, sickness benefits, etc.), which would be replaced by the system operating in the Federal Republic. A transitional period was possible in some instances. The result of the *Einigungsvertrag* was not a unification on the basis of equality. Instead, the institutions of one state disappeared. There was no attempt to see if anything from the

East German system was worth incorporating into the new united Germany. There was no recognition of anything that the East Germans had achieved in forty-five years. Article 4.6 stated that the Basic Law would remain in force until the united German people decided on a new constitution. The question of ownership of nationalized or sequestered property was also addressed. The land reform and the nationalization of industry that had taken place between 1945 and 1949 were not rescinded, but property that had been taken by the state after 1949 was to be returned to its owners and compensation made to the East Germans who had used the property in the intervening period for money that they had invested in it. This aspect of the agreement and the additional laws passed on this matter have led to many problems and great resentment among the East Germans. Article 25 of the agreement dealt with the most important question of privatization. The *Treuhand* (Trusteeship Office) was to organize the selling of state enterprises to the private sector and use some of the profits to help make other enterprises competitive so that they could be privatized. The success of the *Treuhand* is disputed: its work is hailed as a triumph by West Germans but highly criticized by many East Germans, who feel that 'their' factories have been given away.

Artikel 25

Treuhandvermögen

(1) Die Treuhandanstalt ist auch künftig damit beauftragt, gemäß den Bestimmungen des Treuhandgesetzes die früheren volkseigenen Betriebe wettbewerblich zu strukturieren und zu privatisieren. Sie wird rechtsfähige bundesunmittelbare Anstalt des öffentlichen Rechts. Die Fach- und Rechtsaufsicht obliegt dem Bundesminister der Finanzen, der die Fachaufsicht im Einvernehmen mit dem Bundesminister für Wirtschaft und dem jeweils zuständigen Bundesminister wahrnimmt.[8]

The Basic Law itself underwent some amendments. The East German *Länder* are now included in the preamble and Article 23 has been removed. Article 51 has been amended, as follows: 'Jedes Land hat mindestens drei Stimmen, Länder mit mehr als zwei Millionen Einwohnern haben vier, Länder mit mehr als sechs Millionen Einwohnern fünf, Länder mit mehr als sieben Millionen Einwohnern sechs Stimmen.' Article 146 nows reads: 'Dieses Grundgesetz, das nach Vollendung der Einheit und Freiheit Deutschlands für das gesamte deutsche Volk gilt, verliert seine Gültigkeit an dem Tage, an dem eine Verfassung in Kraft tritt, die von dem deutschen Volke in freier Entscheidung beschlossen worden ist.'[9]

Questions on the Source Texts

Text A

1. What is meant in the Federal Republic by *ein demokratischer sozialer Bundesstaat*?
2. Why are human rights regarded as so important in the Basic Law and what rights do they include?
3. How do you interpret *Die Freiheit der Lehre entbindet nicht von der Treue zur Verfassung*?
4. In what ways do the people exercise power? (Article 20.2)
5. What is the significance of Article 20.3?
6. What can the German people do if the democratic order is threatened?
7. Explain the practical application of Article 21 with respect to political parties.
8. What was the significance of Article 23, both in 1949 and for the reunification process in 1990?
9. What do you understand by *Bundesrecht bricht Landesrecht*?
10. How are powers governing relations with foreign states divided between *Bund* and *Länder*?
11. What is the Bundesrat and how is it composed?
12. Enumerate the functions of the federal president and explain how and why they differ from those set out in the Weimar constitution.
13. What is the composition of the federal government and what are its duties?
14. How is the chancellor elected? What responsibilities does he have? How does this compare with the Weimar constitution?
15. What are the areas that lie in the sole jurisdiction of the federal government?

Text B

1. Pick out the sections that indicate the SED did not anticipate a permanent division of Germany at that time.
2. Give examples where the SED did not observe the constitution.
3. In what areas did the East German state implement the constitution?
4. What did the constitution say about the economic system and about property?
5. What was the role of the Volkskammer supposed to be, and what happened in practice?

Text C

1. What role has the SED assigned for itself?
2. What were the most important changes with respect to German unification and the Soviet Union between the 1968 constitution and the 1974 amendments?
3. In Article 24 what do you think was the significance of *dessen freie Wahl entsprechend den gesellschaftlichen Erfordernissen*? Why do you think that voluntary work is now described as a 'duty'?

Notes

1. The Young Plan, named after the American Owen Young who chaired a conference in Paris in 1929 on the settlement of German First World War reparations, laid down that Germany was to pay two billion Marks reparations annually up to 1988. This was bitterly resented by the Germans and a plebiscite was instigated by the German Right. Only 13.8 per cent voted against the Young Plan, however.
2. For a deeper discussion see Rudolf Schuster (ed.), *Deutsche Verfassungen* (Munich, Goldmann, 1976), 11–19.
3. The CDU/CSU and the SPD each had twenty-seven seats, the FDP five, the Zentrumspartei (which still stood under its own name at that time), the Deutsche Partei and the KPD had two each.
4. Hans Kremendahl, 'Die Bundesrepublik Deutschland: Ein demokratischer und sozialer Bundesstaat?', *Politik – kurz und aktuell*, 13 (West Berlin, 1974), 24.
5. Simon Bulmer, 'Territorial Government', in Gordon Smith et al. (eds.), *Developments in West German Politics* (London, Macmillan, 1989), 40–1.

6. Later to be known as *Zivildienst*, i.e. work in the community looking after the elderly, the handicapped etc.
7. Under the original BGB a woman could take up employment only if her husband agreed, and could not represent her child in a court of law. The BGB is still in force in the Federal Republic, but all paragraphs that discriminate against women have been removed.
8. Günter Bannas et al., *Der Vertrag zur deutschen Einheit. Ausgewählte Texte* (Frankfurt/Main and Leipzig, Insel Verlag, 1990), 69.
9. *Der Vertrag zur deutschen Einheit. Ausgewählte Texte*, 46–8 (Artikel 4).

Bibliography

In German

Benz, Wolfgang (ed.), *Die Bundesrepublik Deutschland. Geschichte in drei Bänden. Band 1, Politik* (Frankfurt-am-Main, Fischer Taschenbuch Verlag, 1984).
Ellwein, Thomas and J. Hesse, *Das Regierungssystem der Bundesrepublik Deutschland* (Opladen, Westdeutscher Verlag, 1987).
Erbe, Günter et al. (eds.), *Politik, Wirtschaft und Gesellschaft in der DDR* (Opladen, Westdeutscher Verlag, 1979).
Ludz, Peter C. et al. (eds.), *DDR-Handbuch* (Cologne, Wissenschaft und Politik, 1979).

In English

Beyme, Klaus von, *The Political System of the Federal Republic of Germany* (Aldershot, Gower, 1983).
Beyme, Klaus von and M. Schmidt (eds.), *Policy and Politics in the Federal Republic of Germany* (Aldershot, Gower, 1985).
Conradt, David P., *The German Polity* (New York and London, Longman, 1993).
Edinger, Lewis, *Politics in West Germany* (Boston, Little, Brown, 1977).
Padgett, S. and T. Burkett, *Political Parties and Elections in West Germany: The Search for a New Stability* (London, Hurst, 1986).
Paterson, William and David Southern, *Governing Germany* (Oxford and Cambridge, Mass., Blackwell, 1991).

Scharf, C. Bradley, *Politics and Change in East Germany* (Boulder, Westview, and London, Pinter, 1984).

Smith, Gordon, William Paterson and Peter H. Merkl (eds.), *Developments in West German Politics* (London, Macmillan, 1989).

Part II:

The Political Parties

General introduction to German political parties since 1945

The historical setting

The year 1945 has been called in Germany *das Jahr Null*. Five and a half million Germans had died in the war, millions more had been wounded and millions were in prisoner-of-war camps. In the next few months and years, as a result of the Potsdam Agreement, more than six million Germans were driven from their homes in the Eastern Provinces (East Prussia, Silesia and Pomerania), Poland and Czechoslovakia. Towns and cities lay in ruins – indeed most of the major cities had been more than 70 per cent destroyed. Over 3.6 million dwellings had been totally destroyed or badly damaged and 7.5 million Germans had no roof over their head. The infrastructure had collapsed. Food and clothing were extremely scarce and most people were undernourished. The currency was, in effect, worthless and was replaced by cigarettes and a barter system. Prostitution and crime were rife. The health of the nation was very bad and the mortality rate – especially among infants and the elderly – was high. In the city of Dresden in the summer of 1945, for instance, 73 out of every 100 babies born died within months.[1] The Germans were in a state of shock and morale was extremely low. Somehow out of the total collapse of a modern, highly industrialized society order had to be created and a new beginning made. The political parties and their leaders were to play a significant role in this process.

Conservative, liberal and socialist parties had developed in Germany during the nineteenth and early twentieth centuries, and a large number of small, fringe parties had sprung up during the Weimar Republic, but the advent of the national socialists to power in 1933 put an end to democratic party politics. For twelve years German politicians had been unable to participate in political activities, had been imprisoned or, in some cases, forced into exile or even murdered. In 1945 there was a political vacuum, with few political leaders and no political infrastructure. The population had to be helped to overcome the legacy of twelve years of nazi dictatorship and ideology. The Allies had insisted on the total, unconditional surrender of Germany, and occupation of her territory, over which they assumed supreme governmental power. After the conference at Potsdam from 17 July to 2 August 1945, Truman, Stalin and Attlee signed the Potsdam Agreement, which was to be of fundamental importance to the ensuing development of Germany. Under the Political Principles that were agreed, there was to be uniformity of treatment of the Germans throughout the country, and the Allied Control Council which was set up by the Allies was to oversee this. Germany was to be disarmed and demilitarized, and her arms industry destroyed. German political life was to be restructured on a democratic basis. This covered the education and judicial systems, self-government, the creation of political parties and the development of the basic freedoms of speech, the press and religion. The Germans were not allowed to set up a central government at that time; instead, a decentralized political structure was to be created. The country was to undergo a thorough denazification process. Under the economic principles set out in the Agreement, Germany was to be treated as a single economic unit. Reparations were to be taken from Germany by the Allies – the Russians would take theirs from their zone and would receive 15 per cent of some of the industrial plant from the Western zones in return for food and materials.[2] The Western Allies broke their word on this as the Cold War developed, and from 1947 the Russians – who, of the four allies, had suffered the heaviest human and material losses during the war – had to take all their reparations from their own zone. This considerably set back the East German economy.

Much of the beginning of political life in Germany after 1945 lay in the hands of the Allies, and it soon became clear that the Western powers and the Russians had different concepts of democracy and of the systems that they wanted to create in their zones. It was also soon clear that the wartime alliance between the West and the Russians had broken down, and relations were becoming increasingly confrontational. The division of the world into two hostile blocs (the Cold War) put an end to any hope of rapid German unification and changed the lives of Germans in East and West irrevocably. The Germans were too important – strategically, economically and politically – for either bloc to permit the creation of a neutral reunified Germany or to risk a reunified Germany joining the other bloc. This situation was to continue until one of the blocs collapsed. Only at that point did it become possible for the Germans to come together again in one state.

The setting up of political parties began in the Soviet Zone shortly after Germany's surrender, with the KPD (Kommunistische Partei Deutschlands, 11 June), SPD (Sozialdemokratische Partei Deutschlands, 15 June), CDU (Christlich Demokratische Union, 26 June) and the LDPD (Liberal-Demokratische Partei Deutschlands, 5 July). On 9 July 1945 five *Länder* governments were created there, and on 25 July eleven central German administrative authorities were set up. In the Western zones the organization of political parties was authorized at the end of 1945 and resulted in the creation of the CDU, CSU (Christlich-Soziale Union), SPD and FDP (Freie Demokratische Partei). *Länder* were established in the American zone in late 1945 and in the British and French zones in 1946.

Within the next few years a liberal, Western-style democracy began to emerge in West Germany, and although based on capitalism – or as it soon came to be called, the market economy – it had a strong social dimension. There was a commitment to supporting the weak, distributing the costs that the war had imposed on the millions of refugees (*Lastenausgleich*, particularly from 1952) and to building a more just society. Yet many aspects of life were not changed or reformed, and this led to the period being described as *die Restauration*. For instance, there were few reforms in the education system, except for the removal of nazi ideology and the more high-profile former nazi teachers and university staff. Similarly, nazi and racist laws were annulled but the legal system was only partly and slowly modernized.

In East Germany, during the same period, massive changes took place. Partly they were instigated by the Russians, but to a great extent it was the German communists, and initially socialists themselves, who were most keen to introduce them. Many of them had suffered considerably under the nazis or had been in exile during the nazi period. They were convinced anti-fascists, anti-militarists and, to a great extent, anti-capitalists. They were determined to smash those forces in Germany that had backed the nazis – the industrialists, big business, the financial institutions – and to break the power of the large landowners, the so-called *Junker*. Thus, as early as September 1945, all landowners who had supported the nazis and all those owning more than 100 hectares (250 acres) were dispossessed of a total of 5.3 million hectares. Of this land 2.2 million hectares were given to 559,089 farm labourers, farmers with small acreage and Germans expelled from the Eastern Provinces by the Russians and the Poles.[3] In 1945 the factories of former nazis were sequestered by the Russians (similar steps were taken in the Western zones in fulfilment of the Potsdam Agreement) but this was only the beginning of the wide-scale nationalization of industry, the mines and natural resources, banks and insurance companies. The education system was changed radically. Fifty thousand teachers who had been in the nazi party or nazi teachers' association were dismissed and replaced by teachers from an 'anti-fascist or working-class background'. This ensured that teachers themselves were active supporters of policies which weakened middle-class privileges in education and led to the ending of the *Gymnasium* (grammar school) system. Changes were initiated in the legal system, health service and social security. The communists pushed through a merger with the social democrats in February 1946 – with the argument that it was the division of the Left that had allowed the nazis to come to power, and that unity was essential to overcome the massive problems facing the country. The party that emerged, the Sozialistische Einheitspartei Deutschlands (SED), was to run the country from then to the end of 1989.

By 1949, when it was clear to both the Western Allies and the Russians that Germany was not going to be reunited in the foreseeable future, but that it was stable and that their respective German allies were in control, two separate German states came into being – the Federal Republic of Germany on 7 September and the German Democratic Republic on 7 October.

West German politics were to be dominated from that point up to 1966 by the conservative (CDU/CSU) and liberal (FDP) coalition, and for most of that time under the leadership of Konrad Adenauer (CDU). This was a period of considerable political stability and of exceptional economic success. The *Wirtschaftswunder* (the 'economic miracle') was to become known well outside Germany's borders. The currency reform on 20 June 1948 in the Western zones had laid the basis for the new Deutsche Mark, the massive amount of Marshall Aid given by the United States to West Germany (for which West Germans were highly grateful; see Adenauer's speech to the American Congress, text E, p.70) had made possible the investment to rebuild German industry, and the population had committed all its energies to rebuilding the country. In addition,

German industry was now becoming one of the most modern in the world, its work-force was highly skilled, its products were of high quality and its after-sales service was good, with the result that West Germany became a highly successful exporter. She also consistently had a large balance of payments surplus. During this period West Germany joined the European Coal and Steel Community in 1952, the European Economic Community in 1957 and the Western European Union in 1954. She regained her sovereignty (though with certain special rights still reserved to the Western Allies) and became a member of NATO in 1955. She set up her armed forces, the Bundeswehr, in the same year. Remilitarization was rejected by many in the population at large, however, and there were many demonstrations in the mid- to late 1950s. In September 1955 a major plank of West German foreign policy was introduced. Shortly after the foundation of the West German state, the government had announced that since East Germany's elections were not free and fair and thus not representative of the people living there, the Federal Republic was the only legitimate representative of the East Germans (*Alleinvertretungsanspruch*). In 1955 the Federal Republic went a step further and stated that it would not take up or maintain diplomatic relations with any state that recognized the GDR. This became generally known as the Hallstein Doctrine, named after Walter Hallstein, a foreign-policy adviser to Chancellor Adenauer. The policy was not dropped until 1972, but in the meantime had a highly negative effect, politically and economically, on East Germany.

In East Germany the economy was very much slower to pick up, burdened as it was by reparations and by not being able to benefit from aid or investment from the Americans. The 1950s witnessed an even deeper commitment on the part of the SED to building a 'socialist system' (*Aufbau des Sozialismus*). Those years saw the partial nationalization of medium-sized firms; the creation of agricultural co-operatives (*Landwirtschaftliche Produktionsgenossenschaften*, LPG) out of both land received during the 1945 land reform and land not affected by that reform; and further changes in education and the health and social security systems. The abolition of the *Länder* and existing regions and their replacement with fifteen *Bezirke* was a further step in the centralization of power under the SED. In the late 1940s and early 1950s East Germany had become increasingly Stalinist and repressive. This, coupled with a low standard of living, were two of the factors lying behind the 1953 uprising (which began on 17 June as a strike over wages and work-loads by building workers in

East Berlin and was put down by force by the Russians and the SED in four days). These factors were also the main reasons for hundreds of thousands of East Germans leaving their country each year to start a new life in West Germany. Recruitment of skilled workers and professionals by West German firms and West German propaganda also played a role. (Between 1949 and 1961 2,686,942 East Germans had gone over to West Germany.[4]) This loss of predominantly young, active, highly trained people led to the building of the Berlin Wall, begun on 13 August 1961, and to nearly seventeen million East Germans being sealed off from the West.

In common with the experience in a number of Western countries such as the United States, France and Great Britain, the 1960s were to leave a lasting mark on the Federal Republic. The market economy fosters initiative, competition, investment and growth and, indeed, needs them in order to survive and prosper. Scientific and techno- logical developments are of key importance in this. The 1950s had witnessed the beginnings of a symbiosis of market and technological change, partly as a result of competition between the two world systems and the accompanying arms race. The 1960s saw a further development of this. West Germany, and particularly West Berlin, became the show-place of the West. Millions of new jobs were created in consumer-goods industries such as the production of tele- visions, washing machines and refrigerators. The car industry began to boom. Increasing numbers of people travelled by air. A leisure industry developed rapidly. The old industrial base in coal, steel and heavy industry gave way to a rapid diversification into the new indus- tries and services. The nature of work influences how people live and consume, and has implications for society as a whole and for its values. There are implications for politics as well when the tradi- tional working class begins to disappear, has new aspirations and loosens its loyalty to one particular party. West Germany was in a state of transition. Rising standards of education and, above all, greater access to a wide range of information through television were creating a much better-informed public that was prepared to ask questions about what was happening in society and what the politi- cians were doing, or failing to do. This process began in the 1960s, particularly among young, educated people, but has continued at an increasing pace since then.

Events in the United States formed a catalyst for so much that happened among the young in Western Europe in the mid- to late 1960s. The struggle for democracy and racial equality in the USA waged by the Civil Rights movement, the anti-Vietnam War protests, the preaching of 'flower power' rather than 'power through the barrel of a gun', and the nascent feminist and environmental movements all had a tremendous attraction for young West Europeans, who had already grown up with the USA in many respects as their model, and who saw so much that needed changing in their own countries. A generation became politicized and, since the systems under which they lived were in the main conservative, they naturally sought alternatives and solutions in left-wing politics, in many cases in Marxism. In West Germany and France students reacted to university systems that were outdated and in some respects irrelevant. In Germany protests led to reforms within the universities. In France students and workers together almost brought the government down in 1968. The young saw that they had influence and could effect changes. Protest movements sprang up everywhere in West Germany and covered many different views and causes.

On the political front, a particular concern among protest groups in the 1960s in West Germany was the growing power of the extreme right (examined in chapter 7). A further issue that attracted opposition was the creation of the Grand Coalition of CDU/CSU and SPD in 1966. It was feared that, with only the FDP in opposition, democracy was under threat. The Außerparlamentarische Opposition (APO) was formed from among the protest groups and attracted particularly students, academics and other intellectuals. It particularly opposed the passing of the *Notstandsgesetze* (Emergency Powers Laws) in 1968 which it regarded as a dangerous extension of the powers of the state, and was active in organizing demonstrations.

Some of the most radical elements in the various protest movements wanted the destruction of the economic and political system in the Federal Republic. Yet it was increasingly clear towards the end of the 1960s that the system was strong and certainly not about to fall as a result of student demonstrations or the activities of the APO. In 1968 some extremists began to turn to terrorism to further their aims. The Rote Armee Faktion (RAF) came into being in 1971. The names that were to be most associated with it were Andreas Baader, Ulrike Meinhof, Gudrun Ensslin and Horst Mahler. The theory underpinning their terrorism was that if the state could be provoked into undemocratic actions itself, then its repressive nature would be clear for all to see and would lead to mass action to overthrow the system. The so-called Baader–Meinhof gang carried out arson, bombings, kidnappings and murder across West Germany. They aroused public anxiety and revulsion but no sympathy among the vast majority of the population. In effect, their actions were not only criminal and abhorrent but also totally unproductive, since they moved the political climate towards the right. They themselves either died or were given long prison sentences as a result of their activities. The *Radikalenerlaß* (Act against Radicals) or *Berufsverbot,* as it was called by its opponents, was, in part, a reaction to their activities. Under this act no one with extremist connections could work as a *Staatsbeamte* (civil servant). Screening took place both of candidates for jobs and of those already in employment. It is estimated that some 10,000 people, most of them communists or far-left supporters, either failed to obtain a job or lost one as a result, and hundreds of thousands of people underwent screening.

In 1966 the SPD had its first chance to share power in the running of the Federal Republic when it joined the 'Grand Coalition'. Only three years later it was able to form a government in coalition with the FDP and begin a highly important dialogue with the Eastern bloc on reducing tension and improving bilateral relations. The successes achieved and the treaties that were signed were perhaps the most important contribution that the SPD made to post-1945 Germany and will be examined later. Yet the SPD was to stay in government only up to 1982, and since then the CDU/CSU have remained in power.

The East Germans, too, profited from better relations with West Germany and the general relaxation of tension between East and West. The 1970s were the best years in the history of the GDR. The standard of living rose, a considerable amount of money was poured into education, social security, culture and sport. There was a rising feeling of optimism within the population. With the new *Ostpolitik* and the ending of the Hallstein Doctrine, the GDR received official recognition from most of the states in the world and was able to trade with many of them. Meanwhile the West Germans went from strength to strength. They had an internationally well-respected political system and played an important role in the 'Helsinki Process', the Conference on Security and Co-operation in Europe – an international forum in which the thirty-five member states of North America and Europe could discuss security issues, economic co-operation between East and West and human-rights issues. (The CSCE, by laying emphasis on human rights, helped foster the dissident movements in Eastern and Central Europe that were, in turn, to play an important role in the collapse of the Eastern bloc.) West Germany had a stable currency and a very high standard of living and social security provision. It was the country against which the East Germans measured themselves, and whose life-style was so attractive.

The end of the 1970s saw the beginning of a new round in the East–West confrontation which was to have a considerable effect on the Eastern bloc and on Germany itself. In 1976–7 the Russians decided to replace their medium-range rockets with the more modern SS 20s, which each carried three nuclear warheads. The SPD chancellor, Helmut Schmidt, pressed the Americans and NATO for a response. The result was the NATO 'Twin-Track Decision' (*Doppelbeschluß*) of 12 December 1979. American Cruise and Pershing II rockets would be stationed in Western Europe (Britain, Italy and the Federal Republic) at the end of 1983 if no agreement had been reached by that time. Agreement was not reached, and American rockets were stationed in Germany and other parts of the NATO alliance. The danger of a nuclear war was increased, and people in both parts of Germany in particular became increasingly afraid that if war broke out their country would be totally destroyed. Peace movements developed in both East and West Germany and, as far as the GDR was concerned, this was the beginning of the dissident groups which were to play an important role in the collapse of the GDR in 1989–90. More importantly, however, Ronald Reagan's decision to increase the pace of the arms race was disastrous for the East. The communist bloc's economies were nowhere near as strong as those of the West and were, in any case, inefficient and beset with problems. Money spent on arms could not be used to increase or even maintain the standard of living and services. Dissatisfaction spread throughout the bloc. In East Germany this was very evident in the 1980s, despite the millions of DM lent to the GDR by the Federal Republic. People in the GDR became alienated, especially the young.

In 1985 Mikhail Gorbachev came to power in the Soviet Union and, within a very short time, introduced *perestroika* (economic reforms) and *glasnost* (openness, particularly in government). He and his supporters hoped to modernize the economic and political system, release new energy to help solve the severe economic situation and develop a system of security in Europe that would lead to a de-escalation of the arms race and the Cold War. A new beginning was to be made, but still on the basis of socialism and accompanied by the construction of the 'European House' in which the Soviet Union could find her justified place. Gorbachev's ideas found an echo in the Eastern bloc and had some parallels in Western Europe (for example, the Stockholm discussions under the chairmanship of the Swedish prime minister, Olaf Palme, in the early 1980s, and the dialogue between the SPD and the SED between 1982 and 1987, as will be discussed later). Since 1945 all attempts at change in individual countries of the Eastern bloc – Hungary in 1956, Czechoslovakia in 1968 and Poland in 1980 – had failed because the Soviet Union intervened and suppressed them. This time the move for change was taking place in the heart of the Soviet Union herself, and if it succeeded it would allow change throughout the states that were under Soviet influence. The SED was alarmed because it fully recognized that the GDR only existed because of Soviet support. Yet it also expected that the task confronting Gorbachev would be too great and that his reforms would falter or even fail. The policy that the party adopted was to 'wait and see', and not itself to embark on reforms that could possibly weaken the GDR. Events in the summer and autumn of 1989 overtook it.

The opening of Hungary's borders with the West in August 1989 allowed thousands of East Germans to cross them and reach West Germany. The pictures of happy East Germans being welcomed in the West were shown every day on West German television and could be seen by over 90 per cent of East Germans. The SED did not know how to react. Honecker, the general secretary of the party, was suffering from cancer, and for some of the most critical weeks in the history of the East German state the leadership was rudderless and paralysed. It was increasingly confronted by its citizens seeking asylum in West German embassies in Prague and Warsaw, by its dissidents issuing statements and demands and having the West German media convey their words back to the East German public, and also, slowly but surely, by demonstrations on the streets. The GDR reached its fortieth anniversary on 7 October, but thereafter the collapse was rapid and complete. The warning that Gorbachev gave at the anniversary celebrations, 'Wer zu spät kommt, wird vom Leben bestraft', had itself come too late.

The spokespeople of the hundreds of thousands who demonstrated regularly in the streets of East Berlin, Leipzig and Dresden were members of the dissident groups that had developed around the issues of peace and disarmament, conscientious objection, protection of the environment and the women's question. There were also writers such as Christa Wolf and Stefan Heym, and church people such as Pastor Schorlemmer and Rainer Eppelmann. University staff, doctors, actors, artists and members of the SED all turned out to speak at demonstrations. The tenor was to maintain a separate GDR state, rather than to reunify with the Federal Republic, to reform it and build a democratic system (for example, see text A, p.176–9). On 17 December 1989, according to a public opinion survey carried out by the Zweites Deutsches Fernsehen in East Germany, some 73 per cent of the people wished to remain in an independent, sovereign GDR.

By the spring of 1990 the SED had disappeared, a new party, the Partei des Demokratischen Sozialismus had been constituted and the much-hated *Staatssicherheit* (state security) which had done so much over the years to stifle opposition and discussion, was in the process of being wound up. A plethora of 'reformed' or new parties had come, or were coming into being. These ranged from the CDU, LDPD, NDPD and DBD to the SPD, Demokratischer Aufbruch (DA), Neues Forum (NF), Unabhängiges Frauenverband (UFB) and the Greens. The parties and groups formed the *Runder Tisch* on 7 December 1989 and from then on were to meet regularly. The aim was to run the country up to a general election and begin rebuilding its political life. The economy was spiralling downwards. A population that had lived for forty-five years with certainties and inflexibility was now confronted by a political vacuum and the insecurity of not knowing what the future would bring. The idea of reunification became an increasingly attractive possibility. People did not believe the East Germans could turn their economy around by themselves, and they had little faith in the new political parties that were just starting to find their feet and had no political experience. Nor did they believe that the West German government would bail them out without a change in the GDR system. Millions of East Germans had also visited West Berlin and West Germany after the borders were opened, and they had seen the affluence, they had experienced the warm welcome from the ordinary West Germans, their 'brothers and sisters'. In addition to all that, Chancellor Kohl assured them that unification would give them, in a short space of time, all the things that the West Germans had.

The elections to the Volkskammer took place on 18 March 1990. The electioneering that preceded it had been dominated by the West German party machines and their leading politicians. The East Germans themselves had little idea how to organize an election or fight a campaign. Those parties that had no strong West German party to support them lost out. The Greens were helped by the West German Greens, but their resources were puny in comparison with those that could be given by the West German CDU or SPD. Also the East German Greens made it clear that they wanted to maintain their independence from their friends in the West.

The major issue at the elections was unification with the Federal Republic. The conservative parties wanted unification as soon as possible. The SPD was more cautious and initially felt that a confederation lasting for some years would allow an orderly and successful transition to unity. By the time of the election, however, the party had swung over to speedy unification. The Greens, PDS and the parties that had emerged from the dissident groups, such as Neues Forum, were totally opposed, for they did not want to import the West German system into the GDR: they wanted the opportunity to find a 'third way' between the communism that they had lived under and the market economy of the West. Furthermore, they feared that all the things in the East German system (such as full employment, large state subsidies for pre-school education and support for the arts) that they wanted to keep would be lost on reunification. The outcome of the election was a clear majority of votes for the Allianz für Deutschland, which had been formed by the conservative parties that were fighting the election. Conservatives formed the last Volkskammer government (see appendix III, p.240). They had a mandate to bring about unification speedily. The Deutschmark was introduced in June and replaced the East German Mark. The GDR joined the Federal Republic under a *Beitritt* agreement (Accession Treaty), which was possible under Article 23 of the Basic Law, and ceased to exist on 3 October 1990. With that a new situation was created for the political parties – a situation that is still unfolding.

The electoral system

Elections are a crucial part of the democratic process. On the one hand they produce parliaments, regional governments, local councils and recruit political élites. On the other hand they legitimize the political system in the eyes of the electorate, they mobilize the electorate for social values, political aims and programmes, and they raise political consciousness. They also allow periodic participation in politics by the individual elector, with the minimum outlay of time and effort, and they channel political conflicts.[5] Elections have legitimizing, controlling (i.e. of government by opposition), competitive and representative functions.

The electoral systems in the two parts of Germany were vastly different. The West Germans had choice – they could change their government, could choose whether or not to vote and could actively campaign for their political views. The East Germans did not have such choices: they could not change their government, nor could they oppose it, and they were expected to vote. Yet however they might have voted, they had no impact on election results, as will be seen. After unification the West German system was extended to the whole country.

The election system that developed in West Germany is unusual. For elections to the Bundestag the voter is given two votes on the ballot paper to fill in. The first (*Erststimme*) is for the direct election of a member to represent one of the 328 constituencies. Half of the 656 members (the number had been increased by 138 after unification) are elected in this manner – the candidate who receives the most votes is elected by simple majority. The second (*Zweitstimme*) is for the *Parteiliste*, that is, the party and the list of candidates that it is putting up in the *Land*. In this case, all the second votes given to this party across the whole Federal Republic are multiplied by the total number of seats in the Bundestag (that is, by 656). This figure is then divided by the total number of valid votes cast in the election. As an example, party A receives 12,233,756 votes out of the total second votes cast – 42,596,287. This figure of 12,233,756, multiplied by 656 (seats in the Bundestag), equals 8,025,343,936. This is divided by 42,596,287. The result is 188.405 and gives the party 188 seats. This calculation is carried out for each of the parties. The second step entails calculating how party A's 188 seats are distributed across the sixteen *Landeslisten*. If party A received 1.3 million *Zweitstimmen* in a given *Land* which is represented by nineteen seats, and eleven are filled by directly elected candidates, then eight seats are left to be distributed according to the *Zweitstimme* votes. These seats are filled from the *Landesliste*. The electoral process can lead to so-called *Überhangmandate*. A party may have gained more directly elected members than it is entitled to on the basis of its list votes, so that the number of parliamentarians may rise above 656. At the first elections after reunification there were an additional six members of the Bundestag as a result, and at present there are sixteen additional members as a result of the 1994 election.[6]

The order in which candidates are ranked in the *Land* lists is decided upon by the party itself. In the event of a member of the

Bundestag dying in office or resigning, the seat is given to the next candidate on the *Land* list. There is no system of by-elections.

The normal rule, under which a party has to obtain 5 per cent of the votes cast or three directly elected members in order to be represented in Parliament, was modified in the first election after reunification, particularly in order to help the new parties that had come into existence in East Germany. There were separate 5 per cent thresholds for the areas covered previously by the two states. In subsequent elections 5 per cent has to be achieved across the whole of Germany, or three direct mandates.

Land elections are carried out on the basis of the *Landesverfassung*, the *Landtagswahlgesetz* and the *Landtagswahlordnung*. They normally take place at the end of the legislative period, i.e. every four years in most *Länder*, but, if necessary, can be brought forward according to the law in each *Land*. The 5 per cent clause is now used in all the *Länder*, with the exception of Berlin, Brandenburg and Schleswig-Holstein, where votes below 5 per cent count as long as one directly elected seat has been secured. There is generally a mixture of proportional and direct representation which varies from *Land* to *Land*.

At the lower level there are *Kreistage* and *Gemeinde-* or *Stadträte*. Elections take place on the basis of proportional representation. Lists of candidates are made out for each constituency, and the voter has as many votes as there are candidates. The voter can give up to three votes for a candidate. The total votes are then distributed according to the d'Hondt formula (which is similar to the Hare/Neimeyer system described on p.42).

Direct elections to the European Parliament take place every five years and are on the basis of proportional representation (Hare/Niemeyer formula) and lists of candidates. In contrast to the Bundestag elections, each elector has one vote, which he gives to a party or electoral group. The 5 per cent clause operates.

The electoral system in East Germany was completely different. Only in 1946 were Western-style elections, i.e. parties competing freely for the electors' votes, allowed in East Germany. The newly formed SED did not fare well, so a new election system was devised which resulted in the SED gaining a monopoly of power. The SED was to receive 25 per cent of the Volkskammer seats, the CDU, NDPD, LDPD and the DBD 10 per cent each, and the remaining 35 per cent were allocated to mass organizations such as the trade unions. The SED was in a minority, but since the representatives of the mass organizations were also members of the SED there was a guaranteed majority for the SED in parliament.

The law on political parties

The parties are governed, in particular, by the provisions of the Law on Political Parties which was passed by the Bundestag on 24 July 1967, in conformity with Article 21, paragraph 3 of the Basic Law.[7] The Law on Parties is divided into seven sections. Section I covers the constitutional status and functions of the parties; Section II, their internal organization; Section III, nomination of candidates for election; Section IV, election expenses; Section V, conditions for party accounts; Section VI, legal provision for the imposition of a ban on parties that are unconstitutional. Finally, Section VII makes provision for tax relief on donations to parties and party membership fees.

Section I (paragraph 2) defines more fully than the Basic Law the manner in which the parties are to contribute to the formation of the political will of the people by:

> bringing their influence to bear on the shaping of public opinion; inspiring and furthering political education; promoting an active participation by individual citizens in political life; training talented people to assume political responsibilities; participating in federal, *Land* and local government elections by nominating candidates; exercising an influence on political trends in parliament and the government; initiating their defined political aims in the national decision-making processes; and ensuring continuous, vital links between the people and the public authorities.[8]

In practice the major parties support flourishing foundations – the Konrad Adenauer Stiftung (CDU), Hans Seidel Stiftung (CSU), Friedrich Ebert Stiftung (SPD), Friedrich Naumann Stiftung (FDP) and Heinrich Böll Stiftung (the Greens). These foundations are committed to research, publication and dissemination of information on a wide range of political issues, train party officials and support allied interest groups. All of the foundations also receive large subsidies from the state, e.g. in 1991 amounting to 553 million DM. In accord with Section I, paragraph 3, the parties all put forward their aims in their political programmes. Parties are defined as 'associations of citizens who set out to influence either permanently or for a long period of time the formation of public opinion at federal or *Land* level and to participate in the representation of the people in the Bundestag or the regional parliaments'. Under Section II, a party must have written statutes and a written programme. Parties are subdivided into regional associations. Party bodies are the members' meeting (as represented by the Party Congress, *Parteitag*), the executive committee (*Vorstand*) and the regional associations (*Landesverbände*). The executive committee must be elected at least every two years and must be made up of at least three members. Candidates for election to Parliament must be chosen by secret ballot (Section III).

Another important aspect of the Law on Parties concerns the banning of unconstitutional parties. The Constitutional Court rules on whether the activities of a party are in accord or otherwise with the Basic Law, and the *Land* government then appoints the authorities that have to implement the ruling. After a party has been banned it becomes illegal to set up a new organization to pursue the unconstitutional aims of the original party. In practice the law has not been invoked often. The neo-nazi Sozialistische Reichspartei was banned, and it was succeeded by the National Demokratische Partei which was not banned. The KPD was banned in 1956, but despite the ban on substitute organizations many of its members went into the Deutsche Friedens-Union and the Deutsche Kommunistische Partei (DKP, founded in 1968). After unification the PDS has been examined for possible anti-constitutional activities but has been found to be acting within the constitution.

The question of party financing is always of importance in a democracy, and the parties in Germany are dealing with large sums of money. In 1993, for example, the CDU had an income of 225,854,000 DM and outgoings of 192,903,000 DM, the SPD 280,768,000 DM income and 250,742,000 DM outgoings, while Bündnis 90/Die Grünen had 36,655,000 DM income and 40,030,000 DM outgoings. The PDS also spent above its income (27,356,000 DM income, 28,283,000 DM expenditure).[9] The Law on Political Parties defines carefully what financing is permissible. There are two sources of finance. Firstly, through membership fees, contributions by individual members, fund-raising campaigns and donations from the business community and, in some parties, from the candidates themselves contributing to the campaign expenses. Secondly, from the public purse. Under the first heading, rarely does income cover the high levels of expenditure required for a modern political party to function adequately across all the range of its activities, for example, operational costs, publicity, election campaigning, personnel, research. This is particularly the case for the smaller parties. Furthermore, the smaller parties with correspondingly smaller numbers of members and lower possibilities of fund-raising, despite lower outgoings on administration, could not be adequately represented if they relied on the private sector. It is for these reasons that the parties receive subsidies from public funding – and on a scale unmatched in other Western democracies. In the 1990 Bundestag election, for instance, state funding of election expenses covered: for the SPD 37.2 per cent of outgoings, for the CDU 41.8 per cent, for the CSU 36 per cent, for the FDP 50.4 per cent, and for the Greens 33.3 per cent.[10]

In terms of membership the SPD has traditionally had the highest number of paid-up members since the 1940s. It is followed by the CDU, which was slow to realize the importance of recruiting members. The CSU recruits only in Bavaria. In 1994, for instance, membership stood at: SPD, 849,374; CDU, 670,000; CSU, 176,250; FDP, 90,000 Bündnis 90/Greens, 43,869; PDS, 123,751.[11] The membership of all the parties, with the exception of Bündnis 90/Greens, dropped between 1992 (total 2,070,290) and 1994 (1,954,044). The situation in East Germany was that the SED had, on average, 2.3 million members up to 1989, the CDU had between 70,000 in the 1960s and 140,000 members in 1977, the LDPD fluctuated between 198,920 in 1950 and 82,000 in 1982, the NDPD had some 91,000 members. The funding of these parties was by the state and by membership dues, and neither membership figures nor the method of funding was comparable with that in West Germany. Since unification, membership of the main parties in East Germany has remained, in most cases, low. For instance, in 1992: SPD, 31,000; CDU, 111,000; FDP, 65,000; PDS, 185,000; Bündnis 90, 2,000.[12] It should not be forgotten, however, that not only party members contribute to fund-raising activities.

In 1952 business associations began to organize the collection of funds in support of the conservative and liberal parties in West Germany. The main contributors came from industry, trade, insurance companies and the banks. The level of contribution was generally linked with turnover or number of employees and was tax-deductible. In 1958 the SPD appealed to the Constitutional Court to remove the right to tax deduction, and the court agreed, since the parties were not being treated equally (the SPD received almost no funding from business concerns). Thereafter trade associations took over the role of distributing money to the parties on the basis that they could contribute up to 25 per cent of their dues, which themselves were tax-free. Individual firms also make donations, but some have recently begun to donate to conservative, liberal and social democrat parties alike (for instance, Daimler Benz in 1993 contributed to the CDU, CSU, SPD and FDP, and Deutsche Bank to the CDU and FDP). The Law on Political Parties lays down that the parties must give information on companies which donate more than 200,000 DM or individuals who contribute above 20,000 DM.

Public funding of party activities began in 1959, with the aim of supporting political education, but benefited only the parties that were represented in the Bundestag. After an appeal to the Constitutional Court by the smaller parties, the decision was made in 1966 to fund all parties, but only in support of election costs. The Law on Political Parties specifies (Section IV) that parties which take part in the Bundestag elections are reimbursed from the Federal funds by a flat rate per person eligible to vote (*Wahlkampfkostenpauschale*). The total amount is distributed across the parties that gain 0.5 per cent of the valid second votes in the previous election or 10 per cent of the valid first votes in a district if a *Land* list was open for the given party in that *Land*. After reunification, and partly as a result of an appeal made by the East German Bündnis 90 and the Greens to the Constitutional Court, the law was amended in 1993. Funds are granted to each party on the basis of votes received in the previous election and are paid at the rate of 1.30 DM per vote for the first five million votes (so as to give support to the smaller parties) and 1.00 DM for each vote above that figure. (In 1967 the flat rate was 2.50 DM for each vote. This was increased to 5 DM and maintained at that level up to 1993.) A further subsidy of up to 50 per cent of receipts by a party from dues and private donations could be given. A ceiling of 230 million Marks' subsidies per annum was imposed. At the 1994 Bundestag elections the parties received subsidies amounting to: CDU/CSU, 92 million DM; SPD, 89 million DM; FDP, 14.4 million DM; Bündnis 90/Greens, 9.6 million DM; PDS, 10.6 million DM. The positive aspect of the system is that smaller parties have a fair chance of fighting an election, but on the negative side the subsidies seem overgenerous at a time when Germany is struggling with the economic integration of East Germany, has 4.6 million unemployed and wishes to meet the convergence criteria for membership of the European Single Currency.

Notes

1. K.-H. Schöneburg et al., *Vom Werden unseres Staates 1945–1949* (East Berlin, Staatsverlag der DDR, 1966), 37.
2. Ernst Deuerlein et al., *Potsdam und die Deutsche Frage* (Cologne, Verlag Wissenschaft und Politik, 1970).
3. Schöneburg et al., *Vom Werden unseres Staates 1945–1949*, 83–7.
4. Hartmut Zimmermann (ed.), *DDR Handbuch* (Cologne, Verlag Wissenschaft und Politik, 1984), 418–20.
5. Wichard Woyke, *Stichwort Wahlen* (Opladen, Leske + Budrich, 1994), 18–21.
6. Michael Bechtel, 'Wahlen im Demokratischen Staat', in *Informationen zur politischen Bildung, Wahlen '94* (Bonn, Bundeszentrale für politische Bildung, 1994), 20.
7. *Federal Law Gazette*, 24 July 1967, part I (Bonn, 1967), 773.
8. Inter Nationes (ed.), *The Law on Political Parties* (Bonn-Bad Godesberg, 1978), 14–15.
9. *Taschenbuch des Öffentlichen Lebens* (Bonn, 1996), 905.
10. Woyke, op. cit., 103–4.
11. *Taschenbuch des Öffentlichen Lebens*, 905.
12. *Der Spiegel*, 16/1992.

1. Christlich Demokratische Union (CDU)/ Christlich-Soziale Union (CSU)

A. Christlich Demokratische Union

History and development

The CDU is a conservative party that was newly created after 1945 but had antecedents in the Zentrumspartei which had existed under the Kaiser and during the Weimar Republic and had been a predominantly Catholic party. This party had consistently attracted between 13.6 per cent (1920) and 11.2 per cent (1933)[1] of the vote in Reichstag elections and participated eighteen times in coalition governments, but it was only one of a number of parties competing for the support of the middle-class and landowning sections of the population.[2] In 1945 it was decided that a new party must be formed that would unite large sections of the conservative and liberal population. As Jakob Kaiser, one of its leaders, was to say, 'Wir waren alle in der politischen Arbeit der Jahre zwischen 1933 und 1945 klar geworden, daß eine Parteizersplitterung, wie sie vor 1933 vorherrschte, nicht mehr stattfinden dürfte.'[3] This would be the only way that the SPD and the KPD could be effectively opposed. As in Britain, France and other parts of Europe there was considerable support for left-wing parties in the aftermath of the Second World War. Additionally, the German communists and social democrats had maintained some sort of political organization, mainly in exile, during the nazi period and could be expected to mobilize and organize swiftly after the defeat in 1945. In late 1945 in many parts of Germany (Berlin, Cologne, Frankfurt-am-Main, Munich and Schleswig-Holstein) Christian political groups came into being. They displayed a number of common features – political commitment based on Christian ethics, a determination to oppose dictatorship and to build democracy in Germany, a belief in the rule of law and the rights of the individual. The various groups participated at a meeting in Bad Godesberg in December 1945 and decided on an association of autonomous groups under the name Christlich Demokratische Union. (In fact, it was not until 1952 that the CDU finally set up a central headquarters in Bonn, so jealously had the *Land* associations (*Landesverbände*) guarded their freedom and independence.) The new party would welcome conservative and liberal Protestants, in other words it was to be a non-denominational Christian party whose policies were to be based on Christian ethics. (It should be remembered that immediately after the war all the Churches played an important role in Germany since they represented an oasis of hope and calm, offering practical help in the midst of chaos and despair.) Later, as West Germany became more secular, support for the party remained, even among non-churchgoers. From the outset, the CDU aimed to attract support from all classes and was not to be regionally based. Nevertheless, in Bavaria, which traditionally had maintained a degree of separate identity from the rest of Germany, the Christian Democrats called themselves the Christlich-Soziale Union and remained a predominantly Catholic party. Membership of the CDU rose rapidly, so that by the end of 1946 some 300,000 people had joined. By now the man from the Rhineland, Konrad Adenauer, had become its leader, having beaten off the challenge from the Berlin-based Jakob Kaiser (Kaiser had been the chairman of the Catholic trade unions during the Weimar Republic.[4] After 1945 he wanted a socialist element introduced into the CDU. He also believed it was essential to have a headquarters for the CDU in Berlin and strong organizations in each of the zones. In fact the CDU set up nothing more than a co-ordinating office in Frankfurt-am-Main in 1948.) This, in the longer term, was to be one of the factors which determined that Bonn would become the capital of the Federal Republic in 1949.

The first basic programme was put forward by the CDU council in the British Zone at Ahlen in 1947.[5] It called for the creation of a mixed economy, with the nationalization of the coal industry and control of the steel and chemical industries exercised by government, workers and co-operatives. Basically, Adenauer and others on the right of the CDU were opposed to this policy, and from that year onwards the CDU backed the capitalist or market system, albeit with a strong social-welfare underpinning. Adenauer himself became increasingly pro-market, pro-Western and anti-communist, and helped set a stamp on the party that it has kept ever since.

The period from 1949 to 1969 saw the CDU permanently in government, and the system that had developed during the years of CDU rule led to the Federal Republic being called the 'CDU state'. So successful had the CDU been that they, in effect, forced the social democrats to change course at their congress in Bad Godesberg in 1959 and come more into line with the mainstream of CDU policies in an attempt to win a greater share of the electorate. Yet by the 1960s problems began to arise for the CDU. The first economic recession started to take hold. Grass-roots Catholics were no longer so successful in mobilizing support for the CDU, society was becoming more secular, the Churches themselves were not so closely allied to the CDU. In addition, the building of the Berlin Wall showed the limits of a very important aspect of Christian Democrat policy, namely its *Ostpolitik* and its dealings with the GDR. German society was also going through considerable structural changes which were to have an impact on the political scene. As in other Western industrialized societies, increasingly large numbers of jobs were being created in the tertiary sector, and the traditional working class and the number of self-employed began to shrink. This led to a more differentiated and pluralistic society, to new social-interest groups and to new norms and values. The Christian Democrats were much slower to perceive these changes than the SPD and FDP. Catholics no longer saw the SPD as Marxist, were no longer constrained from voting SPD for ideological or religious reasons, and began to vote for the Social Democrats, especially in 1969 and 1972 in the working-class areas of the Ruhr and Saarland. The CDU/CSU appeared now to be outdated, too conservative, unwilling to meet new challenges. The 1970s, the years in which the CDU/CSU were in opposition, were used to modernize the management of the party, modernize the approach to the electorate and develop programmes that were binding. Success came in the 1980s.

The years 1980–2 were marked by a recession and splits between the governing parties, the SPD and FDP. At the elections in 1983 the CDU/CSU presented themselves as the parties most likely to deal successfully with economic problems. They promised to roll back the state so as to release market forces, encourage investment, increase profits and jobs. They appealed to the growing sector of middle-class voters in professions created by new technology and in the service industries. They promised *eine Atempause* in social policy, not more taxes to pay for more social services and benefits but support for the philosophy that the individual should do more for him- or herself (along the lines of the Catholic social teaching known as 'subsidiarity'). Helmut Kohl promised to push back the state to its 'original functions'. There were parallels with what was happening in Britain under Prime Minister Thatcher and in the United States under President Reagan.

In 1983 the CDU/CSU received their best electoral results since 1957 with 48.8 per cent of the vote. They were fortunate that as they came to power the economy was moving out of recession again and they reaped the political benefit. They were not, however, able to 'push back the state' as far they would have liked – the West Germans were too used to having a high level of social security. Where the CDU/CSU did make – or even merely propose – cutbacks they made themselves unpopular with many of the electorate. In the 1987 elections the governing coalition was returned to power but with a drop in votes, and indeed the CDU lost 3.7 per cent and received its lowest percentage since 1949. The CSU, however, remained buoyant. The loss of support was due to a number of causes. Some of the young and women voters defected to the SPD and the Greens because of discontent with the CDU/CSU on their policies towards the environment, rearmament/peace and women's rights. The CDU lost to the SPD also because of the continuing high level of unemployment among manual workers. There was some defection to the FDP. Some support from the Right was lost because the government had not pushed back the state or changed the social package radically enough, nor was it deemed to have been sufficiently firm with the unions. Finally, the turn-out in rural areas was lower than usual. The importance of the 1987 elections, coupled with a weakening position in four *Land* elections that year, was that the CDU had to rethink its strategy for winning certain groups, such as young people and women. It also began to 'modernize' its programme by laying much more emphasis on the environment, the gaining of equal rights for women and the maintenance of peace and security. Whether these changes would have won the coalition government the next elections, given that the CDU was still losing ground at *Land*, city and European elections in 1988–9, is now a matter of speculation, for the sudden collapse of the Eastern bloc and the GDR provided a completely new set of issues, which will be examined later.

In the first fifteen to twenty years after the war, most party members were male, middle-class and over thirty-five years old. Catholics predominated – for instance, in 1971 they made up some

75 per cent. After a recruitment drive in the early 1970s and a rise in membership from 329,000 in 1970 to 664,000 (1977), the composition changed slightly. The number of women rose to about one-fifth, younger people began to join and the percentage of Catholics dropped to 59 per cent. Members still tend to be concentrated in the strongly Catholic *Länder* such as Baden-Württemberg and Westphalia.

The CDU in East Germany

The CDU was the only party in East Germany to have exactly the same name as a West German party, but it was to undergo a very different development. A call was made on 26 June 1945 by former members of the Catholic trade unions, the Zentrumspartei and surviving members of the 1944 plot to kill Hitler, for a Christian, democratic party to be formed. On 10 July 1945 the Soviet Military Administration (SMAD) gave permission for the creation of the CDU in its zone. Despite all the difficulties, the new party had already gained 100,000 members by the end of August 1945. In the coming months the CDU worked closely with the communists, social democrats and the liberals of the newly formed LDPD to help alleviate some of the suffering in the Soviet Zone and build up German local government and administrations. The CDU supported nationalization of natural resources, the placing of the monopolies under state control, the creation of a single trade-union movement, and land reform; yet it was this last policy that was to bring the first split within the CDU and between the CDU and the left-wing parties. The CDU and LDPD wanted compensation to be paid to the former landowners, or the land to be given back to them after normality had been restored to Germany and all hunger and need had been overcome. The SMAD was instrumental in removing the leaders of the CDU, Hermes and Schreiber. The new leader was Jakob Kaiser, but he in turn was removed by the SMAD in 1947 for rejecting the Oder–Neiße Line as the new eastern frontier of Germany, and for calling for American Marshall Aid to be made available to the Soviet Zone. Kaiser was replaced by Otto Nuschke on 19 September 1948 as party chairman. From then on the CDU moved increasingly under the influence of the SED and its policies. In the years from 1945 to 1948 it had, in any case, been purged of those members who were active opponents of the SED's policies, and from 1947 its representatives no longer took part in meetings with the CDU from the Western zones.

The CDU, at its party congress in October 1952, committed itself to the *Aufbau des Sozialismus*. It stated: 'The Christian must see the correctness of the basic economic analysis of Marxism-Leninism . . . The CDU thus supports this regime and works steadfastly with it.'[6] The CDU did not condemn the SED for discrimination against Christian students at the universities, or for the suppression of the 1953 uprising. It remained silent over the building of the Berlin Wall and the intervention of the Warsaw Pact countries in the suppression of the reform movement in Czechoslovakia in 1968. When the Churches spoke out in 1954 against the introduction of the *Jugendweihe* (a secular rite that had parallels with church confirmation), the CDU did not support them publicly. Similarly, when the Churches protested against the introduction of civil defence and paramilitary courses into the school curriculum in 1978 or spoke out for church members who were in difficulties with the security service for protest activities in the 1980s, there was no public support from the CDU. Only once, in 1972, did some CDU members of the Volkskammer vote against the abortion law.

The CDU had, in fact, other roles to fulfil. In common with the LDPD, the NDPD and the DBD, it helped to give the appearance of the GDR being a multi-party state, and helped build or maintain links with parties in West Germany and, in particular, abroad. It helped to integrate certain sections of the population, Christians, craftsmen, farmers and small-scale entrepreneurs – particularly in the early years – into the mainstream of SED activities. Many people who did not want to become members of the SED but wished to appear 'socially and politically active' for career or other reasons, also joined the CDU, LDPD, NDPD or DBD. The CDU helped build bridges between the SED and the Churches in the 1960s. The party was active internationally in supporting the SED on the question of peace and stability in Europe, and, domestically in its peace campaigns and demonstrations against Western nuclear weapons. Much of its rhetoric was couched in the same language as was used by the SED (see texts A and B, pp.75, 76).

The CDU had fifty-two members in the Volkskammer. In the first GDR government the CDU took the posts of deputy prime minister, foreign minister, minister of post and telegraphs and minister of health. It was represented in the Council of State and the Council of Ministers.[7] The party had a central and a number of regional and local newspapers and owned two publishing houses.

With the collapse of the GDR in 1989 the West German CDU was placed in a difficult position. The CDU leaders in the East were too compromised by their close contacts with the SED and the former regime to be credible partners. The West German CDU thus set its hopes on the newly formed Deutsche Soziale Union and the Demokratischer Aufbruch,[8] but with the chairman of the DA, Wolfgang Schnur, uncovered as a secret collaborator with the Stasi, that party lost some of its image. The West German CDU had to come back to supporting the East German CDU, both financially and in the preparation and fighting of the first free Volkskammer election in March 1990.[9] Furthermore, the East German CDU had, by then, to a large extent carried out its own 'purge' of its former leaders. It had 'come in from the cold'.

The CDU since 1990

The importance of the collapse of East Germany and the unification process for the image of the CDU had certain parallels with the 'Falklands factor' in Prime Minister Thatcher's second victory. Chancellor Kohl was able to appeal to popular sentiment and play the 'national card'. He was also able to show himself as an outstanding statesman. The collapse of the Eastern bloc presented him with an ideal situation for the seizing of possibly the only chance of reuniting Germany. Less than three weeks after the opening of the Berlin Wall Chancellor Kohl produced his Ten-Point Plan for the eventual unification of Germany (28 November 1989). In it he envisaged the signing of treaties between the Federal Republic and the GDR that would help to bridge the gap between them. Then after perhaps five years they would form a number of confederational structures and institutions. Thereafter a *Staatenbund* (confederation) would be created, and at some point in the future this could lead to a *Bundesstaat*, a single federal state.[10] Events overtook these proposals, however. With the continuing political and economic collapse of the GDR in the spring of 1990, the demonstrable signs that increasing numbers of East Germans were keen on unification (as the slogan on the streets changed from *Wir sind das Volk* to *Wir sind ein Volk*) and, above all, Gorbachev's acceptance that unification could take place, Chancellor Kohl's plan had to be radically changed. He backed the creation of the Allianz für Deutschland (Alliance for Germany) which brought all the conservative parties together, he actively campaigned throughout Germany, garnering massive support for the Alliance, and particularly for the CDU. He was seen by East German voters as a man of integrity who promised them what they wanted: the Deutschmark, economic success and stable government. The CDU/CSU had been successful for the West Germans over many decades; why should they not be equally successful for the East Germans? Why support the SPD, who were not in power in Bonn and had not been for eight years, and who were advocating a much slower process of unification?

Just as Ludwig Erhard had personified the market economy in the 1950s and Willy Brandt the *Ostpolitik* in the 1970s, Chancellor Kohl personified German unification in 1990. A good part of the electoral success of the CDU/CSU in the first all-German elections was built around this personification, the emotional climate after unification and the optimism of many East Germans that they would enjoy rapid improvement in their lives. In fact, the election manifesto did not present much new policy. There was to be modest economic growth and inflation was to be kept low. State-owned industries in East Germany were to be privatized and investment there would come from borrowing. Law and order became an issue, with both CDU and CSU promising a hard line. The election results showed a small drop for the CDU (down 0.5 per cent) but a slight gain (1.4 per cent) for the government coalition (CDU/CSU/FDP). The new government had an overall majority of 134 seats.

By 1991 the government was forced to introduce more taxes, including increases on oil and petrol and a new one of 7.5 per cent on income, the *Solidarbeitrag*, in order to help finance the restructuring of East Germany. This was to be unpopular with the West Germans, who had not been told how much they would personally have to pay for unification, and who had evidently forgotten how much unification had profited the West German economy by providing new markets and new opportunities for banks, insurance agencies, the car industry and the retail chains. The government was unpopular over its policy towards asylum-seekers. Most people, especially in West Germany, felt that too many economic migrants were coming to Germany and claiming asylum status to which they were not entitled. (This large-scale migration had helped the new extreme right-wing party, the *Republikaner*, to gain votes.)[11] The government did subsequently tighten the law, and the number of people entering the country in this manner dropped. In East Germany, despite the purge in 1990, the CDU was perceived by many voters as still having too many people in it who had been associated with the CDU in the former GDR. In 1991 there was a series of losses for the CDU in *Land* elections, which in turn led to the CDU/CSU losing its majority in the Bundesrat.

The 1994 Bundestag elections on 16 October saw a drop in support for the CDU/CSU, as well as for the FDP, but increases for SPD, Bündnis 90/Greens and the PDS (see appendix V, p.242). The euphoria in East Germany had gone, and since there was no established tradition of party loyalties the electorate was much more volatile than in the West. The major problem was the high level of unemployment. The East Germans had always experienced full employment – men and women, young and old, fit and handicapped, they had all had work. Psychologically, they were totally unprepared for unemployment or job insecurity, and financially they had few savings to fall back upon. Out of a work-force of 8.5 million in the GDR, 40 per cent were to become unemployed, have to change their jobs, be forced to commute (or even move) to West Germany, or take part in training programmes that often did not lead to their reintegration into the work-force. Those who had work still often did not earn as much as West Germans did for the same work. There was insecurity about increases in rent for their accommodation, and there was much resentment of West German claims for return of property in which East Germans had often lived for decades, and in which they had invested money and effort. The population now began to miss provisions, such as free pre-school education, that it had always taken for granted under the SED regime. It was the government, and particularly the CDU, that many blamed for their plight. Human nature being what it is, memories of the economic situation that united Germany inherited in 1990 had blurred during the intervening four years. Since the situation in East Germany has not changed much since 1994, given that unemployment has risen (to almost 4.7 million across Germany by February 1997) and the the government is calling for austerity to meet the criteria necessary for Germany to join the single European currency in 1999, the present outlook for the CDU/CSU in the 1998 elections is highly uncertain.

Konrad Adenauer – a portrait

Konrad Adenauer was born in Cologne on 5 January 1876. He studied law and economics and embarked on a legal career. In 1906 he joined the Zentrumspartei. He was mayor of Cologne from 1917 to 1933, when he was removed from office by the nazis. He was also a member and president of the Prussian council of state (*Staatsrat*). In 1945 the Americans appointed him mayor of Cologne, but when the British took over (Cologne lay in their zone of occupation) he was dismissed again – they found him difficult to get on with and he stood up too strongly for German interests for their liking. Adenauer joined in creating the new CDU party and as early as 1946 he became party chairman. On 1 September 1948 he was elected president of the Parliamentary Council. On 15 September 1949 Adenauer was elected the first chancellor of the Federal Republic of Germany, yet with the slimmest of majorities – one vote. He was a highly successful chancellor, particularly in anchoring West Germany into the Western bloc – economically through the Coal and Steel Pact and the European Economic Community, and militarily through NATO and the creation of the Bundeswehr as a highly reliable military partner in the Western Alliance. He was re-elected chancellor on numerous occasions and remained in power up to 1963, giving the fledgeling Federal Republic and its democracy both stability and economic success at a highly important stage in its development. It is not surprising that the period 1949–63 is known as the Adenauer era. Important for this period were the deepening of relations and rapprochement with France and the attempt to make good to the state of Israel some of the terrible losses suffered by the Jews of Europe in the Holocaust.

Helmut Kohl – a portrait

Helmut Kohl was born on 3 April 1930 in Ludwigshafen on the Rhine. In the 1950s he studied history and political sciences at universities in Frankfurt-am-Main and Heidelberg and was awarded a doctorate. In 1946 he was one of the founders of the Junge Union, the CDU youth movement, and held a number of offices in it and in the CDU itself. In 1959 he was elected to the *Landtag* for Rhineland-Palatinate. In 1963 he became leader of the CDU group in the *Landtag*. In 1969 he took over as minister president of Rhineland-Palatinate. At the second attempt Helmut Kohl became chairman (*Parteivorsitzender*) of the CDU in 1973 and did much to streamline and modernize the party in the following years. He was put up by the CDU/CSU as their candidate for chancellor in 1976 but was beaten by Helmut Schmidt. (He had, none the less, achieved 48.6 per cent of the votes.) Kohl then gave up his office as minister president and moved to Bonn to head the CDU parliamentary group. On 1 October 1982 he became chancellor. He was to be confirmed in that office in subsequent elections in 1983, 1987, 1990 (when he was for the first time elected by West and East Germans) and 1994. He was the right person in the right place in 1989–90, and will undoubtedly go down in history as the chancellor who reunited the German people in peace and not at the expense of Germany's neighbours (text F, p.72–5). Chancellor Kohl has decided to contest the 1998 Bundestag elections and run again for chancellor. If he succeeds he is likely to continue to work hard for European union.

Sources

CDU in West Germany and unified Germany

Text A: 'Prinzipen der Ökologischen und Sozialen Marktwirtschaft', in CDU, *Freiheit in Verantwortung. Das Grundsatzprogramm* (Bonn, 1994), 40–4

Die Ökologische und Soziale Marktwirtschaft ist ein wirtschafts- und gesellschaftspolitisches Programm für alle. Sie hat ihr geistiges Fundament in der zum christlichen Verständnis des Menschen gehörenden Idee der verantworteten Freiheit und steht im Gegensatz zu sozialistischer Planwirtschaft und unkontrollierten Wirtschaftsformen liberalistischer Prägung. Wir treten für die Ökologische und Soziale Marktwirtschaft ein, weil sie wie keine andere Wirtschafts- und Gesellschaftsordnung unsere Grundwerte Freiheit, Solidarität und Gerechtigkeit verwirklicht. Ihre Grundlagen sind Leistung und soziale Gerechtigkeit, Wettbewerb und Solidarität, Eigenverantwortung und soziale Sicherung. Sie verbindet den Leistungswillen des einzelnen mit dem sozialen Ausgleich in unserer Gesellschaft und schafft im Rahmen ihrer ökologischen Ordnung die Voraussetzungen für die Bewahrung der Schöpfung.

Wir vertrauen auf die schöpferischen Fähigkeiten des Menschen, sich in Freiheit und Verantwortung zu entfalten. Wir wissen, daß der Mensch seine Fähigkeiten mißbrauchen und ohne Rücksicht auf soziale und ökologische Belange wirtschaften kann. Deshalb muß unser Staat Rahmenbedingungen setzen, um die Kräfte der Selbstregulierung in der Wirtschaft zu stärken und alle am Wirtschaftsleben Beteiligten auf die Beachtung sozialer und ökologischer

Erfordernisse zu verpflichten. Dabei sind die Prinzipien des Wettbewerbs und der sozialen sowie ökologischen Ordnung miteinander verbunden und bedingen sich wechselseitig . . .

Markt und Wettbewerb sind zentrale Elemente unserer Wirtschaftsordnung und ermöglichen Freiheit durch Dezentralisation von Macht. Der freiheitlichen Demokratie entspricht der Markt als Organisationsform der Wirtschaft. Wettbewerb fördert den Leistungswillen des einzelnen und dient damit zugleich dem Wohl des Ganzen. Markt und Wettbewerb ermöglichen eine effiziente und preisgünstige Versorgung mit Gütern und Dienstleistungen, sorgen für eine auf die Wünsche der Konsumenten ausgerichtete Produktion, fördern Innovationen und zwingen zur ständigen Rationalisierung. Mehr Staat und weniger Markt führen demgegenüber vielfach zur Verminderung der Leistungsbereitschaft der Leistungsfähigen und damit zu weniger Wohlfahrt und weniger Freiheit für alle. Allerdings kann der Markt nicht allein aus sich soziale Gerechtigkeit bewirken. Die Leistungsgerechtigkeit des Markts ist nicht identisch mit der sozialen Gerechtigkeit. Die Ökologische und Soziale Marktwirtschaft fügt deshalb Marktordnung und Ordnung der sozialen Leistungen zu einem ordnungspolitischen Ganzen zusammen. Dabei muß der Grundsatz gelten: Soviel Markt wie möglich, um Eigeninitiative, Leistungsbereitschaft und Selbstverantwortung des einzelnen zu stärken, und soviel Staat wie nötig, um Wettbewerb und die soziale und ökologische Ordnung des Marktes zu gewährleisten.

Zu einer freiheitlichen und sozialen Wirtschaftsordnung gehört das sozial verpflichtete Privateigentum. Privateigentum an Produktionsmitteln ist Bedingung für die wirtschaftliche und sorgsame Nutzung knapper Güter sowie für die Leistungsfähigkeit und Produktivität der Wirtschaft. Die Vertrags-, Gewerbe-, und Niederlassungsfreiheit sowie die Freiheit der Berufswahl sind ebenso grundlegende Voraussetzungen für freie wirtschaftliche Betätigung wie die Chance des Gewinns und das Risiko des Verlustes.

Soziale Ordnung

Wirtschafts- und Sozialordnung sind untrennbar miteinander verbunden. Sie begrenzen und ergänzen sich gegenseitig. Eine Wirtschaftspolitik ohne soziale Gerechtigkeit gefährdet den sozialen Frieden und führt zugleich zu volkswirtschaftlichen Verlusten und gesellschaftlicher Instabilität. Unsere soziale Ordnungspolitik verbindet die Prinzipien der Humanität und Wirtschaftlichkeit sowie der Leistungs- und Verteilungsgerechtigkeit. Sie zielt auf die Stärkung der Eigenverantwortung auf persönliche Hilfe und aktive Solidarität.

Wir gestalten unsere soziale Ordnungspolitik nach den Prinzipien der Solidarität und der Subsidiarität. Wir wollen gemeinschaftlich die Risiken absichern, die der einzelne nicht allein und aus eigener Kraft tragen kann. Grundlegende Elemente unserer sozialen Ordnung bleiben Versicherungspflicht und Leistungsgerechtigkeit sowie Dezentralisierung und Selbstverwaltung in den Sozialversicherungen.

Unsere Sozialordnung beruht zu einem erheblichen Teil auf der Solidarität zwischen den Generationen. Angesichts der tiefgreifenden demographischen Veränderungen dürfen wir diesen Generationsvertrag nicht überlasten. Es entspricht unserem Verständnis von Solidarität und Subsidiarität, angesichts des gewachsenen Wohlstandes die Absicherung von zumutbaren Risiken in die Eigenverantwortung des einzelnen zu übertragen.

Von besonderem Wert für unsere soziale Ordnung und für den Erfolg unserer Wirtschaft ist die soziale Partnerschaft. Ein Vergleich mit vielen anderen Industrieländern zeigt, wie hoch die produktive Kraft des sozialen Friedens einzuschätzen ist. Zur sozialen Partnerschaft in der Ökologischen und Sozialen Marktwirtschaft gehören vor allem Mitbestimmung, Selbstverwaltung in der Sozialversicherung, Vermögensbeteiligung der Arbeitnehmerinnen und Arbeitnehmer und die Tarifautonomie.

Die Tarifautonomie ist ein wichtiger Faktor unseres sozialen Friedens. Die Idee der Partnerschaft erfordert funktionsfähige Gewerkschaften und Arbeitgeberverbände. Die Tarifpartner tragen besondere Vertantwortung für Vollbeschäftigung, Geldwertstabilität und Wachstum und damit für das Gemeinwohl. Zu den grundlegenden Elementen unserer sozialen Ordnung gehören ferner ein wirksamer Arbeitnehmerschutz, die Mitbestimmung und Vermögensbeteiligung der Arbeitnehmer und die soziale Partnerschaft ebenso wie die Gleichberechtigung von Frau und Mann.

Ökologische Ordnung

Wir Christliche Demokraten erweitern die Soziale Markwirtschaft um eine ökologische Dimension. Stärker als bisher wollen wir die Kräfte und Steuerungsmechanismen der Marktwirtschaft einsetzen, um einen schonenden Umgang mit Natur und Umwelt zu erreichen.

Ziel der Ökologischen und Sozialen Marktwirtschaft ist es, eine Synthese von Ökonomie, sozialer Gerechtigkeit und Ökologie zu schaffen.

Unsere Verantwortung für die Schöpfung muß auch unser wirtschaftliches Handel leiten. Wir müssen die Vernetzung von Mensch, Natur und Umwelt zum Prinzip unseres Handelns machen. Grundlage der ökologischen Ordnung sind das Verursacher- und das Vorsorgeprinzip. Wir wollen, daß in Zukunft jeder, die Kosten unterlassener Umweltvorsorge und der Inanspruchnahme von Umwelt tragen muß, die aus seinem Verhalten als Produzent oder Konsument entstehen. Das ist nur dann gewährleistet, wenn sich diese Kosten in ökologisch ehrlichen Preisen niederschlagen. Damit setzen wir Signale und schaffen Anreize zu umweltschonendem Verhalten.

Marktwirtschaftliche Anreize und das gesetzliche Ordnungsrecht sind die Instrumente zur Verwirklichung dieser Ziele. Über beide Instrumente kann die Knappheit der Naturgüter erfaßt werden. Ausgehend von der Verantwortung des einzelnen in der Ökologischen und Sozialen Marktwirtschaft treten wir dafür ein, zunächst alle Chancen zur Kooperation zu nutzen, bevor staatliche Regelungen eingesezt werden müssen. Wir werden auch künftig das ökologische Ordnungsrecht mit gesetzlichen Ge- und Verboten, Grenzwerten, Auflagen und Genehmigungsfordernissen zur wirkungsvollen Abwehr von unmittelbaren Gefahren für Mensch und Umwelt benötigen ...

Wir Christliche Demokraten werben für ein neues Verständnis von Wohlstand und Wachstum. Wesentlicher Bestandteil des Wohlstandes ist eine gesunde und lebenswerte Umwelt. Wachsum bedeutet weitaus mehr als nur die Mehrung von Gütern und Dienstleistungen. Unser neues Verständnis von Wachstum schließt die schonende Nutzung der natürlichen Ressourcen durch den Einsatz modernster Produktionsmethoden und den Weg ökologisch ehrlicher Preise für die Inanspruchnahme von Umwelt ein.

Vocabulary

die Prägung	character, nature, hallmark
die Grundwerte	basic values
die Schöpfung	creation (relig.)
der Belang (-e)	importance, significance
entfalten	to develop
die Rahmenbedingungen	framework conditions
der Wettbewerb	competition

wechselseitig	mutually
preisgünstig	cheap
die Gewerbefreiheit	freedom of trade
die Niederlassungsfreiheit	freedom to establish (a business)
die Geldwertstabilität	stability of the currency
schonend	taking care of, caring
das Verursacherprinzip	the firm (etc) causing the damage pays the costs
das Vorsorgeprinzip	principle of precautions taken to prevent damage
unterlassen	neglected
die Inanspruchnahme (no plural)	claims, damages
die Grenzwerte	limits
die Auflage	condition
die Mehrung	increase
die Dienstleistungen	services

Text B: 'Die Vereinbarkeit von Familie und Beruf verbessern', in CDU, *Das Grundsatzprogramm. Freiheit in Verantwortung* (Bonn, 1994), 23–5

Wir treten dafür ein, daß Frauen und Männer Familie und Beruf besser vereinbaren können. Frauen haben den gleichen Anspruch wie Männer, Familie und Beruf zu vereinbaren. Viele Frauen und zunehmend auch Männer widmen sich vorübergehend oder ganz der Arbeit in der Familie und der Kindererziehung. Dies bedeutet Sicherheit und Geborgenheit für Kinder. Die vielfältigen Anforderungen in diesem Bereich bringen persönliche Bereicherung aber auch eine große Arbeitsbelastung und noch immer finanzielle Nachteile mit sich.

Jährlich werden mehr Stunden Haus- und Familienarbeit als Erwerbsarbeit geleistet. Wir Christliche Demokraten setzen uns dafür ein, daß diese Leistung stärker anerkannt wird. Die in Haus- und Familienarbeit erworbenen Kompetenzen müssen als Qualifikation bewertet werden. Auch Mütter und Väter, die ihre Kinder alleine erziehen, müssen stärker als bisher die Unterstützung der Gesellschaft erfahren. Das Erziehungsgeld, der Erziehungsurlaub, sowie die Anerkennung von Erziehungs- und Pflegezeiten in der Rentenversicherung sind Schritte zur Verwirklichung unseres Ziels der sozialen Anerkennung und Absicherung von Familienarbeit und müssen weiter ausgebaut werden. Es ist eine Aufgabe sowohl der Tarifpartner in Wirtschaft und öffentlicher Verwaltung als auch der Politik, die Rahmenbedingungen für die Vereinbarkeit von Familie und Beruf zu verbessern. Betriebe und Gemeinden müssen mehr und flexiblere Betreuungseinrichtungen für Kinder der verschiedenen Altersgruppen bereitstellen. Die bessere Vereinbarung von Familie und Beruf liegt auch im Interesse der Entwicklung der Kindergeneration.

Wir treten für eine Ausweitung des Elternurlaubs und unbezahlte Freistellungszeiten, auch für die Pflege von Angehörigen, ein. Es müssen mehr qualifizierte Teilzeitarbeitsplätze und flexiblere betriebliche und tarifvertägliche Arbeitszeitregelungen für Frauen und Männer geschaffen werden. Wir wollen dazu beitragen, daß die Arbeitswelt familiengerechter wird. Erziehungsarbeit bedeutet nicht den endgültigen Verzicht auf Erwerbsarbeit. Wir wollen Wahlfreiheit auch dadurch ermöglichen, daß wir den Wiedereinstieg in den Beruf erleichtern. Wir setzen uns für ein breites Angebot an Weiterbildungsmöglichkeiten ein, damit auch während der Familienphase der Kontakt zum Berufsleben erhalten bleibt.

Vocabulary

vereinbaren	to co-ordinate
der Anspruch	right
vorübergehend	temporarily
die Bereicherung	enrichment
die Erwerbsarbeit	paid employment
das Erziehungsgeld	child allowance
die Pflegezeit	time spent in caring for someone

Text C: CDU-Bundesgeschäftsstelle, *Wir sichern Deutschlands Zukunft. Regierungsprogramm von CDU und CSU* (Bonn, 1994), 48–50

Das Ende des Ost-West-Konflikts hat unseren Frieden und unsere Freiheit sicherer gemacht. Zugleich sehen wir uns aber einer Vielzahl neuer weltpolitischer Risiken und Gefährdungen gegenüber: Dazu gehören kriegerische Auseinandersetzungen – auch mitten in Europa – die dadurch ausgelösten Flüchtlings- und Wanderungsbewegungen, grenzüberschreitende Gefährdungen der inneren

Sicherheit und weltweite Belastungen der Umwelt. Kein Staat kann diese Herausforderungen allein bewältigen. In Europa werden wir Frieden und Freiheit, wirtschaftlichen Wohlstand und soziale Sicherheit, innenpolitische Stabilität und eine intakte Umwelt nur durch gemeinsames und solidarisches Handeln auf Dauer bewahren können.

CDU und CSU sind daher entschlossen, den Prozeß der europäischen Einigung kraftvoll und zielstrebig voranzubringen. Die Europäische Union ist der Kern einer stabilen Friedens- und Freiheitsordnung.

Deutschland kann nur im Bündnis mit seinen Freunden und Partnern seine Sicherheit gewährleisten. CDU und CSU wollen die Atlantische Allianz weiter stärken. Sie bleibt unverzichtbarer Garant für Sicherheit und Stabilität in ganz Europa. Jedem Sonderweg, der uns aus der westlichen Staatengemeinschaft herausführen würde, erteilen wir eine klare Absage. Wir bekennen uns zu unserer Verantwortung als Mitglied der Vereinten Nationen und in der Einen Welt.

Europa vereinen staat Sonderwege gehen

Wichtigstes Ziel der Europapolitik von CDU und CSU ist es, die Europäische Union auf der Grundlage des Maastrichter Vertrages zu festigen und weiterzuentwickeln.

– Wir wollen den Aufbau der Europäischen Union im Inneren wie nach außen vorantreiben. Die politische und wirtschaftliche Integration muß ergänzt werden durch eine gemeinsame Außen- und Sicherheitspolitik, damit Europa auch in diesen Bereichen handlungsfähig wird. Die deutsch-französische Freundschaft bleibt dabei Motor der Integration und Schlüsselfaktor europäischer Sicherheit,

– CDU und CSU haben Föderalismus und Subsidiarität als Struktur- und Ordnungsprinzipien Europas durchgesetzt. Die Europäische Union darf nur Aufgaben übernehmen, die nicht auf der Ebenen der Regionen und Mitgliedstaaten gelöst werden können. Wo nötig, müssen auch Kompetenzen zurückverlagert werden.

Wir werden dafür sorgen, daß Europa nicht von Bürokratie und Zentralismus bestimmt wird. Die Europäische Union muß freiheitlich, demokratisch, föderal und subsidiär als ein 'Europa der Bürger' gestaltet werden. Diese Grundsätze wollen wir im Hinblick auf die Regierungskonferenz 1996 umsetzen. Insbesondere fordern wir eine klare Abgrenzung der Zuständigkeiten zwischen europäischer Ebene, Bund und Ländern.

– Zur Stärkung ihrer Handlungsfähigkeit muß die Europäische Union institutionell weiterentwickelt werden. Dabei wollen wir die Rechte des Europäischen Parlaments stärken.

– Wir wollen die Zusammenarbeit in der Innen- und Rechtspolitik verstärken. CDU und CSU setzen sich für den raschen Ausbau von EUROPOL zu einem Europäischen Polizeiamt mit den notwendigen Handlungsmöglichkeiten ein. Wir fordern einheitliche Sicherheitsstandards an den Außengrenzen der Europäischen Union und Rauschgiftkontrollen sowie Rechtshilfe und Auslieferungsverfahren nach gemeinsamen Regeln. CDU und CSU treten dafür ein, in der Europäischen Union einheitliche Maßstäbe durchzusetzen, nach denen straffällig gewordene Ausländer rasch in ihre Heimatländer abgeschoben werden können.

– Wir wollen eine gemeinsame Asylpolitik und eine gerechtere Verteilung der entstehenden Lasten zwischen den Mitgliedstaaten der Europäischen Union. Die Anerkennung von Asylanträgen sollte nach einheitlichen Maßstäben erfolgen. Flüchtlinge müssen gleichmäßiger als bisher auf die Mitgliedstaaten verteilt werden.

– Wir wollen die Wettbewerbsfähigkeit deutscher Unternehmen durch gemeinsame europäische Anstrengungen zum Ausbau der Kommunikations- und Verkehrsinfrastruktur, durch die Förderung von Forschung und Entwicklung sowie durch den Abbau wettbewerbsverzerrender Regelungen in der Europäischen Union verbessern. Der deutschen Landwirtschaft muß im gemeinsamen europäischen Markt eine zukunftsfähige Entwicklung ermöglicht werden.

– CDU und CSU wollen durch eine gemeinsame, stabile europäische Währung wirtschaftliches Wachstum fördern und insbesondere auch die Wettbewerbsposition der deutschen exportorientierten Wirtschaft verbessern. CDU und CSU treten dafür ein, daß sich die Währungspolitik im geeinten Europa an dem bewährten Modell der Deutschen Bundesbank orientiert. Am Ziel der Währungsunion halten wir fest; sie wird dann in Kraft treten, wenn die Stabilitätsbedingungen des Maastrichter Vertrages ohne Abstriche erfüllt sind.

– Wir wollen der sozialen Dimension Europas neue Impulse geben. Auch in der Sozialpolitik gilt: Europa lebt von seiner Vielfalt. Das heißt, in Deutschland erreichte Standards werden nicht vermeintlichen Harmonisierungszwängen geopfert. Mit CDU und CSU wird es ein soziales Dumping in Europa nicht geben. Vielmehr geht es darum, Schritt für Schritt soziale Mindestbedingungen in den Ländern der Gemeinschaft zu verwirklichen.

– Die deutschen Heimatvertriebenen, Flüchtlinge und Aussiedler haben einen wesentlichen Beitrag zum Aufbau von Staat und Gesellschaft geleistet. CDU und CSU treten für das Recht auf die Heimat als unabdingbares Menschenrecht ein und verurteilen jede Form von Vertreibung. Zu einer freiheitlichen, friedlichen und gerechten Ordnung in Europa gehören Volksgruppenrechte und Minderheitenschutz. Bei der Aussöhnung mit unseren östlichen Nachbarn kommt den Heimatvertriebenen, den in Mittel-, Ost- und Südosteuropa lebenden Deutschen sowie der jungen Generation eine besondere Aufgabe zu.

– Wir halten am Recht der Spätaussiedler fest, nach Deutschland zu kommen.

Vocabulary

grenzüberschreitend	cross-border
bewältigen	to overcome
intakte Umwelt	sound environment
zurückverlagert	moved back
Rauschgiftkontrollen	drug (narcotics) controls
die Währungspolitik	fiscal policy
ohne Abstriche	without cuts
die Währungsunion	currency union
der Minderheitenschutz	protection of minorities

Text D: 'Unsere Verantwortung für die eine Welt. Zu Frieden und Sicherheit beitragen', in CDU, *Freiheit in Verantwortung. Das Grundsatzprogramm* (Bonn, 1994), 91–5

Oberstes Ziel unserer Friedens- und Sicherheitspolitik ist es, Freiheit und Frieden als Voraussetzung für ein menschenwürdiges Leben zu sichern und zu fördern. Internationaler Dialog, Konfliktverhütung, und Krisenmanagement, Ausbau der internationalen Rüstungskontrolle und weltweite Verminderung der Rüstungspotentiale sind zentrale Elemente unserer Politik.

Sicherheit bedeutet für uns mehr als militärische Sicherung. Unser Verständnis von Sicherheitspolitik richtet sich auf alle politischen, wirtschaftlichen, ökologischen, militärischen und kulturellen Anstrengungen, die das friedliche Zusammenleben der Völker zum

Ziel haben. Hierzu gehören der völkerrechtliche Schutz der Menschen- und Bürgerrechte, die Beilegung religiöser und ethnischer Konflikte, die Verhinderung ökologischer Zerstörungen und die Bekämpfung der international organisierten Kriminalität.

Die wirtschaftliche Entwicklung und die Überwindung sozialer Spannungen sind wichtige Voraussetzungen zur Lösung von Nationalitätenkonflikten. Eine wesentliche Bedingung für den Frieden ist die allseitige Bereitschaft zum Gewaltverzicht und zur bedingten Achtung der Menschen- und Bürgerrechte ebenso wie der Schutz von ethnischen und religiösen Minderheiten. Wir treten für das Selbstbestimmungsrecht der Völker und im Rahmen dessen für ein internationales Volksgruppen- und Minderheitenrecht, das Recht auf die Heimat, eigene Sprache und Kultur ein. Völkervertreibungen jeder Art müssen international geächtet und verletzte Rechte anerkannt werden.

Wir Deutschen sind bereit und in der Lage, unserer gewachsenen außenpolitischen Verantwortung gerecht zu werden. Deutschland muß wie alle anderen Partner der europäischen Verteidigung an den gemeinsamen Aufgaben im Rahmen des NATO-Bündnisses teilnehmen und die Rechte und Pflichten, die es mit dem Beitritt zu den Vereinten Nationen übernommen hat, in vollem Umfang wahrnehmen können. Wir wollen, daß sich Deutschland im Rahmen der Charta der Vereinten Nationen an Aktionen der UNO, NATO, WEU und KSZE zur Wahrung und Wiederherstellung des Friedens beteiligen kann.

Wir sind uns des hohen Beitrages bewußt, den unsere Bundeswehr zum Erhalt des Friedens und der Freiheit leistet. Die Bundeswehr trägt entscheidend dazu bei, die politische Handlungs- und Bündnisfähigkeit Deutschlands zu erhalten. Ihr Verfassungsauftrag spiegelt die Wertgrundlage deutscher Sicherheitspolitik wider. Die Bundeswehr schützt Deutschland und seine Staatsbürger vor politischer Erpressung und äußerer Gefahr; sie fördert die militärische Stabilität und die Integration Europas. Die Bundeswehr verteidigt Deutschland und seine Verbündeten, sie dient dem Frieden und der internationalen Sicherheit im Einklang mit der Charta der Vereinten Nationen; sie hilft bei Katastrophen und unterstützt humanitäre Aktionen. Die Bundeswehr muß mit ausreichenden Mitteln ausgestattet sein, um ihren Auftrag erfüllen zu können. Wir treten für die Aufrechterhaltung der Wehrpflicht ein. Es ist Bürgerpflicht, für Freiheit und Sicherheit einzutreten. Als Bürger in Uniform verdienen die Soldaten der Bundeswehr unsere volle Unterstützung.

Wir wollen, daß die Europäische Union künftig eine größere Verantwortung im Rahmen der europäischen Friedenssicherung übernimmt. Bei der Wahrung von Sicherheit und Frieden in und für Europa bleiben wir auch in Zukunft auf die Partnerschaft mit unseren nordamerikanischen Verbündeten und deren militärische Präsenz in Europa angewiesen. Wir wollen mit unseren Freunden und Partnern ein Netz europäischer Sicherheit knüpfen, in dem sich NATO, WEU und KSZE ergänzen.

Die Verteidigung der Mitgliedsstaaten der NATO bleibt auch in Zukunft der primäre politische und militärische Zweck des Bündnisses. Dazu gehört die Beibehaltung der nuklearen Schutzgarantien für die Mitgliedstaaten. Deutschland bleibt als nichtnuklearer Staat auch weiterhin auf den Schutz durch die westlichen Nuklearstaaten, vor allem die USA, angewiesen. Der Schutz vor nuklearer Erpressung ist durch die weltweite Verbreitung von Technologien, die auch anderen Staaten die Verfügungsgewalt über Massenvernichtungsmittel ermöglicht, für Deutschland und Europa von großer Bedeutung ...

Unsere Partnerschaft mit den USA liegt auch angesichts der stark gestiegenen Bedeutung der internationalen Wirstchafts-, Finanz- und Handelspolitik in deutschem Interesse. Die Fortentwicklung der Institutionen Weltbank, Internationaler Währungsfonds und GATT erfordert die vertrauensvolle Zusammenarbeit mit den USA.

Vocabulary

die Voraussetzung	precondition
die Konfliktverhütung	conflict prevention
der Gewaltverzicht	renunciation of force
das Selbstbestimmungsrecht	right to self-determination

Text E: 28 May 1957: Erklärung des Bundeskanzlers Adenauer vor dem amerikanischen Repräsentantenhaus (Bonn, *Bulletin 1957*, no. 100, 1 June 1957), 898–9

Die Bundesrepublik Deutschland ist ein junger Staat – noch keine acht Jahre alt – und er ist noch unfertig: er ist solange unvollständig, als die Wiedervereinigung mit den 17 Millionen Deutschen in der sowjetisch besetzten Zone nicht vollzogen ist. Erst seit drei Jahren sind wir souverän, sind wir selbst Herren unserer politischen Entscheidungen.

Als der totalitäre Nationalsozialismus zusammenbrach, nachdem er der Welt und dem deutschen Volk unsägliche Schmerzen zugefügt hatte, hinterließ er ein Chaos: Millionen von Toten und Krüppeln, zehn Millionen Menschen, die man aus ihrer angestammten Heimat, den deutschen Ostgebieten, vertrieben hat, verbrannte Städte, zerstörte Industrien und Verkehrswege, eine ruinierte Wirtschaft, eine nur noch in den Gemeinden notdürftig funktionierende Verwaltung, ratlose Menschen und vor allem eine der Gefahr eines zerstörenden Nihilismus ausgesetzte Jugend.

Das deutsche Volk ging an die Arbeit, bei seinen ersten Schritten gestützt durch die westlichen Besatzungsmächte, die im Laufe der Zeit unsere Verbündeten und Freunde wurden. Es baute seine Häuser wieder auf, seine Fabriken, seine Läden, seine Straßen und Bahnen. Die Deutschen arbeiteten hart und sie waren diszipliniert. Sie fanden unschätzbare Hilfe von außen, private und öffentliche, vor allem vom amerikanischen Volk. Das vor zehn Jahren in Angriff genommene große Werk des Marshall-Plans wird in Europa unvergessen bleiben. Es ist mir ein Herzensbedürfnis für dieses alles in dieser Stunde zu danken.

In bewußter Abkehr von allen totalitären Gedanken und Bestrebungen begannen wir, in dem Teile Deutschlands, in dem die demokratischen Freiheitsrechte wiederhergestellt werden konnten, unseren Staat, die Bundesrepublik Deutschland, zu errichten. Wir schufen ihn auf der unverrückbaren Grundlage der Demokratie – mit den berühmten Worten Abraham Lincolns: 'Eine Regierung des Volkes, durch das Volk, für das Volk'.

Freiheit, Achtung der unveräußerlichen Rechte der Persönlichkeit und das Prinzip des Rechtsstaates waren die Grundlagen unserer Verfassung. An die besten Traditionen unseres Volkes konnten wir dabei anknüpfen. Unsere Wirtschaft ordneten wir auf der Grundlage des Wettbewerbs und der sozialen Gerechtigkeit. 'Soziale Marktwirtschaft' nennen wir diese Wirtschaftsordnung, die freies Unternehmertum mit sozialer Verantwortung verbindet. Die Folgen der materiellen Zerstörung versuchten wir durch einen tiefgreifenden 'Lastenausgleich' auf viele Schultern gerecht zu verteilen.

Die größten Probleme aber waren uns durch die Umwelt gestellt, durch die internationale Lage. Die Welt, in die unser Staat, die Bundesrepublik, hineingewachsen war, war in zwei Lager geteilt. Diese Lage stellt unser Volk vor die bedeutendste Entscheidung, die es zu treffen hatte. Es entschied ohne Zögern – und das ist der Sinn der Wahlen zum ersten Bundestag 1949 – für die Freiheit gegen die

Sklaverei, für die Würde des Einzelmenschen gegen das Kollektiv, für das Recht gegen die Willkür. In unserem freigewählten Parlament ist schon seit 1953 kein einziger Kommunist.

In wiederholten Entscheidungen haben die Deutschen der Bundesrepublik mit großer Mehrheit die unauflösliche Zugehörigkeit des deutschen Volkes zur freien Welt bekräftigt. Ausdruck dieser Gesinnung ist vor allem auch unser Bekenntnis zur Einigung Europas. Wir traten daher dem Straßburger Europarat und der OEEC bei. Wir beteiligten uns an der Schaffung der Europäischen Kohle- und Stahlgemeinschaft, an dem Versuch der Schaffung einer Europäischen Verteidigungsgemeinschaft und einer europäischen politischen Gemeinschaft, und wir hoffen daß der Gemeinsame Markt und EURATOM bald von den Parlamenten aller sechs Länder ratifiziert sein werden.

Wir haben uns all diesen Werken in dem Bewußtsein angeschlossen, daß sie eine unlösliche Bindung an die Welt der Freiheit bedeuten. Schon als im Jahre 1948 in unserem 'Parlamentarischen Rat' unsere Verfassung entworfen wurde, sahen wir eine Bestimmung vor, nach der durch ein einfaches Gesetz Teile unserer Souveränität auf eine europäische Gemeinschaft übertragen werden können. Das war eine Absage an die Vorstellung, daß der Nationalstaat ein zur politischen Ordnung Europas heute noch geeignetes Prinzip sei. Dieses Prinzip ist Europa in der Vergangenheit in vielen Kriegen teuer zu stehen gekommen.

Mit der freien Welt teilen wir die Gefahr, die dieser drohen: Gefahren für den Frieden. Als ein Land, durch dessen lebendigen Organismus jetzt eine Trennungslinie geht, die ein Teil des Eisernen Vorhangs, ist, sind wir uns dieser Gefahren besonders bewußt. Wir bedürfen deshalb der Sicherung. Diese Sicherung finden wir in dem mächtigen nordatlantischen Bündnis, da in der moralischen, politischen, wirtschaftlichen und militärischen Kraft der Vereinigten Staaten seinen Hauptrückhalt hat. Die NATO ist ein in Einklang mit den Grundsätzen der Vereinten Nationen stehendes Instrument zur Wahrung der Freiheit, das die westliche Welt sich geschaffen hat, nachdem die Sowjets einen mit soviel Sorgfalt wie Idealismus ausgedachten Sicherheitsmechanismus der Vereinten Nationen weitgehend lahm gelegt haben. Auch wir haben nichts anderes als die Verteidigung unserer Freiheit im Sinn, wenn wir uns nach Kräften bemühen, unseren Beitrag zu der militärischen Rüstung des Bündnisses zu leisten.

Niemand in Deutschland, bei Gott niemand, spielt mit dem

Gedanken der Gewaltanwendung oder des Krieges, auch nicht in der Frage der deutschen Wiedervereinigung, die uns doch so brennend am Herzen liegt. Das Grauen der Bombennächte des zweiten Weltkrieges, die furchtbaren Verwüstungen unserer Heimat sind noch frisch in unser aller Erinnerung.

Wenn heute zwischen dem amerikanischen und dem deutschen Volk ein Verhältnis verständnisvollen Einvernehmens, ja – ich wage zu sagen – herzlicher Freundschaft besteeht, so ist das nicht die Folge eines zufälligen Zusammentreffens vorübergehender Interessen, sondern es beruht auf einer Gemeinsamkeit tiefer Überzeugungen. Es beruht auf der einzigen Macht, die freie Menschen dazu bringt, ihr Schicksal dauerhaft miteinander zu verbinden, auf Vertrauen. Das deutsche Volk bringt Ihnen dieses Vertrauen entgegen. Bewahren Sie ihm Ihr Vertrauen, darum bitte ich Sie.

Vocabulary

unsäglich	unspeakable
die Besatzungsmächte	occupying powers
unverrückbar	unshakeable
unveräußerlich	inalienable
ohne Zögern	without hesitation
die Willkür	arbitrariness, arbitrary act
die Wahrung	preservation, safeguarding
die Gemeinsamkeit	commonality, common ground

Text F: 'Tag der Deutschen Einheit (3. Oktober 1990). Ansprache von Bundeskanzler Dr. Helmut Kohl über Rundfunk und Fernsehen am 2. Oktober 1990', in Bundesministerium für innerdeutsche Beziehungen (ed.), *Texte zur Deutschlandpolitik, Reihe III/Band 8b – 1990* (Bonn, Deutscher Bundesverlag, 1991), 698–700

Liebe Landsleute!
In wenigen Stunden wird ein Traum Wirklichkeit. Nach über vierzig bitteren Jahren der Teilung ist Deutschland, unser Vaterland, wieder vereint. Für mich ist dieser Augenblick einer der glücklichsten in meinem Leben; und aus vielen Briefen und Gesprächen weiß ich, welche große Freude auch die allermeisten von Ihnen empfinden.

An einem solchen Tag richten wir unseren Block nach vorn. Doch bei aller Freude wollen wir zunächst an jene denken, die unter der Teilung Deutschlands besonders zu leiden hatten. Familien wurden grausam auseinandergerissen. In den Haftanstalten wurden politische Gefangene eingekerkert. Menschen starben an der Mauer.

Das alles gehört glücklicherweise der Vergangenheit an. Es soll sich niemals wiederholen Deshalb dürfen wir es auch nicht vergessen. Wir schulden die Erinnerung den Opfern. Und wir schulden sie unseren Kindern und Enkeln. Solche Erfahrungen sollen ihnen für immer erspart bleiben.

Aus dem gleichen Grunde vergessen wir auch nicht, wem wir die Einheit unseres Vaterlandes zu verdanken haben. Aus eigener Kraft allein hätten wir es nicht geschafft. Viele haben dazu beigetragen. Wann je hatte ein Volk die Chance, Jahrzehnte der schmerzlichen Trennung auf so friedliche Weise zu überwinden? In vollem Einvernehmen mit unseren Nachbarn stellen wir die Einheit Deustchlands in Freiheit wieder her.

Wir danken unseren Partnern, wir danken unseren Freunden. Wir danken insbesondere den Vereinigten Staaten von Amerika, allen voran Präsident George Bush. Wir danken unseren Freunden in Frankreich und in Großbritannien. Sie haben in schwierigen Zeiten stets zu uns gehalten. Sie haben jahrzehntelang die Freiheit des Westteils von Berlin geschützt. Sie haben unser Ziel unterstützt, die Einheit in Freiheit wiederzuerlangen. Ihnen bleiben wir auch in Zukunft in Freundschaft verbunden.

Dank schulden wir auch den Reformbewegungen in Mittel-, Ost- und Südosteuropa. Vor gut einem Jahr ließ Ungarn die Flüchtlinge ausreisen. Damals wurde der erste Stein aus der Mauer geschlagen. Die Freiheitsbewegungen in Polen und der Tschechoslowakei haben den Menschen in der DDR Mut gemacht, für ihr Recht auf Selbstbestimmung einzutreten. Jetzt gehen wir daran, eine dauerhafte Aussöhnung zwischen dem deutschen und dem polnischen Volk zu verwirklichen.

Wir danken Präsident Gorbatschow. Er hat das Recht der Völker auf den eigenen Weg erkannt. Ohne diese Entscheidung hätten wir den Tag der Deutschen Einheit nicht so bald erlebt.

Daß dieser Tag schon jetzt kommt, ist besonders jenen Deutschen zu verdanken, die mit der Kraft ihrer Freiheitsliebe die SED-Diktatur überwanden. Ihre Friedfertigkeit und ihre Besonnenheit bleiben beispielhaft.

Wir Deutschen haben aus der Geschichte gelernt. Wir sind ein friedens-, wir sind ein freiheitsliebendes Volk, und nie werden wir unsere Demokratie den Feinden des Friedens und der Freiheit schutzlos ausliefern. Für uns gehören Vaterlandsliebe, Freiheitsliebe und der Geist guter Nachbarschaft immer zusammen. Wir wollen zuverlässige Partner, wir wollen gute Freunde sein. Dabei gibt es für uns alle auf der Welt nur einen Platz: an der Seite der freien Völker.

Gute Nachbarn wollen wir auch im Innern sein. Aufgeschlossenheit für den Nächsten, Achtung vor dem Andersdenkenden und Verbundenheit mit unseren ausländischen Mitbürgern gehören auch dazu. Unsere freiheitliche Demokratie muß von Vielfalt, von Toleranz, von Solidarität geprägt sein.

Solidarität müssen wir vor allem als Deutsche jetzt untereinander beweisen. Vor uns liegt – jeder weiß dies – eine schwierige Wegstrecke. Wir wollen diesen Weg gemeinsam gehen. Wenn wir zusammenhalten und auch zu Opfern bereit sind, haben wir alle Chancen auf einen gemeinsamen Erfolg.

Die wirtschaftlichen Voraussetzungen in der Bundesrepublik sind heute ausgezeichnet. Noch nie waren wir besser vorbereitet als jetzt, die wirtschaftlichen Aufgaben der Wiedervereinigung zu meistern. Hinzu kommen Fleiß und Leistungsbereitschaft bei den Menschen in der bisherigen DDR. Durch unsere gemeinsamen Anstrengungen, durch die Politik der Sozialen Marktwirtschaft, werden schon in wenigen Jahren aus Brandenburg, aus Mecklenburg-Vorpommern, aus Sachsen, aus Sachsen-Anhalt und aus Thüringen blühende Landschaften geworden sein.

Die wirtschaftlichen Probleme, dessen bin ich gewiß, werden wir lösen können: gewiß nicht über Nacht, aber doch in einer überschaubaren Zeit. Noch wichtiger ist jedoch, daß wir Verständnis füreinander haben, daß wir aufeinander zugehen. Wir müssen ein Denken überwinden, daß Deustchland immer noch in ein 'Hüben' und ein 'Drüben' aufteilt.

Über vierzig Jahre SED-Diktatur haben gerade auch in den Herzen der Menschen tiefe Wunden geschlagen. Der Rechtsstaat hat die Aufgabe, Gerechtigkeit und inneren Frieden zu schaffen. Hier stehen wir alle vor einer schwierigen Bewährungsprobe. Schweres Unrecht muß gesühnt werden, doch wir brauchen auch die Kraft zur inneren Aussöhnung.

Ich bitte alle Deutschen: Erweisen wir uns der gemeinsamen Freiheit würdig. Der 3. Oktober ist ein Tag der Freude, des Dankes und der Hoffnung. Die junge Generation in Deutschland hat jetzt – wie kaum eine Generation vor ihr – alle Chancen auf ein ganzes Leben in Frieden und Freiheit.

Wir wissen, daß unsere Freude von vielen Menschen in der Welt geteilt wird. Sie sollen wissen, was uns in diesem Augenblick bewegt: Deutschland ist unser Vaterland, das vereinte Europa unsere Zukunft. Gott segne unser deutsches Vaterland!

Vocabulary

einkerkern	to imprison
die Besonnenheit	level-headedness
die Fleiß	industriousness
aufeinander zugehen	meet each other
Hüben und Drüben	this side and that
die Bewährungsprobe	test
sühnen	atone, expiate

CDU in East Germany

Text A: 'Rahmenplan für die Arbeit der CDU in Vorbereitung des 14. Parteitages', in Sekretariat des Hauptvorstandes der Christlich-Demokratischen Union Deutschlands (ed.), *Dokumente der CDU, Band 11 – 1976–1981* (East Berlin, Union Verlag, 1981), 19–20

Vor unserer Partei wie vor allen in der Nationalen Front der DDR vereinten Kräften steht die Aufgabe, in der Deutschen Demokratischen Republik weiterhin die entwickelte sozialistische Gesellschaft zu gestalten und so grundlegende Voraussetzungen für den allmählichen Übergang zum Kommunismus zu schaffen. Alle Mitglieder zu noch bewußterem schöpferischen Einsatz bei der Verwirklichung dieser Aufgabe zu gewinnen und politisch zu befähigen, ist das Hauptziel unserer Parteiarbeit in Vorbereitung des 14. Parteitages.

Treue zum Sozialismus bedeutet und verlangt in der neuen Entwicklungsetappe nicht nur die tatkräftige Mitarbeit an seiner Stärkung, sondern zugleich die bewußte Bejahung und Mitgestaltung seiner kommunistischen Perspektive. Indem der Sozialismus planmäßig und dadurch die höhere Phase der neuen Gesellschaftsordnung vorbereitet wird, werden seine Vorzüge – seine Menschlichkeit, seine friedenssichernde und völkerverbindende Kraft, die durch ihn gewährleistete soziale Sicherheit und Geborgenheit für alle, seine lebendige Demokratie und die ständige Verbesserung des Lebens der Werktätigen – immer wirksamer zur Geltung kommen.

Text B: 'Anschlag auf das elementarste Menschenrecht', in Christlich-Demokratische Union Deutschlands (ed.), *Dokumente der CDU, Band 11* (op. cit.), 78-9

Das Präsidium des Hauptvorstandes der CDU nahm in seiner Sitzung am 16. August 1977 zu der Absicht der USA-Regierung Stellung, die Neutronenbombe zu produzieren. Es erklärt: Die Entwicklung dieser Waffe, die das Leben vernichtet, aber Sachwerte unversehrt lassen soll, ist ein Anschlag auf das elementarste Menschenrecht, das Recht zu leben. Sie entlarvt abermals den barbarischen Charakter des Imperialismus, der den Profit höher stellt als die auf Frieden und Entspannung gerichteten Interessen der Völker.

Es ist eine ebenso zynische wie durchsichtige Lüge, wenn der Bau dieser neuen Massenvernichtungswaffen mit einer von den sozialistischen Ländern drohenden Gefahr begründet wird. Die Staaten der sozialistischen Gemeinschaft kennen kein höheres Ziel als die Festigung des Friedens. Ihnen sind aggressive Pläne wesensfremd. Ihre Friedenspolitik, die entscheidend zum Ergebnis der Konferenz von Helsinki* beitrug und unserem Kontinent die längste Friedensperiode dieses Jahrhunderts sicherte, wird durch immer neue konstruktive Vorschläge für Abrüstung und Entspannung bestimmt . . .

Kein christlicher Bürger darf zu solchen imperialistischen Plänen schweigen. Seine Stimme und seine Aktion müssen sich mit denen aller anderen friedliebenden Kräfte vereinen.

*The meeting of the thirty-five states at which they signed the Helsinki Agreement and created the CSCE.

Vocabulary

tatkräftig	energetic, active
die Geborgenheit	security
die Neutronenbombe	nuclear bomb that kills people but leaves property etc. undamaged
die Sachwerte	real value, property
unversehrt	untouched
entlarven	expose
durchsichtig	transparent
die Massenvernichtungswaffen	weapons of mass destruction

Questions on the Source Texts

CDU in West Germany and unified Germany

Text A

1. Explain the following terms and expressions:
   Ökologische und Soziale Marktwirtschaft
   verantwortete Freiheit
   Solidarität
   die Kräfte der Selbstregulierung in der Wirtschaft
   Prinzipien des Wettbewerbs
   Freiheit durch Dezentralisierung der Macht
   Die Leistungsgerechtigkeit des Marktes ist nicht identisch mit der sozialen Gerechtigkeit
   Subsidiarität
   soziale Partnerschaft
2. What are the main features of the market and competition?
3. Why is social justice so important?
4. What are the main tenets of ecological policy and what does the CDU suggest should be the role of the state in protecting the environment?
5. What is the new CDU concept of growth?

Text B

1. Identify the words which show that the CDU supports women staying at home to look after their children.
2. Why is the party none the less supporting a better integration of activities in the home with paid employment?
3. What measures is the CDU suggesting to help both women and men to combine family duties with work outside the home?

Text C

1. Explain the terms:
   Heimatvertriebene
   Spätaussiedler
2. What are the CDU's main attitudes towards (i) European integration; (ii) the single currency; (iii) centralism and federalism;

(iv) asylum-seekers in a united Europe?
3. What practical steps towards further co-operation in Europe does the CDU suggest?
4. What is the CDU attitude to Germans living outside the borders of the Federal Republic?

Text D

1. Explain the following words and phrases:
   Krisenmanagement
   internationale Rüstungskontrolle
   der völkerrechtliche Schutz der Menschenrechte
   international organisierte Kriminalität
2. What are the main elements of CDU security policies?
3. What elements does the party include in its definition of 'security'?
4. What proposals does the CDU make with respect to ethnic minorities?
5. How does the CDU perceive Germany's new military role?
6. What is the function of the Bundeswehr?
7. How are nuclear weapons perceived by the party?
8. Why is it important for Germany to have a 'partnership' with the USA?

Text E

1. Explain the following phrases and terms:
   eine der Gefahr eines zerstörenden Nihilismus ausgesetzte Jugend
   Marshall Plan
   Europarat
   Europäische Kohle- und Stahlgemeinschaft
   EURATOM
   der Eiserne Vorhang
2. In Adenauer's opinion, why did the West Germans decide to ally themselves with the West?
3. What does Adenauer have to say about the division of Germany?
4. Examine his attitude towards the USA.
5. What role does he want Germany to play in Europe?

Text F

1. Examine the rhetoric of the text.
2. What generalizations are made here?
3. What is the significance of the order of naming of the partners, USA, France and Britain, for their contribution to German unification?
4. What role did the communist bloc countries play in reuniting Germany?
5. The recognition by the chancellor of the significance of the East German dissidents for hastening the collapse of the GDR was honoured by what part of the electoral law in the first all-German elections in December 1990?
6. What did Chancellor Kohl say about 'tolerance'?
7. What did this speech promise the East Germans? To what extent do you think the promises have been kept?
8. Why should Chancellor Kohl say that a united Europe is Germany's future?

CDU in East Germany

Text A

1. What points do you find surprising for a conservative and Christian party?
2. What role is the party and its members to play in East Germany?
3. What does it describe as the 'positive aspects' of the system in the GDR?

Text B

1. What words and phrases show that the CDU was using the vocabulary of the communist system?
2. What image of the communist bloc's attitude to peace does the text convey? Give examples where reality did not coincide with this peaceful image.

Notes

1. Tony Burkett, *Parties and Elections in West Germany* (London, Hurst, 1975), 27.
2. Gerhart Binder, *Das Kaiserreich. Die Weimarer Republik* (Munich, Goldmann Verlag, undated), 172.
3. Werner Konze et al., *Jakob Kaiser. Der Widerstandskämpfer* (Stuttgart, Kohlhammer Verlag, 1967), 231.
4. For details of this activity see Erich Kosthorst, *Jakob Kaiser. Der Arbeiterführer* (Stuttgart and Berlin, Kohlhammer Verlag, 1967).
5. Helmut Kistler, *Die Bundesrepublik Deutschland, Vorgeschichte und Geschichte 1945–1983* (Bonn, Bundeszentrale für politische Bildung, 1992), 67–70.
6. K.-H. Schöneburg, R. Mand, H. Leichtfuß and K. Urban, *Vom Werden unseres Staates*, 2 (East Berlin, Staatsverlag der DDR, 1968), 286–8.
7. See, for example, Sekretariat der Volkskammer (ed.), *Die Volkskammer der Deutschen Demokratischen Republik, 8. Wahlperiode* (East Berlin, Staatsverlag der DDR, 1982), 65, 85, 103, and CDU members of Volkskammer committees, 126–42.
8. Uwe Thaysen, *Der Runde Tisch oder: wo blieb das Volk?* (Opladen, Westdeutscher Verlag, 1990), 126–8.
9. The West German party foundations gave 7.5 million DM to the Volkskammer election campaign. This money was given via the Ministerium für innerdeutsche Beziehungen, Bonn, to the parties in the GDR. The Christian Democrats received 4.5 million DM, whereas the Greens received nothing; Zeno and Sabine Zimmerling, *Neue Chronik der DDR, 4/5* (East Berlin, Verlag Tribüne, 1990), 241.
10. See 'Zehn-Punkte-Programm zur Überwindung der Teilung Deutschlands und Europas. Rede des Bundeskanzlers Helmut Kohl vor dem Deutschen Bundestag am 28. November 1989', *Bulletin* (Presse und Informationsamt der Bundesregierung), 29 November 1989.
11. For a useful overview of the Republikaner see Günter Minnerup, 'Franz Schönhuber and the Re-nationalization of German Politics', in *Debatte*, no. 2 (Oxford and New York, Berg, 1993), 71–94.

Bibliography

Publications in German

Adenauer, Konrad, *Erinnerungen*, 6 vols. (Stuttgart, Deutsche Verlags-Anstalt, 1965–8).
Buchstab, G. and K. Gotto (eds.), *Die Gründung der Union* (Munich, Olzog Verlag, 1990).
Gabriel, Oscar W. and Angelika Vetter, 'Die Chancen der CDU/CSU in den neunziger Jahren', in *Aus Politik und Zeitgeschichte*, 2

February 1996 (Bonn, Bundeszentrale für politische Bildung), 9–19.

Haungs, Peter, 'Die Christlich Demokratische Union Deutschlands und die Christlich-Soziale Union in Bayern', in Hans-Joachim Veen (ed.), *Christlich-demokratische Parteien und konservative Parteien in Westeuropa, 1* (Paderborn, 1983), 9–194.

Haungs, Peter, 'Die CDU: Krise einer modernisierten Volkspartei?', in H.-G. Wehling (ed.), *Parteien in der Bundesrepublik* (Stuttgart, Kohlhammer, 1990), 30–40.

Haungs, Peter, 'Die CDU: Prototyp einer Volkspartei', in Alf Mintzel and Heinrich Oberreuter, *Parteien in der Bundesrepublik Deutschland* (Opladen, Leske + Budrich, 1992).

Kleinmann, Hans-Otto, *Geschichte der CDU, 1945–1982* (Stuttgart, Deutsche Verlags-Anstalt, 1993).

Osterheld, Horst, *Konrad Adenauer. Ein Charakterbild* (Bonn, Eichholz Verlag, 1975).

Perger, Werner, 'Die CDU', *Aus Politik und Zeitgeschichte*, 5 (Bonn, 1992).

Schmidt, J. (ed.), *Die CDU* (Opladen, Leske + Budrich, 1990).

Publications in English

Broughton, David, 'The CDU-CSU in Germany: Is there any Alternative?', in David Hanley (ed.), *Christian Democracy in Europe: A Comparative Perspective* (London and New York, Pinter, 1994), 101–20.

Chandler, William M., 'The Christian Democrats', in Peter H. Merkl (ed.), *The Federal Republic of Germany at Forty* (New York, New York University Press, 1989).

Chandler, William M., 'The Christian Democrats and the Challenge of Unity', in Stephen Padgett (ed.), *Parties and Party Systems in the New Germany* (Aldershot and Brookfield, Dartmouth Publishing Company, 1995), 129–46.

Conradt, David, 'The Christian Democrats in 1990: Saved by Unification?', in Russell J. Dalton (ed.), *The New Germany Votes* (Oxford and Providence, Berg, 1993), 59–75.

Paterson, William, E., 'The Christian Union Parties', in H. G. Peter Wallach and Georg K. Romoser (eds.), *West German Politics in the Mid-Eighties: Crisis and Continuity* (New York, Praeger, 1985).

Pridham, Geoffrey, *Christian Democracy in West Germany: The CDU/CSU in Government and Opposition, 1945–1976* (London, Croom Helm, 1977).

Prittie, Terence, *Adenauer: A Study in Fortitude* (London, Tom Stacey, 1972).

Schwarz, Hans-Peter, *Konrad Adenauer: A German Politician in a Period of War, Revolution and Reconstruction*, vol. 1, *1876–1952* (Providence and Oxford, Berghahn, 1995).

CDU in East Germany

Ditfurth, Christian von, *Blockflöten. Wie die CDU ihre realsozialistische Vergangenheit verdrängt* (Cologne, Kiepenheuer & Witsch, 1994).

Lapp, P. J., *Die Blockparteien im System der DDR* (Melle, Verlag Ernst Knoth, 1988).

Further information may be obtained from:
CDU
Bundesgeschäftsstelle
Abt. Öffentlichkeitsarbeit
Konrad-Adenauer-Haus
Friedrich-Ebert-Allee 73–5
D-53113 Bonn
Tel (0228) 544-0
Fax (0228) 544-216

B. Christlich-Soziale Union

From its beginnings in 1945 the CSU has always shown some differences from the CDU. Initially it was in favour of a strongly centralized, democratically led party whereas, as already explained, the CDU was for a loose association of semi-autonomous groups. The CSU set out to attract Bavarian Catholic voters and members rather than to be non-denominational. Its leaders were Catholic, and in 1947 90.2 per cent of members and 91.3 per cent of its voters were Catholic. It was a party of the middle class that found the Christian social wing of the CDU, as represented through the Ahlener Programme, unacceptable. It committed itself totally to the capitalist/market system before the CDU did. The CSU was soon to be exposed to political competition in its homeland by the Bayernpartei (BP), a protest party that had come into being as large numbers of German expellees from the Eastern Provinces were settled in Bavaria, and did not disappear until the 1960s. The CSU share of the vote at the *Landtag* election of 1950 was only 27.4 per cent in comparison with 52.3 per cent in 1946. It rose slightly to 38.8 per cent in the 1954 *Landtag* elections and was the largest party. From 1956 the party began to modernize itself and change its image.

The 1960s were successful years for the CSU as the party contained and then slowly pushed back its competitors. Part of the reason for the CSU success was the way that from 1957, and particularly under its minister president, Hanns Seidel (1955–61), the so-called 'architect of modern Bavaria', it had developed the industrial and technological base of Bavaria and then had maintained a flourishing entrepreneurial base in the small and medium-sized firms. The party also successfully married the traditional culture and ideology of Bavaria with the new modern economy. Furthermore, the 1960s witnessed the CSU uniting the various Catholic political factions that had been feuding for many decades and thus consolidating the party's own position.

From the 1960s onwards the CSU has been a well-organized, astutely led party which very early introduced new technology into its administrative work. In the 1970s it changed its image from that of a party of farmers, small-time entrepreneurs and craftsmen, with its central support in the small towns and villages, to the party of the wage-earner, of officials, white- and blue-collar workers, as well as of the farmers. It remains a Catholic party. It has formed every Bavarian *Land* government, without the need of a coalition partner, since 1966 and can be regarded as the *Staatspartei*, the party of the state of Bavaria. This is one part of its dual function – the other is to represent Bavarian interests at the heart of federal government when the CDU is in power. What the CSU can never become, however, is anything more than a minority party at federal level. It is doomed to exist always as a junior coalition partner.

In the Bundestag the CDU and CSU form a joint parliamentary group, with the CSU taking up a more right-wing stance than the CDU. When Christian Democrats are in government the CSU is always represented in the cabinet. The two parties agree jointly on a candidate for chancellor, although this has caused friction in the past, for example, between Helmut Kohl and Franz Josef Strauß in 1976 (see 'Franz Josef Strauß – a Portrait', below.) This led to a break in the tacit agreement that the CDU would not put up candidates for election in Bavaria and the CSU would confine its activities to its own *Land*. Strauß, who enjoyed considerable popularity in Bavaria, wanted to be adopted as CDU/CSU candidate for chancellor. The CDU feared that his radical conservative image and rhetoric would lead to defeat, and thus backed Helmut Kohl instead. The CSU announced that it would leave the CDU/CSU party group in the Bundestag. The implication could have been that the two parties would stand in each other's territories and mutually weaken their chances. The CSU gave way and relations returned to normal. In fact Strauß was put up as CDU/CSU chancellor candidate in 1980, but without success.

The CSU since 1990

The reunification of Germany, which the CSU had steadfastly supported for forty-five years, has brought problems for the party. There had been some hopes in the CSU that the CDU would agree to its fielding candidates in Saxony and Thuringia. In fact, the CSU ended up supporting the Deutsche Soziale Union throughout East Germany, and when the DSU failed abysmally (6.3 per cent) in 1990, CSU surrogate expansion was effectively ended. Support for the DSU formally ended in April 1993. With the expansion of the Bundestag to accommodate members from East Germany, the CSU, statistically, has lost influence. This means that the CSU theoretically has less leverage in Bonn and less room to press Bavarian interests at the heart of government. This raised the question once more of the possibility of the CSU standing in all the *Länder* in elections to the Bundestag. After much debate the idea was dropped again – the danger of the CDU standing in Bavaria and splitting the CSU vote was too high, and there was also the risk of a loss of Bavarian identity if the party extended its activities across Germany. The strength of the CSU in federal politics is that it has always been a coalition partner with the CDU, whereas the FDP has not, and the CSU receives more votes in Bavaria than the FDP does nation-wide.

At present the CSU has four ministerial posts in the Bundestag, one of the most influential but most difficult being that of minister of finance, held by Theo Waigel.

Franz Josef Strauß – a portrait

Franz Josef Strauß was born on 6 September 1915 in Munich. He studied history, Latin and Greek after leaving school. He spent the Second World War as a soldier and at the end of hostilities the Americans made him deputy *Landrat* in Schongau in Bavaria. He was one of the founders of the CSU. He was general secretary of his party from 1949 to 1952, from that year to 1961 he was its deputy chairman, and from 1961 its chairman. He was a member of the Bundestag from 1949 to 1978. He was Federal *Minister für besondere Aufgaben,* 1953–5, and took over the newly created Ministry for Atomic Energy. In October 1956 he was moved to the Ministry of Defence and was highly instrumental in the creation and development of the Bundeswehr. He was involved in the so-called *Spiegelaffäre* which led to his resignation at the end of 1962. (The *Spiegel* magazine had published criticism of the Bundeswehr on 10 October. Its offices were subsequently raided by the police, its editor and the author of the article were arrested. There was political and public outrage at what was seen as an attempt to muzzle the press. The FDP left the coalition government in protest.) Strauß became minister of finance in the

Grand Coalition government from 1966 to 1969. Throughout the 1970s Strauß was strongly opposed to the *Ostpolitik* of the SPD/FDP coalition government. Paradoxically, it was this highly conservative and right-wing politician who conducted successful negotiations with the SED and apparently was the go-between and motor for billions of Deutschmarks being granted as credit by the West German banks to the GDR in 1983, with the federal government acting as guarantor. The reason for this bailing out of the East German economy was to keep relations between the Federal Republic and the GDR strong and stable when general instability in East–West relations had arisen as a result of the 'second round' of the Cold War. In 1978 Strauß became minister president of Bavaria. He remained an influential political figure up to his death on 3 October 1988.

Sources

Text A: 'Die CSU kann auf bewährten Grundsätzen aufbauen', in CSU, *Grundsatzprogramm* (Munich, 1994) 15–16

Die Christlich-Soziale Union muß die Grundlagen ihres politischen Denkens und Handelns nicht korrigieren. Die politischen Leitideen von freiheitlichem Rechtsstaat und Sozialer Marktwirtschaft haben sich als überlegen erwiesen. Subsidiarität und Föderalismus waren für die CSU stets die unverzichtbaren Pfeiler einer freiheitlichen Staats- und Gesellschaftsordnung. In allen europäischen Ländern setzt sich die Erkenntnis durch, daß ein in Freiheit geeintes Europa nur auf der Grundlage dieser Bauelemente entstehen kann.

Mittelpunkt der Politik der CSU sind weiterhin der Mensch und seine Freiheit. Denn der Mensch ist nach dem christlichen Menschenbild zur Freiheit, zur Selbstverantwortung bestimmt. Er lebt in der Spannung zwischen Selbstbestimmung und Solidarität. Zur Verantwortung des Menschen gehört, daß er seine Freiheit nicht auf Kosten anderer auslebt, seine Interessen mit dem Gemeinwohl in Übereinstimmung bringt, sich seinen Mitmenschen verpflichtet weiß und solidarisch handelt. Der freie, in seinem Gewissen gebundene, selbst- und mitverantwortliche Bürger, nicht der Untertan und nicht der verantwortungslose Individualist, sind Maßstab unserer Politik. In dieser Wertgebundenheit will die CSU unsere freie und offene Gesellschaft gestalten.

Christliches Menschenbild, Selbstverantwortung in Solidarität und Subsidiarität als die Markenzeichen christlich-sozialer Politik sind als Grundlagen und Ordnungsprinzipien für Staat und Gesellschaft aktueller denn je.

Pp. 52–4

Eine freiheitliche Wirtschafts- und Gesellschaftsordnung ist der Garant der persönlichen Freiheit. Eine auf dem Grundsatz der Vertragsfreiheit aufbauende Privatrechtsordnung ist das Fundament der Marktwirtschaft. Die Freiheit, etwas zu beginnen und aufzubauen, über Privateigentum zu verfügen, gehört zu den unabdingbaren Voraussetzungen sinnvoller Selbstverwirklichung. Privates Eigentum muß rechtlich so abgesichert sein, daß es in seiner materiellen Substanz generationsübergreifend verfügbar bleibt.

Die Soziale Marktwirtschaft hat sich der Planwirtschaft in jeder Hinsicht als überlegen erwiesen. Sie bündelt die schöpferischen Kräfte des Menschen, ihre materielle Ergiebigkeit ist nicht nur die Quelle individuellen Wohlstands, sondern auch Voraussetzung für sozialen Frieden und Humanisierung der Arbeitswelt. Sozialer Friede und ein angemessenes Niveau sozialer Sicherheit sind notwendige Rahmenbedingungen für eine erfolgreiche Volkswirtschaft.

Die Durchsetzung der Sozialen Marktwirtschaft gegen den erbitterten Widerstand der Sozialisten war eine epochale politische Leistung Ludwig Erhards.* Sie ist auch das Modell für den wirtschaftlichen Neuaufbau in Osteuropa. Zur Sozialen Marktwirtschaft gibt es in einer freiheitlichen Gesellschaft keine Alternative.

Die Soziale Marktwirtschaft ist die Wirtschaftsordnung sozial und ökologisch verantworteter Freiheit. Sie entspricht den Idealen einer freiheitlichen Gesellschaft und entspringt der europäischen kulturellen Tradition. Sie gewährt den Unternehmern den Freiraum für den optimalen Einsatz der Produktionsmittel in ihrer persönlichen Verantwortung und auf eigenes Risiko, sie eröffnet den Arbeitnehmern die Chance auf gesellschaftlichen Aufstieg und mehr Einkommen durch Leistung; sie sorgt aber auch für Chancengleichheit und Verminderung sozialer Spannungen.

Die Soziale Marktwirtschaft ist eine anpassungsfähige lebendige Ordnung. Sie war und ist immer offen für notwendige soziale

---

*Minister for Economics under Adenauer, highly influential in the currency reform and the *Wirtschaftwunder*.

Korrekturen. Sie kann auch am besten sachgerechte Antworten auf die wachsenden ökologischen Herausforderungen geben. Es ist Aufgabe der Wirtschaftspolitik, die ökonomische und gesellschaftliche Dynamik mit den gesicherten ökologischen Notwendigkeiten im Einklang zu bringen.

Der Staatsanteil am Bruttosozialprodukt ist in Grenzen zu halten, um die Innovationsfähigkeit der Unternehmen, das Schaffen von Arbeitsplätzen und das Wachstum des privaten Unternehmenssektors zu begünstigen und die Erhaltung unserer wettbewerbsorientierten Wirtschaftsordnung sicherzustellen.

Nach Auffassung der CSU ist die Soziale Marktwirtschaft auch das Ordnungsprinzip für die Europäische Wirtschafts- und Währungsunion, das möglichst unverfälscht durchgesetzt werden muß.

Vocabulary

generationsübergreifend	can be passed from one
verfügbar bleibt	generation to another
epochale	epoch-making
durch Leistung	through hard work
sachgerecht	proper (properly used)
das Bruttosozialprodukt	gross national product

Text B: 'Familie: Fundament unserer Gesellschaft', in CSU, *Grundsatzprogramm der Christlich-Sozialen Union in Bayern* (including *Profil der CSU*) (Grünwald, Atwerb Verlag, 1993), 27, 31–2

Ehe und Familie haben sich über Jahrhunderte des gesellschaftlichen, sozialen und wirtschaftlichen Wandels als Urzelle der Gesellschaft bewährt. In Familien suchen und erfahren Menschen Liebe, Geborgenheit, Lebenssinn, gegenseitige Hilfe und Unterstützung.

Ehe und Familie stehen im Mittelpunkt unserer Politik. Sie sind natürliche Lebensformen und Grundpfeiler einer freien und solidarischen Gesellschaft. Deshalb fördert die CSU Ehe und Familie und hält an ihrem verfassungsrechtlichen Schutz fest. Kinder sind eine Bereicherung für Familie und Gesellschaft. Kinder bedeuten Zukunft . . .

Lebensschutz hat höchsten Rang

Unser christliches Menschenbild und unsere Verfassung verpflichten den Staat, menschliches Leben zu schützen und zu fördern. Die Menschenwürde und das Recht auf Leben und körperliche Unversehrtheit stehen allen zu – dem geborenen Menschen ebenso wie dem ungeborenen Kind.

Lebensschutz ist die Aufgabe des Rechtsstaates. Das Recht auf Leben hat als Grundrecht auch grundsätzlich Vorrang vor anderen Rechten.

Recht auf Leben für das ungeborene Kind

Das ungeborene Kind ist Mensch von Anfang an und hat ein Recht auf Leben. Ungeborene Kinder wollen leben und angenommen sein. Geborene und ungeborene Kinder müssen daher willkommen sein, nicht nur den Eltern, sondern auch den Nachbarn, Vermietern und Arbeitgebern. Die CSU kämpft für eine kinderfreundliche Gesellschaft. Kinder sind Glück und Zukunft für uns alle. Deshalb hat die CSU mit ihrer Familienpolitik ein Netz sozialer Hilfen für Kinder und Familien geknüpft. Dabei steht im Mittelpunkt, Schwangere durch weitere Hilfe zu ermutigen, ein Kind anzunehmen.

Abtreibung ist Tötung menschlichen Lebens. Eine Fristen-regelung, die die Tötung ungeborener Kinder generell bis zu einer bestimmten Schwangerschaftswoche erlaubt, öffnet der Willkür Tür und Tor. Die CSU hält am Lebensrecht ungeborener Kinder fest.

Zum Schutze des Grundrechts auf Leben darf der Gesetzgeber auf das Strafrecht nicht verzichten. Das Strafrecht scheidet Recht von Unrecht. Die Strafdrohung ist zur Bildung von Wertbewußtsein und zur Verhaltungsorientierung unerläßlich.

Die CSU will einen Strafrechtsschutz *für* das Leben, *nicht gegen* die Frau. In einer schwaren Not- oder Konfliktlage kann die Fort-setzung einer Schwangerschaft für eine Frau unzumutbar werden. In diesem Fall kann nach Beratung eine Schwangerschaft straffrei abge-brochen werden. Die Beratung dient der Sorge und Hilfe für die Schwangere und dem Schutz des ungeborenen Kindes.

Gleiche Verantwortung für Vater und Mutter

Vater und Mutter tragen die gleiche moralische und rechtliche Verantwortung für das Leben und den Schutz des ungeborenen

Kindes. In schwierigen Lebenssituationen oder Konfliktlagen darf die schwangere Frau weder in ihrer Verantwortung alleingelassen noch zu einer unverantwortlichen Entscheidung gegen das Lebensrecht des Kindes gedrängt werden. Nach Auffassung der CSU ist strafwürdig, wer die Frau in einer schweren Konfliktlage zur Abtreibung nötigt.

Eine besondere Verantwortung für das Leben des Ungeborenen kommt gerade auch dem Arzt zu, der die Frau medizinisch betreut. Die CSU betont ausdrücklich die Verantwortung der Ärzte, hier gemäß ihrem Eid, Leben zu schützen, zu beraten und zu behandeln.

Wer das Recht ungeborener Kinder bedenkenlos zur Disposition stellt, leistet der möglichen Diskriminierung und Ächtung Behinderter und schwer Pflegebedürftiger in der Gesellschaft Vorschub.

Wo der Schutz menschlichen Lebens gesellschaftlichen oder Nützlichkeitserwägungen untergeordnet wird, verliert auch der kranke und alte Mensch sein Recht auf Leben und sterben in Würde. Auch aus unheilvoller geschichtlicher Erfahrung gilt deshalb für die CSU die Mahnung: Wehret den Anfängen! Das Recht auf Leben ist unteilbar. Staat und Gesellschaft haben die Pflicht, das Leben der Behinderten zu achten und schützen. CSU-Politik steht in der Verantwortung gegenüber der ganzen Schöpfung.

Text C: 'Die CSU betreibt Politik aus christlicher Verantwortung. *Profil der CSU*', in *Grundsatzprogramm*, 141–5

Die CSU begründet ihre Politik und ihr Selbstverständnis aus der Verantwortung vor Gott und gegenüber dem Nächsten. Das Recht auf Leben und die Würde des Menschen sind ihre Leitbilder. Auf christlicher Grundlage entwickelt sie schöpferische Kraft für die Gestaltung des politischen Lebens und erhält die Motivation zum Einsatz für die Schöpfung, für Gerechtigkeit, Frieden und Freiheit. Die CSU geht vom christlichen Menschenbild und von der christlichen Wertordnung aus. Deshalb weiß sie von der Begrenztheit und Unvollkommenheit des Menschen, und deshalb weiß sie, daß die politische Gestaltung der Welt letzte Vollkommenheit nicht erreichen kann. Deshalb lehnt die CSU politische Ideologien ab, die sich als irdische Heilslehren ausgeben. In der Zusammenarbeit von Christen der beiden großen Konfessionen liegt eine der starken Wurzeln der CSU. Die CSU geht von der weltanschaulichen Neutralität des

Staates auf der Wertordnung unserer Verfassung aus. Aus der christlichen Grundlage ihrer Politik leitet die CSU keinen politischen Absolutheitsanspruch ab. Sie steht allen offen, deren politischen Vorstellungen mit der christlichen Wertorientierung vereinbar sind . . .

Die CSU ist eine konservative Partei

Die CSU ist einer dauerhaften Wertordnung verpflichtet. Sie steht auf der Grundlage abendländischen Denkens sowie des geschichtlichen und kulturellen Erbes unseres Volkes. Tradition und Heimat, Sprache und Kultur geben dem einzelnen Geborgenheit und der Gemeinschaft Identität. Dies ist Grundlage für offenes Denken, für abgewogenen Fortschritt, für notwendige Veränderung und ein verantwortbares Wachstum. Für die CSU ist Fortschritt nicht Selbstzweck, er muß stets im Dienste der Menschen und nachfolgenden Generationen stehen. Es gilt: Veränderung nicht um jeden Preis und nicht zu jedem Ziel, sondern nur zum Besseren. Die CSU ist deshalb auch eine konservative Partei . . .

Die CSU ist eine bayerische Partei

Neben ihrer deutschen Verantwortung und europäischen Orientierung ist die Liebe zur bayerischen Heimat und ihren Menschen ein tragendes Element im Selbstverständnis der CSU. Sie schöpft ihre Identität aus einer mehr als tausendjährigen bayerischen Staatlichkeit und sieht in der Zukunftsgestaltung der bayerischen Heimat einen vorrangigen Auftrag. Die Stimme Bayerns im geeinten Deutschland und im sich einigenden Europa Gehör zu verschaffen, ist die besondere bayerische Verpflichtung der CSU. Als überzeugter Anwalt eines lebendigen Föderalismus tritt die CSU für die Durchsetzung dieses staatlichen Ordnungsprinzips auch in Deutschland und Europa ein. Wir arbeiten für ein modernes Bayern, das sich wirtschaftlich leistungsfähig und dynamisch, sozial gesichert, umweltfreundlich und ebenso traditionsbewußt wie fortschrittlich im weltweiten Wettbewerb behauptet. Unser Ziel ist klar: Bayern muß auch künftig liebenswerte Heimat für seine Bürger bleiben. Gerade die starke Verankerung der CSU in Bayern hält ihr alle deutschen Optionen offen.

Vocabulary

das Selbstverständnis	self-evidence
das Leitbild (-er)	model
schöpferisch	creative
die Schöpfung	creation (religious)
die Wertordnung	codex of values
die Begrenzheit	limitation
die Unvollkommenheit	shortcoming, imperfection
die Konfession	church, religious belief
abendländisch	western
die Geborgenheit	sense of security
die Staatlichkeit	statehood

Text D: Dr Edmund Stoiber, minister president of Bavaria, 'Rede zum neuen Grundsatzprogramm', October 1993, in *Grundsatzprogramm der Christlich-Sozialen Union in Bayern* (Munich, 1993), 166–7

Die europäischen Nationen müssen auf Souveränität verzichten. Denn nur wenn Europa in der Außen- und Sicherheitspolitik als Kontinent handlungsfähiger wird, werden wir unsere Rechte und Interessen in der Welt angemessen wahren. Der Binnenmarkt ohne Grenzen kann nur funktionieren mit einem gemeinsamen sozial- und umweltpolitischen Mindeststandard. Hinzukommen muß eine europäische Kriminalitätsbekämpfung, eine europäische Asyl- und Einwanderungspolitik, damit wir den Wohlstandsgewinn nicht mit einem Sicherheitsverlust bezahlen müssen.

Wir brauchen aber keinen Souveränitätsverzicht und keine EG-Kompetenzen in den Fragen, in denen es nicht um die Lösung grenzüberschreitender Probleme, in denen es nicht um Fragen der Wettbewerbsgleichheit im Binnenmarkt geht. Der Kernpunkt ist: In Brüssel muß nicht verordnet werden, welche Arbeitsräume der Dorfmetzger von Waakirchen* vorhalten muß. Es muß nicht in Brüssel entschieden werden, ob der kleine Bauunternehmer in Viechtach* für seine Baustellen einen Sicherheits- und Gesundheitsbeauftragten bestellen muß. Wir wehren uns gegen diesen zentralistischen Eurokratismus, weil er die europäische Integration

---

*Villages in Bavaria.

diskreditiert. Er fördert die Integration nicht. Wir wollen eine durchgehende Demokratisierung der EG-Institutionen, damit europäische Entscheidungsprozesse durchschaubar und politische Verantwortungen zurechenbar werden. Wir wollen eine Stärkung des Europäischen Parlaments, wir wollen eine dem Parlament und dem Ministerrat gegenüber verantwortliche europäische Regierung. Und wir wollen, daß das Parlament und der EG-Ministerrat als Organ der Mitgliedstaaten gemeinsam das Legislativorgan der Europäischen Gemeinschaft werden.

'Das Bild von Deutschland in der Welt', in *Grundsatzprogramm der Christlich-Sozialen Union*, 132–4

Deutschlands Ansehen in Europa und der Welt wird entscheidend davon bestimmt, welches Bild von Deutschland, seiner Geschichte, seiner Kultur und Gegenwart von der auswärtgen Kulturpolitik vermittelt wird.

Die auswärtige Kulturpolitik – oft als dritte Säule der Außenpolitik bezeichnet, aber vielfach als fünftes Rad am Wagen behandelt – steht nach der Vereinigung Deutschlands ebenfalls vor neuen Herausforderungen. Dabei kann sie, besonders auch im östlichen Europa und in Übersee, an bedeutende Traditionen anknüpfen. Die großen Leistungen deutscher Künstler, Gelehrter, Forscher und Philanthropen sind in vielen Ländern der Erde unvergessen. Das Interesse an der deutschen Sprache ist größer als je zuvor. Der internationale Kulturaustaussch fördert dauerhafte und tragfähige Beziehungen zwischen den Völkern.

Sowohl das große deutsche Kulturerbe als auch die wesentlichen Schöpfungen unserer Gegenwartskultur müssen den Menschen im Ausland zugänglich gemacht werden, die sich dafür interessieren. Für Präsentationen im Ausland ... sollen international oder zumindest national angesehene Persönlichkeiten oder Ensembles gewonnen werden ...

Im Hinblick auf die Verbreitung der deutschen Sprache bedeutet dies, daß stärkere Anstrengungen unternommen werden müssen, um durch Sprachkurse, Literaturhilfe (auch im wissenschaftlichen Bereich) und durch eine größere Anzahl von Deutschlehrern das gestiegene Interesse an der deutschen Sprache vor allem in Ost- und Südosteuropa zu befriedigen. Dies muß nicht in erster Linie durch neue Haushaltmittel erfolgen, sondern kann durch Umschichtungen und neue Prioritätensetzungen in der auswärtigen Kulturpolitik erreicht werden.

Ein bevorzugter Adressat der deutschen auswärtigen Kulturpolitik sind die im Ausland lebenden Deutschen und die in Mittel-, Ost- und Südosteuropa lebenden deutschen Volksgruppen. Die zunehmende Aufgeschlossenheit unserer östlichen und südöstlichen Nachbarn für Europa muß zunehmend genutzt werden, das unverlierbare, jahrhundertalte deutsche Kulturerbe in der angestammten Heimat zu bewahren.

Vocabulary

verzichten	to forgo
der Sicherheits- und	
Gesundheitsbeauftragte	health and safety officer
zurechenbar	including

Questions on the Source Texts

Text A

1. Explain the following terms:
   auf dem Grundsatz der Vertragsfreiheit aufbauende Privatrechtstordnung
   Europäische Wirtschafts- und Währungsunion
2. According to the CSU, in what ways does the market economy guarantee personal freedom?
3. How has the market economy proved itself superior to the planned economy and what are its strengths?
4. To what extent do you agree with the CSU that the market economy derives from the European cultural tradition?
5. What reasons are given for controlling state participation in the economy?
6. What relationship does the CSU suggest between the market economy and European integration?

Text B

1. What is the role of the family, according to the CSU, with respect to its members and to society as a whole?

2. What is the party's attitude to abortion?
3. What alternatives to abortion does the party suggest?
4. Why is it important for there to be legal penalties with respect to abortion?

Text C

1. What are the roots of the basic values propagated by the CSU?
2. In what sense does the CSU regard itself as a conservative party?
3. In what ways is the CSU a 'Bavarian' party?
4. How does the CSU see Bavaria's role in Germany and Europe?

Text D

1. What arguments does Dr Stoiber put forward for giving up some national sovereignty to European institutions?
2. Where should the line be drawn for non-intervention by Brussels?
3. What reforms in the political institutions of the European Union does he advocate?
4. What does the CSU suggest that Germany should do to develop her image abroad?

Bibliography

In German

Fahrenholz, Peter, 'Die CSU vor einem schwierigen Spagat', *Aus Politik und Zeitgeschichte,* 7 January 1994 (Bonn, 1994), 17–20.

Jesse, Eckhardt, 'Die CSU im vereinigten Deutschland', *Aus Politik und Zeitgeschichte,* 2 February 1996 (Bonn, 1996), 29–35.

Mintzel, Alf, *Geschichte der CSU. Ein Überblick* (Opladen, Westdeutscher Verlag, 1977).

Olzog, Günter and Hans-J. Liese, *Die politischen Parteien in Deutschland* (Munich, Olzog Verlag, 1992), 100–13.

Tempel, Karl G., *Die Parteien in der Bundesrepublik Deutschland* (Berlin, Landeszentrale für politische Bildungsarbeit, 1987), 122–32.

In English

Mintzel, Alf, 'The Christian Social Union in Bavaria', in Max Kaase and Klaus von Beyme (eds.), *Elections and Parties* (London, Sage, 1978).

Further information may be obtained from:
Christlich-Soziale Union in Bayern
Abteilung Öffentlichkeitsarbeit
Franz-Josef Strauß-Haus
Nymphenburger Straße 64–8
D-80335 Munich
Tel. (089) 1243–0
Fax (089) 1243-274 or -258

2. Freie Demokratische Partei Deutschlands (FDP)/ Liberal-Demokratische Partei Deutschlands (LDPD)

A. Freie Demokratische Partei

Like the CDU and CSU, the FDP was a party that was newly founded after 1945 but had roots in Germany's earlier political landscape. Traditionally, since the nineteenth century, the liberals in Germany had had two distinct strands to their ideology – on the one hand, nationalism, linked with the aim of unifying and strengthening the nation, and on the other, the representation of liberal middle-class values and the desire to build a democracy based on those values. In the Weimar period there were two liberal parties representing this basic split, the Deutsche Volkspartei (DVP) and the Deutsche Demokratische Partei (DDP). In 1928 the combined votes of the two parties gave them 18 per cent of the total votes cast for the Reichstag elections but this had dropped to only 2 per cent by 1933 as German politics polarized and radicalized. Many of their voters switched allegiance to the nazis, for they were predominantly Protestant, small-scale entrepreneurs and landowners – the very groups who were most easily recruited to national socialism.

In 1945 liberals began to form political groups and parties, under a variety of names, throughout Germany. It was not until 12 December 1948 that the West German parties merged to form the FDP,[1] and even then the disputes between the two ideological wings of the party had not been finally settled. Traditions had lived on, and the division of Germany and the initial isolation of the groups from each other had acted against the development of a single agreed platform. Over the years, and in some areas, the liberals were near to the social democrats, in others they were strongly anti-left-wing and even nationalistic.

From the outset the basic values of the FDP were freedom, the individual, property and tolerance. Throughout, they have shown flexibility in how they have applied these principles in practical co-operation with their coalition partners, for, although the party has mainly been in coalitions with the CDU and CSU in the Bundestag, there have been a number of times where, both at national and *Land* level, the FDP has joined a coalition with the SPD.[2] As with the CDU/CSU the Free Democrats believe that private property and the private ownership of the means of production are fundamental to the freedom of the individual and a free society. In the 1940s they rejected the initially strongly social elements of the CDU's platform and insisted on the freedom of the market. They wanted the very minimum of state intervention, and in some cases were against the trade unions, for instance in their voting against elements of co-determination in 1951 and 1952.

Their foreign and security policies have undergone a number of changes. In the 1950s they strongly supported the CDU/CSU's efforts to integrate the Federal Republic into West European and Western institutions. For instance, the FDP supported the creation of a European defence community, but, in contrast to the other main parties, the Free Democrats wanted Germany to be reunited before the unification of Western Europe, since they feared that German reunification would then be forgotten. In the late 1950s the FDP supported better relations with the Soviet Union and a declaration that German unity would only be achieved by peaceful means. In the interests of not deepening the division of Germany, the FDP voted against the Federal Republic joining the European Economic Community. In the same year the FDP rejected demands for the Bundeswehr to be armed with nuclear weapons and by 1959 was advocating that a reunited Germany should become neutral, joining neither NATO nor the Warsaw Pact, and develop its *Ostpolitik*. From now on the FDP rejected the Hallstein Doctrine, accepted the Oder–Neiße Line and was in favour of recognizing the GDR as a separate German state (although the two Germanys were not to treat each other as 'foreign countries').

By 1957, under the influence of new leaders, and particularly Walter Scheel (later to become federal president), the FDP began to define itself as a 'party of the centre', a party representing the interests of the monied and educated people. The social changes in the 1960s and the impact of the FDP becoming the only parliamentary opposition during the period of the Grand Coalition brought about a further reorientation of policies. The party worked hard for changes in educational, economic and judicial policies. It became a party for social change and it was thus natural for it to work in coalition with the SPD since it, too, was a party of change. (None the less, at least some in the party were unhappy at a coalition with the SPD in 1969.) By 1971 the FDP, in its highly important *Freiburger Thesen*,[3] had made it clear that it wanted to spread the liberal, democratic ethic through the population and make it part of the political culture of the Federal Republic. By then the composition of the electorate had changed – the traditional supporters of the FDP, the self-employed, had dropped to 35 per cent. The FDP had to appeal more widely. In the following decade it succeeded in developing its image as the party for the 'politically aware' voter.

The formation of the SPD/FDP government in 1969 led to controversy and discussion both within the party and among FDP voters. However, the party, with its new profile, certainly attracted new members, and in fact during the 1970s two-thirds of them had joined after 1972. The increased share of the vote in 1972 showed that the FDP had successfully changed course. Yet by 1977 it was clear that there were limits to the social package of the *Freiburger Thesen*, for the FDP was again calling for a reduction of state subsidies, the privatization of some of the public services and changes in taxation for entrepreneurs. In the area of foreign policy and relations with East Germany, the FDP was able to place two of its most eminent politicians into the office of foreign minister – Walter Scheel and Hans-Dietrich Genscher. They both gave considerable support to the SPD in its *Ostpolitik*, and Genscher played an important role in the CSCE process (see text F, pp.112–13). In coalition with the CDU/CSU the FDP proved to be a guarantee that the progress already made in the dialogue with the communist bloc would continue, and even made that a condition for again forming a coalition with the Christian democrats in 1987. The FDP continued to believe that the only way to overcome communism was to make more political contact at every level, from national government down as far as twin-town contacts.

In 1982, after the FDP left the coalition with the SPD and joined with the CDU/CSU to form a new government there was discontent among the more reform-minded members of the FDP, who would have preferred to stay in a coalition with the social democrats. Many of them resigned from the party after November 1982 but were replaced by an increased number of medium-size entrepreneurs, lawyers and tradespeople. The party increasingly won electoral support from the new technical intelligentsia, the growing middle class working in the service industries and high-status civil servants and administrators. By the Bundestag election in January 1987, the FDP had gained ground again, and recorded 9.1 per cent, in comparison with 7 per cent in 1983. There had been a slightly improved showing in various *Land* elections in 1987, and the party was able to move into a coalition government with the CDU in Rhineland-Palatinate and with the SPD in Hamburg. In 1988 there were losses in Schleswig-Holstein and Baden-Württemberg, followed in 1989 by disaster in West Berlin, where the FDP attracted only 3.9 per cent and was thus no longer involved in the government of the city. In the European election in June 1989 the FDP registered 5.6 per cent. A feeling of pessimism and insecurity was discernible within the party.

The FDP after 1990

The year of reunification turned out to be a remarkable one for the FDP. Their leading figure, Hans-Dietrich Genscher, who was foreign minister, played a major role in the German unification process, particularly in his dealings with the four former Allies and the 'Two Plus Four' negotiations (i.e. the two German states and the Allies) that commenced in February 1990. In East Germany he was felt to be someone who understood the problems there well, and to be very near to his fellow East Germans. In August 1990 the FDP and the East German LDP joined forces but retained the FDP title. The West German FDP had some 67,000 members at that time, but in combination with the LDP membership the figure topped 200,000.[4] The FDP could face the December elections with considerable optimism. The party gained 13.4 per cent of the East German vote and 10.6 per cent in West Germany, which gave them an overall 11 per cent nation-wide. The Free Democrats appealed, in part, to the East Germans because they were perceived to champion the rights of the individual and were opposed to unnecessary bureaucracy.

The successes of 1990 were short-lived, however. In the 1994 Bundestag elections the party received one of its lowest votes ever, 6.9 per cent, and in that year was represented in only four out of sixteen *Land* parliaments. The large number of members in East Germany had dropped, a pattern which applied to other parties as well. The FDP lost its strength in the field of foreign and German–German policy once the country had been unified, it has not sought to establish a new profile and it has failed to develop a new economic policy to help in the solution of the massive problems confronting the country since unification. It has not been able to move on to territory occupied by the Greens, namely, the environment or women's equality. Equally, it has not been able to compete with the SPD's high-profile and long-standing commitment to social policy, or with the CDU/CSU on law and order. Furthermore, the party lost a number of its highly qualified and well-known leaders in rapid succession – Hans-Dietrich Genscher, Otto Graf von Lambsdorff and Jürgen Moellemann. At a time where electoral success is increasingly dependent on personalities, this has proved a problem. Finally, the FDP has not broadened its electoral base since the mid-1980s and it can only command a comparatively small group of loyal voters. A party that relies heavily on floating voters is always in danger of failing to find an issue that will be attractive for the next election.

In the 1994 Bundestag election the FDP received the ministries of Foreign Affairs (Klaus Kinkel, who also became deputy chancellor), Justice (Dr Edzard Schmidt-Jortzig) and Economics (Günter Rexrodt).

By the nature of the electoral system, the major political parties (CDU/CSU and SPD) can never achieve an absolute majority in the Bundestag, and herein lies the importance and influence of the FDP. Since 1949 the FDP has played a part in every government, with the exception of the years 1956–61 and 1966–9, and has been rewarded by its members having some of the major portfolios, such as Foreign Affairs. It was partly responsible for Chancellors Adenauer and Erhard relinquishing power early. By changing coalition partners in the 1980s and ensuring that the CDU/CSU were in power when the GDR collapsed, the FDP has had an impact on the way Germany was reunified, for events would have been different with the SPD at the helm. The FDP can be credited with having a moderating influence on their larger coalition partners. The weakness of the party has always been its inability to break significantly into the support of the Christian and social democrats and develop a stronger liberal base amongst the electorate or society as a whole. The FDP has often had weak leadership and party organization. It has often had splits in its own ranks. The question now is whether the FDP will be 'squeezed' by the other parties and fall below the 5 per cent hurdle, or whether it will continue to bounce back as it has so often done during the last four decades and again fight well above its weight on the German political scene.

B. Liberal-Demokratische Partei Deutschlands

After the creation of the LDPD in July 1945 large numbers of people joined the party in a very short space of time – by spring 1946 there were already 113,000 members, and in December 1950 this rose to a peak of nearly 200,000. In the first local elections in September 1946 the LDPD received 21.1 per cent of the votes, and at the *Land* elections in October of the same year they reached 24.6 per cent, which made them the second largest party in East Germany after the SED.[5] They were committed to basic freedoms, private property and the market. They were Protestants or free-thinkers and they were middle-class. As was the case with the East German CDU, the liberal democrats were brought into line with SED policy within a few years, partly by driving opponents out of the party or by making life so difficult for them that they went as refugees to West Germany, and partly by supporting certain members of the LDPD so that they got into power and then followed the SED line.

By 1947 the party was advocating religious education in schools (this had been banned in 1946 by the SED), it was against the provision of social welfare, on the basis that it sapped the initiative of the individual to provide for him- or herself and it was anti-monopolist. By 1952 the party had committed itself, however, to the 'planned construction of socialism'. Increasingly it became a rubber stamp for SED policies and, in fact, produced no party programme of its own.

As in West Germany, the original members and supporters of the LDPD were from among white-collar workers, tradespeople, the intelligentsia and farmers. The function of the party was, to a great extent, to integrate and mobilize them for the SED and its policies. The LDPD was also useful for maintaining dialogue with liberals, generally at a personal level, in West Germany and other Western countries and for having contacts with the West German middle class. There were intermittent formal contacts between the LDPD and the FDP.

The LDPD had fifty-two members of the Volkskammer, 10 per cent of seats in regional governments, 6.9 per cent at district level and 3.3 per cent in community councils. It had its own daily newspaper, *Der Morgen*, and four regional newspapers, with a total print run of 442,300 copies.

From October 1989 the LDPD received visits from a number of

leading FDP politicians – Wolfgang Mischnik, long-term leader of the FDP, European commissioner Martin Bangemann and Otto Graf von Lambsdorff. There were a number of discussions with Manfred Gerlach, the leader of the LDPD, although he was to disappear from the scene because of his former close relations with the SED. There were considerable contacts at grass-roots level between East and West German liberals during the late autumn. Throughout December 1989 the LDPD was active in reorganizing itself. It announced that it no longer supported socialism but, instead, the market economy. It wanted a free society, with respect for the rights of the individual, and was prepared to support the unification of Germany in the longer term. The party still had 110,000 members, a full organizational structure and 1,500 paid officials from the GDR era. In February the LDPD held a party conference, changed its name to LDP and issued a programme for the Volkskammer elections. Leading West German FDP politicians spoke at the conference. In February an East German FDP formed and represented itself as 'true' liberals who had not collaborated with the SED. Liberals also gathered in another new party, the Deutsche Forum Partei (DFP), but it was very small and without influence. The three liberal parties were persuaded by the West Germans to form the Bund Freier Demokraten (BFD) to fight the forthcoming elections but there was lasting disharmony among the groups despite this. The West German FDP, both at national and local organization levels, played a major role in the Volkskammer elections, yet despite this the BFD achieved only 5.3 per cent of the vote and twenty-one seats in the Volkskammer. The other 'middle-class' party, the NDPD, was almost obliterated at the poll (0.4 per cent). Some of its remaining supporters joined the liberal democrats.

Hans-Dietrich Genscher – a portrait

Hans-Dietrich Genscher was born on 27 March 1927 near Halle/Saale in what was then central Germany – *Mitteldeutschland.* He studied law at Halle and Leipzig universities from 1946 to 1949. After 1945 he joined the newly formed LDPD in the Soviet Zone. In 1952 he moved to West Germany where he began to practise law in 1954. He joined the FDP and became party manager in the Bundestag. From 1962 to 1964 he was manager of the FDP at federal level. In 1965 he became a member of the Bundestag, and from 1968

to 1974 he was the deputy president of his party. In the social democrat–liberal coalition government he became minister of home affairs
in 1969. In 1974 he was appointed foreign minister and deputy chancellor. In 1974 he became chairman of his party. He played a
significant role in German–German policies and never forgot his
fellow East Germans living in the GDR. He played a pivotal role in
the delicate negotiations in 1989/90 that led to the unification of
Germany. He not only understood the situation in the GDR well but
also had considerable status on the international stage and enjoyed
the confidence of his Western partners and of the Soviet Union. He
also gave decisive support to the Helsinki CSCE process throughout
his years in office. He resigned from his post in May 1992.

Sources

Text A: 'Mehr Freiheit und Selbstbestimmung in allen Lebenskreisen', in *Zukunftschance Freiheit. Liberales Manifest für eine Gesellschaft im Umbruch* (Bundesparteitag der F.D.P., 23–4 February 1995, Saarbrücken), 8–10

Wir müssen die politischen Voraussetzungen für den Übergang von
der anonymen Massengesellschaft zu einer an der Persönlichkeit
orientierten und dezentralisierten Gemeinschaft schaffen. In ihr hat
der Einzelne den Freiraum zur sinnvollen Lebensgestaltung, zur
Selbsthilfe, zur Nachbarschaftshilfe, zur Eigenverantwortung und
Mitsprache. Die Liberalen fordern zum Mut auf, die Vernunft zu
gebrauchen, zum Mut, sich der Zukunft zu stellen. Die Angst vor
dem Fortschritt, dem Zögern und Zaudern setzen wir eine
Gesellschaft aktiver Bürger entgegen.

Freiheit ist nie endgültig sicher. Sie ist immer wieder und überall
neu zu erstreiten und zu sichern. Wir wollen die größtmögliche Freiheit des Einzelnen und die daraus erwachsende Verantwortung für die
Gesellschaft. Deshalb gehen wir bei unseren politischen Antworten
von den Lebenskreisen des Einzelnen aus:
- seiner Persönlichkeit
- seiner Beziehung zur Natur
- seinen Tätigkeiten
- seinem sozialen Umfeld und
- seiner Stellung gegenüber Institutionen und Staat.

Die Freiheit des Einzelnen hat dort ihre Grenzen, wo die Freiheit anderer beeinträchtigt wird.

Liberale Politik will mehr Freiheit und Selbstbestimmung in allen Lebenskreisen – denn Freiheit ist unteilbar ...

Die Fortentwicklung der Medien soll mehr Kommunikation und Meinungsvielfalt bringen; wir wollen keine Medienmonopole.

Nicht der Staat, sondern der einzelne Bürger soll entscheiden, was er sehen, hören und lesen will. Der Medienbereich ist deshalb von staatlichen Ge- und Verboten möglichst weitgehend freizuhalten.

Notwendig sind jedoch Rahmenbedingungen, die ein Gleichgewicht zwischen freier Presse, öffentlichen Anstalten und privaten Anbietern herstellen. Hierzu bedarf es vor allem für den Bereich der neuen Medien verbesserter Möglichkeiten der Fusionskontrolle. Medienvielfalt wird Freiheit, Selbstbestimmung und Selbstverantwortung des Einzelnen stärken und mehr Mitwirkungschancen schaffen.

Jungen Menschen müssen dazu die Gefahren eines unreflektierten Konsums der Medien bewußt gemacht werden. Menschenverachtende Darstellungen müssen vor allem durch Selbstkontrolle in den verschiedenen Medienbereichen bekämpft werden, die viel wirksamer als der Staat für einen ethischen Mindestrahmen sorgen kann.

Text B: 'Die offene Bürgergesellschaft', in *Karlsruher Entwurf für eine liberale Bürgergesellschaft 47. Bundesparteitag der F.D.P.*, Karlsruhe, 7–9 June 1996, 27–8

In Deutschland leben zur Zeit mehr als 7 Millionen Ausländer. In Deutschland leben Menschen unterschiedlicher Herkunft und Abstammung. Wie Ausländer hier leben, welchen Rechtsstatus sie haben und wie Deutsche und Zuwanderer miteinander auskommen, ist von maßgeblicher Bedeutung für den Zusammenhalt, den inneren Frieden und die Toleranz in unserer Gesellschaft. Deutschland hat Zuwanderung und braucht Zuwanderung. Ziel muß es sein, Zuwanderer in unsere Gesellschaft zu integrieren, d.h. ein gleichberechtigtes Zusammenleben von Deutschen und Zuwanderern zu erreichen. Die liberale Bürgergesellschaft lädt zur Integration ein. Sie verlangt Bereitschaft zur Eingliederung, ohne jedoch eine gleichmachende Anpassung einzufordern. Liberale stehen für die Vielfalt der Lebensentwürfe, für das Miteinander der Kulturen und Religionen in unserem Land, für die Möglichkeit individueller Selbstverwirklichung innerhalb eines gemeinsamen Rahmens von Normen und Werten.

Systematische Einwanderungs- und Eingliederungspolitik brauchen eine gesetzliche Grundlage. Wir brauchen ein Zuwanderungsgesetz. Eine gesetzliche Grundlage schafft gesellschaftliche Akzeptanz und Verträglichkeit – für Einwanderungswillige und für die aufnehmende Gesellschaft. Unser geltendes Staatsangehörigkeitsrecht wird der Internationalisierung der Gesellschaft nicht gerecht. Ausländern, deren Lebensmittelpunkt auf Dauer Deutschland ist, muß der Zugang zur deutschen Staatsbürgerschaft erleichtert werden. Eine erfolgreiche Integration der Zuwanderung setzt Integrationswillen, den Abbau diskriminierender Hürden und Eingliederungshilfe voraus. In Deutschland geborene Kinder von Zuwanderern erwerben ab der zweiten Generation mit der Geburt die deutsche Staatsangehörigkeit. Im übrigen wird nach einer fünfjährigen 'Probezeit' ein unbefristetes Recht auf Aufenthalt, sofern dieser rechtmäßig ist, verliehen und die Einbürgerung angeboten. Am Ende einer zweiten dreijährigen Zeitspanne steht der Rechtsanspruch auf Einbürgerung.

Vocabulary

der Rechtsstatus	legal status
miteindander auskommen	to get on with each other
der Zuwanderer	immigrant
die Einbürgerung	naturalization

Text C: 'Gleichstellungspolitik. Mehr Chancen für Frauen', in F.D.P., *Liberal denken. Leistung wählen* (Bonn, 1994), 99–101

Für die FDP ist eine aktive und zielorientierte Gleichstellungspolitik eine zentrale Aufgabe, der im vereinten Deutschland große Bedeutung zukommt. In den neuen Ländern ist eine Situation entstanden, in der sich Frauen zunehmend als die Verlierer der Einheit sehen und die zwingend konkrete Maßnahmen erfordert.

Chancengleichheit heißt für die FDP, **Rahmenbedingungen zu schaffen, die es Frauen und Männern ermöglichen, Familie und Beruf selbstbestimmt und sinnvoll zu verbinden** und ihnen gegen besondere Bedrohungen und Diskriminierungen rechtlichen Schutz zu gewährleisten. Dabei ist u.a. sicherzustellen, daß Familienarbeit und Erwerbsarbeit die gleiche gesellschaftliche Anerkennung genießen und ehrenamtliches Engagement in der Gesellschaft entscheidend aufgewertet wird ...

Die F.D.P. lehnt Quoten ab. Das Ziel, **Chancengleichheit für Frauen ohne starre Quoten** und ohne zusätzliche Vorschriften und Regelungen zu erreichen, ist realisierbar, wenn sich Frauen und Männer diesem Ziel gleichermaßen verpflichtet fühlen. Quoten zielen nicht auf die Ursachen der Defizite bei der Gleichstellung ab. **Frauenselbsthilfegruppen und -initiativen sind verstärkt zu fördern.** Hierbei ist insbesondere den Frauen in den neuen Ländern die notwendige Unterstützung zu geben.

Vereinbarkeit von Familie und Beruf

Derzeit sind 53% der Frauen in Deutschland erwebstätig. Dies ist ein deutliches Signal dafür, daß Frauen Berufstätigkeit als einen wichtigen Bestandteil ihres Selbstverständnisses sehen. Auch unter dem Aspekt der Bevölkerungsentwicklung in Deutschland in den nächsten 20 bis 30 Jahren kommt der **Erwerbstätigkeit von Frauen** eine wachsende Bedutung zu.

Deshalb fordert die F.D.P.:
– Nach wie vor bestehende Hemmnisse für die Beschäftigung von Frauen in bestimmten Berufszweigen sind abzubauen.
– Wir wollen eine umfassende und frühzeitige Information und Beratung über **Berufsmöglichkeiten außerhalb 'traditioneller Frauenberufe'.** Dies gilt mit dem Blick auf die neuen Länder, in denen ein großes Potential in technischen Berufen gut ausgebildeter Frauen vorhanden ist.
– Wir wollen die Einsetzung einer Enquete-Kommission beim Deutschen Bundestag, die eine klare Analyse der großen **Beschäftigungsprobleme der Frauen in den neuen Ländern** erarbeitet und entsprechende Lösungsmöglichkeiten aufzeigt.
– Berufe im sozialen und pflegerischen Bereich sind nicht nur ideell, sondern vor allem auch materiell entscheidend aufzuwerten. Die öffentliche Hand ist gefordert, ihren sozialen Pflichtaufgaben nachzukommen. Damit würde auch die Beschäftigungslage vieler Frauen in der derzeit schwierigen Arbeitsmarktlage verbessert.
– **Frauen sind gemäß ihrem Anteil an den Arbeitslosen bei ABM zu berücksichtigen.** Die angebotenen Qualifizierungsmaßnahmen

müssen geeignet sein, Frauen auf dem Arbeitsmarkt wieder einzugliedern. Dazu sind die Qualität zu verbessern sowie die Angebotspalette zu erweitern.

– Die Doppelbelastung durch Familie und Berufstätigkeit trifft nach wie vor im besonderen Frauen und Alleinerziehende. Wir brauchen daher ein **verstärktes Angebot an flexiblen Arbeitsverhältnissen**, um eine höchstmögliche Arbeitszeitsouveränität für Frauen und Männer zu erreichen . . .

Gewalt gegen Frauen

Gewaltsame Übergriffe gegen Frauen sind ein Thema, das in letzten Jahren enttabuisiert und öffentlich gemacht wurde. Zugunsten betroffener Frauen wurde eine Reihe von Gesetzesänderungen durchgeführt, die konsequent fortgeführt werden müssen. Insbesondere sind **Straftaten zu erfassen, die die Intimsphäre von Frauen verletzen**, aber durch das Strafgesetzbuch bisher nicht erfaßt wurden. Dazu gehört u.a. die sexuelle Belästigung von Frauen am Arbeitsplatz, die in wesentlich stärkerem Maße als bisher geahndet werden muß. Die jahrzehntelange vollständige Tabuisierung des Themas Gewalt gegen Frauen in der ehemaligen DDR macht es erforderlich, gerade den Frauen in den neuen Bundesländern umfassende Hilfe und Unterstützung bei der Auseinandersetzung mit Gewalt zu geben. Die Ursachen von Gewalt gegen Frauen sind vielschichtig und bedürfen einer genauen Analyse und einer weiteren verstärkten öffentlichen Auseinandersetzung.

Deshalb fordert die F.D.P.

– Das **Sexualstrafrecht** muß geändert werden. Die Vorschläge zur ausdrücklichen Strafbarkeit der Vergewaltigung in der Ehe müssen endlich umgesetzt werden. Die Diskriminierung der verheirateten Frau beim Schutz gegen Verletzungen ihres sexuellen Selbstbestimmungsrechts ist nicht länger hinnehmbar.

– Die weitgehende **Beschränkung des Gewaltbegriffs** bei Sexualstraftatsbeständen auf körperliche Gewalt ist aufzuheben. Die bisherigen Regelungen werden den Situationen, in denen die Opfer aus Angst auf Gegenwehr verzichten, nicht gerecht . . .

– Wir brauchen ein flächendeckendes Angebot institutionell geförderter **Frauenhäuser**, wobei auch hier der noch vorhandenen Nachholbedarf in den neuen Ländern besonders zu beachten ist und ein Angebot an Mädchenhäusern, das dem steigenden Bedarf gerecht wird. Darüber hinaus sind Möglichkeiten zu schaffen, gewalttätige

Lebenspartner aus der gemeinsamen Wohnung zu entfernen und ihnen Plätze in Übergangswohnheimen anzubieten.
- **Männerselbsthilfegruppen und -initiativen** gegen Gewalt sind verstärkt zu fördern.

§218 StGB

Das Bundesverfassungsgericht hat in seinem **Urteil vom 23. Mai 1993 zu §218 StGB** die Auffassung der FDP zum Beratungsprinzip anerkannt. Das Bundesverfassungsgericht hat ebenso bestätigt, daß ein **wirkungsvoller Schutz des ungeborenen Lebens nur mit der Schwangeren, nicht gegen sie möglich ist** . . .
Deshalb fordert die F.D.P.
- Wir brauchen ein **flächendeckendes Netz von pluralistischen Beratungsstellen**, auch in den neuen Bundesländern.
- Jeder Gynäkologe, der Schwangerschaftsabbrüche ambulant durchführen möchte und in seiner Praxis die hierfür geforderten Voraussetzungen sicherstellt, muß die Niederlassung erhalten.
- Die **Qualität der Beratung** ist durch entsprechend ausgebildetes Fachpersonal unter Wahrung der entsprechenden Forderungen des Bundesverfassungsgerichts zu sichern.
- Sexuelle Aufklärung, Verhütungsberatung und Familienplanung sind für Jugendliche und Erwachsene zu verbessern. Dazu gehört eine **sexuelle Aufklärung** in den Schulen.
- Die Möglichkeiten des **ambulanten Schwangerschaftsabbruchs** sind auszuweiten und zu verbessern.
- Die Abtreibungspille **RU 486** muß auch in Deutschland zugelassen werden.

Vocabulary

ehrenamtlich	voluntary
aufwerten	set more store on, give greater recognition
die Enquete-Kommission	committee of inquiry
die öffentliche Hand	the public purse
ABM	Arbeitsbeschaffungsmaßnahmen (job-creation schemes)
die Angebotspalette	range of jobs on offer
enttabuisieren	remove taboos
die Vergewaltigung	rape

der Gewaltbegriff	concept of the use of force
StGB	Strafgesetzbuch – criminal code
§218	paragraph dealing with abortion
Übergangswohnheime	short-stay hostels
das Beratungsprinzip	compulsory consultation before an abortion can be carried out
die Niederlassung	the setting up of a practice
die Abtreibungspille RU 486	'morning after' contraceptive pill

Text D: 'Für eine gesamteuropäische Friedensregion', in *Liberal denken. Leistung wählen. Das Programm der F.D.P. zur Bundestagswahl 1994*, 120–1

Die F.D.P. setzt sich für den **Ausbau einer gesamteuropäischen Friedensregion** ein. Dauerhaften Frieden in Europa kann es nur geben, wenn die Vereinigten Staaten, Kanada, die Russische Föderation und die neuen unabhängigen Staaten auf dem Gebiet der ehemaligen Sowjetunion einbezogen sind. Deshalb muß die Stabilitätsregion Europa stufenweise ausgedehnt werden. Eine gesamteuropäische Friedensregion muß auf dem Prinzip der kollektiven Sicherheit aufgebaut sein. Eine zentrale Rolle kommt hierfür der **Konferenz für Sicherheit und Zusammenarbeit in Europa (KSZE)** zu. Sie ist das tragende Gerüst für den Ausbau und die Schaffung neuer kollektiver Sicherheitsstrukturen in Europa. Sie kann als einzige auf absehbare Zeit die Funktion einer übergreifenden Sicherheitsbrücke zwischen allen Staaten Europas erfüllen . . .
   Deshalb fordert die F.D.P.
– Der **Ausbau der KSZE** muß konsequent vorangetrieben werden. Die KSZE muß handlungsfähiger werden. Insbesondere müssen ihre Fähigkeiten zur Früherkennung von Krisen und Konflikten weiterentwickelt und ihre Möglichkeiten zur Streitschlichtung und Konfliktprävention ausgebaut werden. Vor dem Hintergrund der zunehmenden gewaltsamen Konflikte in Europa müssen ihre Mechanismen für Konfliktvorbeugung, Krisenmanagement und politischer Kooperation wesentlich verbessert werden . . .
   Eine gesamteuropäische Friedensregion kann nur durch eine sinnvolle Weiterentwicklung und **effektive Arbeitsteilung von Europäischer Union, Nordatlantischem Bündnis, Westeuropäischer Union and KSZE** geschaffen werden. Der neugeschaffene NATO-Kooperationsrat sowie die 'Partnerschaft für den Frieden'

müssen zur Integration und Einbindung der mittel- und osteuropäischer Staaten aktive genutzt werden.

– Die **NATO** ist in einer Zeit des Umbruchs der wichtigste Garant für Stablilität und Sicherheit in Europa. Die F.D.P. bekennt sich zur europäisch-amerikanischen Bindung im nordatlantischen Bündnis. Die integrierten Einsatzverbände der NATO bilden das Rückgrat für zukünftige Friedensaufgaben in Europa. Mittelfristig gesehen müssen aber auch **multinationale Verbände** unter Einschluß mittel- und osteuropäischer Staaten Friedensaufgaben unter UNO- oder KSZE-Mandat erfüllen können. Hierfür kommt dem NATO-Kooperationsrat als wirkungsvollem Instrument der sicherheitspolitischen Zusammenarbeit mit den Staaten des ehemaligen Warschauer Paktes eine wichtige Funktion zu.

– Das **Eurokorps bildet den operativen Kern einer gemeinsamen europäischen Verteidigung** und muß in Zukunft auch für internationale Friedensaufgaben auf der Grundlage von UNO-Beschlüssen ausgerüstet werden.

Text E: 'Eine demokratische und föderale Europäische Union', in *Liberal denken. Leistung wählen, 1994,* 126–7

Die Europäische Union ist und bleibt der Garant für Frieden und Wohlstand in Europa. Das Konzept der europäischen Integration – über die Europäische Gemeinschaft zur Europäischen Union – ist die kreative Idee der Nachkriegszeit. **Die Europäische Union bietet den besten Rahmen, die jeweiligen nationalen Interessen der Mitglieder friedlich und zum gegenseitigen Nutzen in Übereinstimmung zu bringen.** Krieg ist unter den Mitgliedern der Europäischen Union heute nicht mehr denkbar ... **Für Liberale gibt es zur Erweiterung und Weiterentwicklung der europäischen Integration keine Alternative.** Die Europäische Union soll kein zentralistischer europäischer Superstaat, sondern ein **moderner und demokratischer Bundesstaat** werden. Die F.D.P. will ein 'Europa der Bürger' schaffen. Dazu ist es erforderlich, dem Bürger Klarheit und Verständnis über seine Mitwirkungsrechte, über das Subsidiaritätsprinzip und den föderalen Aufbau der Europäischen Union zu vermitteln.

Deshalb fordert die F.D.P.

– Wir wollen eine **europäische Verfassung mit einem Grundrechtekatalog.** Diese Verfassung soll vom Europäischen Parlament erabeitet, von einer hierzu einzuberufenden verfassungsgebenden Versammlung gebilligt und durch ein Referendum in allen Mitgliedsstaaten legitimitiert werden.

– **Die Europäische Union muß endlich demokratischer werden.** Auf der 1996 vorgesehenen Regierungskonferenz, die unter Mitwirkung des Europäischen Parlaments stattfinden sollte, müssen substantielle **Demokratisierungsfortschritte** erreicht werden. Dazu gehören: volles Mitentscheidungsrecht des Europäischen Parlaments, Initiativrecht für das Europäische Parlament und die Wahl des Parlaments nach den Grundsätzen des Verhältniswahlrechts. Das Europäische Parlament muß die vollen Gesetzgebungs- und Haushaltsrechte in denjenigen Bereichen haben, die in die Zuständigkeit der Europäischen Union fallen. Wirtschaftliche und politische Einigung sind für die F.D.P. untrennbar miteinander verknüpft.

– Das im Maastrichter Vertrag verankerte **Subsidiaritätsprinzip** muß konkretisiert und konsequent angewandt werden. Wir brauchen bürgernahe Entscheidungen. Dazu muß eine klare Kompetenz-zuweisung an die Gemeinschaft sowie an die nationalen und regionalen Ebenen erfolgen. Richtig verstandene Bürgernähe sichert dezentralisierte Entscheidungen und verhindert, daß Entschei-dungsverantwortung routinemäßig ohne Ansehen des wirklichen Regelungsbedarfs auf höhere Ebenen verlagert wird. Subsidiarität stärkt Dezentralisierung, Wettbewerb und Eigenverantwortung . . . Konsequent praktizierte Subsidiarität bedeutet auch Deregulierung und Bürokratieabbau in Brüssel für eine effiziente und schlanke Verwaltung und mehr Bürgerfreiheit und Bürgerverantwortung.

**Text F: 'Rede von Dr. Otto Graf Lambsdorff, F.D.P. –
Bundesvorsitzender', in** *Bundesparteitag der Freien
Demokratischen Partei am 11. August 1990,* **Hanover, 6–8**

Der 9. November 1989 hat eine Vorgeschichte außenpolitischer Erfolge, deren erste große Station die maßgeblich von der F.D.P. mitgestaltete Ost- und Entspannungspolitik ab 1969 war.

Was viele damals als falsche Anerkennung östlicher Diktaturen verstanden, war in Wirklichkeit der Grundstein zu ihrer Über-windung.

– Die Mauer fiel auch deshalb am 9. November, **weil sie zwanzig Jahre lang immer durchlässiger gemacht wurde.**

– Mit der Vertragspolitik wurden menschliche Erleichterungen durchgesetzt, wurden Brücken gebaut und Löcher in die Mauer gebohrt.

Wir waren die ersten Mauerspechte.

– **Mit dem KSZE-Prozeß wurden die ehernen Grundsätze liberaler Menschenrechtspolitik in den Osten exportiert.**

– Gegen CDU and CSU mußte damals innenpolitisch durchgesetzt werden, was weltweit die Voraussetzung für Entspannung geschaffen hat und letztlich auch in der UdSSR für ein Klima sorgte, in dem Gorbatschow und nicht Ligatschow an die Macht kommen konnte.

– Dazu beigetragen hat unser Kampf gegen eine Modernisierung von Kurzstreckenraketen, die Deutsche, Polen, Tschechen, Slowaken und Ungarn in Mitteleuropa bedroht hätten.

– Zum Fall der Mauer hat beigetragen, daß gegen die Wünsche der SPD an der einheitlichen Staatsbürgerschaft aller Deutschen festgehalten wurde.

– Als die DDR Mitte des letzten Jahres immer mehr zur stalinistischen Insel in einem sich öffnenden Ostblock wurde, haben die Übersiedler, die Flüchtlinge aus der DDR, einen großen Beitrag geleistet.

– Und der 9. November wäre nicht möglich gewesen, wenn nicht Ungarn als erstes Land im Osten den eisernen Vorhang geöffnet hätte.

– Der Fall der Mauer wäre nicht möglich gewesen ohne die Bereitschaft der tschechosolowakischen Regierung, die Ausreise der deutschen Botschaftsflüchtlinge zu unterstützen.

Questions on the Source Texts

Text A

1. Explain the following terms:
   anonyme Massengesellschaft
   wir wollen keine Medienmonopole
   Fusionskontrolle
2. What are the FDP's views on freedom?
3. What should the relationship be between the state and the media?
4. Are any constraints to be placed on the media in respect of young people?

Text B

1. Explain the following term:
   Zuwanderungsgesetz
2. What reasons does the FDP give for changing the immigration and nationality laws?
3. How would foreigners become German nationals according to these suggestions?

Text C

1. Explain the following terms:
   ideell
   ABM
   flexible Arbeitsverhältnisse
   Arbeitszeitsouveränität
   Frauenhäuser
   Männerselbsthilfegruppen
   Sexuelle Aufklärung, Verhütungsberatung und Familienplanung
2. Why do you think the FDP says that women in East Germany are the losers in the process of German unification?
3. Why does the FDP reject the idea of quotas being set for women in certain jobs and professions? What alternative is suggested?
4. Why should population development in the coming century affect female employment?
5. Women are heavily concentrated in social and caring professions which are low-paid. What does the FDP suggest to correct this problem?
6. What measures does the FDP want to introduce to protect women from sexual harassment and the use of force against them? Do you think these could be effective?
7. Do you agree with the FDP opinion that only by working with the mother can the rights of the unborn child be protected?
8. What changes in the areas of advice to pregnant mothers, sex education and contraception does the FDP want to promote?
9. Enumerate all the measures that the FDP wants to introduce for women in East Germany. Do you think they would solve the problems there?

Text D

1. Explain the following terms:
   gesamteuropäische Friedensregion
   kollektive Sicherheit
   Streitschlichtung
   Krisenmanagement
2. How does the FDP view the role of the CSCE (OSCE) in maintaining peace and security in Europe?
3. What is the importance and role of NATO?
4. How do the Eastern and Central European states fit into the suggested security framework?

Text E

1. What does the FDP mean by the creation of the *Europa der Bürger*?
2. What are FDP suggestions for the democratization of the EU?
3. What new powers should the European Parliament be given?

Text F

1. Explain the following terms:
   Entspannungspolitik
   Diktatur
   Die Mauer
   Vertragspolitik
   Mauerspechte
   Kurzstreckenraketen
2. List the stages of FDP policies that finally helped end the division of Germany.
3. Comment on the passages in the text printed in bold type.

Notes

1. Helmut Kistler, *Die Bundesrepublik Deutschland*, 72–5.
2. For example, in the late 1980s in Hamburg and in the 1990s in Rhineland-Palatinate.
3. F.D.P. Bundesgeschäftsstelle, *Die Freiburger Thesen. Beschluß des*

F.D.P.-Parteitags, Freiburg im Breisgau, 25–7 October 1971. The document covered liberal societal policy, property, wealth creation, co-determination, the environment.
4. Christian Søe, 'Unity and Victory for the German Liberals: Little Party, What Now?', in Russell J. Dalton (ed.), *The New Germany Votes* (Providence and Oxford, Berg, 1993), 99.
5. 'Liberal-Demokratische Partei Deutschlands', in Hartmut Zimmermann (ed.), *DDR Handbuch* (Cologne, Verlag Wissenschaft und Politik, 1985), 828–30.

Bibliography

Publications in German

Dittberner, Jürgen, *FDP – Partei der zweiten Wahl* (Opladen, Westdeutscher Verlag, 1987), 86–96.

Falter, Jürgen W. and Jürgen R. Winkler 'Die FDP vor dem Aus?', in *Aus Politik und Zeitgeschichte*, 6 (Bonn, 1996), 29–35.

Filmer, W. and H. Schwan, *Hans-Dietrich Genscher* (Düsseldorf, Econ Verlag, 1988).

Gerlach, Manfred, *Mitverantwortlich. Als Liberaler im SED-Staat* (Berlin, Morgenbuch Verlag, 1991).

Lapp, Peter Joachim, *Die 'befreundeten Parteien' der SED. DDR-Blockparteien heute* (Cologne, Verlag Wissenschaft und Politik, 1988).

Mischnick, Wolfgang (ed.), *Verantwortung für die Freiheit. 40 Jahre FDP* (Stuttgart, Deutsche Verlags-Anstalt, 1989).

Vorländer, Hans, 'Die FDP nach der deutschen Vereinigung', in *Aus Politik und Zeitgeschichte*, 5 (Bonn, 1992), 14–20.

Vorländer, Hans, 'Die Freie Demokratische Partei', in Alf Mintzel and Heinrich Oberreuter, *Parteien in der Bundesrepublik Deutschland* (Opladen, Leske + Budrich, 1992), 306ff.

Publications in English

Kirchner, Emil J. and David Broughton, 'The FDP in the Federal Republic of Germany: The Requirements of Survival and Success', in Emil J. Kirchner (ed.), *Liberal Parties in Western Europe* (Cambridge, Cambridge University Press, 1988), 62–93.

Roberts, Geoffrey K., 'The Free Democratic Party and the New Germany', in Stephen Padgett, *Parties and Party Systems in the New Germany* (Aldershot and Brookfield, Dartmouth Publishing Company, 1995).

Søe, Christian, 'The Free Democrat Party', in H. G. Peter Wallach and George K. Romoser (eds.), *West German Politics in the Mid-Eighties* (New York, Praeger, 1985), 112–86.

Søe, Christian, 'Unity and Victory for the German Liberals: Little Party, What Now?', in Russell J. Dalton (ed.), *The New Germany Votes* (Providence and Oxford, Berg, 1993), 99–133.

Further information may be obtained from:
F.D.P.
Abt. Öffentlichkeitsarbeit
D-53113 Bonn
Thomas-Dehler-Haus
Adenauerallee 266
Tel. (0228) 547–0
Fax (0228) 547–298

3. Sozialdemokratische Partei Deutschlands (SPD)

The SPD traces its roots back to 1863. The industrialization of Germany began in the first half of the nineteenth century and, as in other industrialized countries such as Britain and France, it was accompanied by bad working conditions, long working days (of up to seventeen hours), health hazards, child labour, poverty and social injustice. Such conditions led to reactions and an attempt to change the situation. The 1848 revolution, however, was a middle-class attempt to wrest power from the upper class and end absolutism, rather than an uprising inspired by the emerging working class.[1] Yet 1848 was important for the development of left-wing politics in Germany, for in that year Karl Marx and Friedrich Engels published the *Communist Manifesto* which was to form the theoretical basis of communism, and also of much of socialism as a whole. Also in 1848 Stephan Born created the first working-class organization in Germany with the Allgemeine Deutsche Verbrüderung, which was the umbrella organization for thirty-two workers' groups. The idea behind the movement was that the workers would gain their rights and emancipation through their own organized efforts. The tension between demands for radical economic, political and social change on the one hand and more gradual evolution on the other was to remain a prominent feature of the German (and not only German) Left from then till today.

On 23 May 1863 Ferdinand Lassalle set up the Allgemeiner Deutscher Arbeiterverein in Leipzig under the motto, 'Freiheit, Gleichheit und Brüderlichkeit. Einigkeit macht stark'.[2] Yet before his party could get off the ground Lassalle was killed in a duel in 1864. Five years later, in August 1869, August Bebel and Wilhelm Liebknecht founded the Sozialdemokratische Arbeiterpartei in

Eisenach. They took over ideas from Marx and Engels as well as Lassalle for their political platform. This party merged with the Lassalle followers at Gotha as the Sozialistische Arbeiterpartei under a programme that had been set out by Lassalle but was radical enough to be accepted by Karl Marx.[3]

Two assassination attempts on the life of the Kaiser were used as a pretence for banning the new party and trade unions in 1878, and it remained illegal for twelve years. The only official activity left open to the social democrats was through their members in the Reichstag.[4] During the twelve-year ban the ideologists of the party such as Eduard Bernstein (1850–1932) and Karl Kautsky (1854–1938) became more radical and Marxist, whereas the members of the Reichstag were moderates. The party renamed itself the SPD at the Erfurt party congress in October 1891, when it also accepted a party programme that was to last up to 1921. The SPD continued to grow in strength up to the First World War, and by 1912 was the largest parliamentary group in the Reichstag with 110 members. The SPD remained a basically Marxist party but was swept along by the popular enthusiasm for the First World War and voted for war credits in 1914. This led to a split in the party in 1916 and the creation of the Unabhängige Sozialdemokratische Partei Deutschlands in 1917. The USPD, in turn, joined with the Marxist Spartakusbund led by Karl Liebknecht[5] and Rosa Luxemburg and supported the German November revolution of 1918.[6]

The SPD took over government after the revolution and the abdication of the Kaiser in a situation that was not of their making, and inherited a demoralized nation, a shattered economy and soon, also, reparations and the loss of German territory. In 1920 the Kommunistische Partei Deutschlands was created, and most of the USPD became members of the KPD, with only a few returning to the SPD. The next thirteen years were to witness constant struggles between the social democrats and the communists, and the disunity of the Left was, in part, helpful to Hitler's rise to power. When the nazis introduced the *Ermächtigungsgesetz* on 30 January 1933 and banned the KPD, only the SPD voted against the act, but neither they nor the unions took any further steps against the nazis. The result was the smashing of the trade unions in 1933 and the banning of the SPD on 22 June of that year. Both communists and social democrats carried on with illegal activities within Germany against the nazis and paid a heavy price for their resistance. Both parties also set up leaderships in exile and prepared for the day that Germany would again be freed from fascism.[7]

After 1945 the German Left developed in very different directions in East and West Germany. In East Germany separate social democrat and communist parties existed for only a very short time, from June 1945 to April 1946. The social democrats, and the traditions and values for which they stood, were wiped out in East Germany, and the communists and Stalinists took over complete control. This situation was not to be reversed until after 1989. In West Germany, the opposite happened and the SPD gained the upper hand, the KPD was banned in 1956 and communists clustered in a number of disparate, radical and extremist parties with very little electoral support (e.g. the Deutsche Kommunistische Partei, founded 25 September 1968, received no more than 118,581 votes (*Zweitstimmen*) at its peak in 1976; the *Deutsche Friedensunion*, founded 1960, gained only a maximum of 609,918 *Zweitstimmen* in 1961). Overtures were made a number of times by the SED to the SPD but were rejected, partly for ideological reasons and partly for pragmatic considerations – the SPD in West Germany did not want to be tarred with the brush of communism or extremism, or accused of supporting East Germany, nor did it want to lose the support of an electorate that showed clearly that it was against the KPD.

The SPD has become a left-wing party that wants to bring about reform of society by democratic rather than revolutionary means. Because of its long-standing links with the working class, its base has remained for much of the period in this section of society. It has come to accept that the capitalist or market economy system has many positive features and that although it 'needs to be reformed', it is in fact possible to reform it rather than destroy it. The aim is to reduce social injustices, remove social tensions and maintain a stable economic and political system. The SPD has come to accept the democratic state in its middle-class interpretation, the private ownership of the means of production, co-operation between classes and social partnership. The party is committed to taking account of the social and political interests of large sections of the population. It is against a policy of confrontation in the international arena and for disarmament. In opposition the SPD is committed to playing a positive role and to being prepared to enter coalitions with other parties.

The SPD in West Germany officially came into being at its conference in May 1946 in Hanover, where it elected Kurt Schumacher as its chairman. Social democrats in all three Western zones, as in the Soviet Zone, had been active for almost a year by then in trying to restore some sort of order to their shattered country and rebuild their party. Schumacher wanted to create a new SPD, but in fact in 1945 the party really repeated the model that had been created in the Weimar period. This was not surprising, since some 90 per cent of the members and party workers in the Western zones had been in the SPD, or organizations associated with it, during the Weimar period, so that the chance of revitalizing the party was missed. It was soon clear that the SPD in the West would not follow the example of the party in the Soviet Zone and unite with the KPD, and in fact it quickly developed a pronounced anti-communist stance as it became clear what was happening in the eastern part of the country. It was also soon clear that the SPD saw the future of West Germany – ultimately of a united Germany – as lying with the West. It thus accepted, with gratitude, the Marshall Aid provided by the United States and supported the fusion of the three Western zones to form what was to become the Federal Republic, even though that meant the inevitable division of Germany for the foreseeable future. There was also a general consensus within the party that socialism must be combined with democracy, and that social democracy should develop within the framework of the nation. It was also recognized that although industrial workers formed the backbone of the SPD, nevertheless it would have to win the support of new social groups, and particularly the middle class, in order to prevent a repeat of Weimar, when that class did not support democracy sufficiently. Furthermore, the strongholds of the SPD in Saxony and Brandenburg now lay in the Soviet Zone and their future relations with the SPD in West Germany were highly uncertain. Yet, in the early years, the SPD failed to win the Catholic workers and was still regarded as a working-class party by the middle class.

In the 1940s the SPD wanted to limit the power of the market, for instance by the nationalization of the basic and key industries, transport, the banks and insurance companies. It supported the large-scale development of public accommodation, a reform of the social security system and pensions. It wanted to plan and control credit and raw materials. It aimed to overcome unemployment. These aims were set out in August 1949 in the *Durkheimer 16 Punkte*.[8] At the first elections for the Bundestag that year, the SPD strongly criticized Ludwig Erhard's economic policy, repeated the call for nationalization, demanded a strengthening of the trade unions and their right to co-determination in the workplace. The party also laid emphasis on labour law. This platform was popular and brought the SPD 29.2 per cent of the votes, in comparison with the CDU/CSU's 31 per cent.

For the next seventeen years the SPD was in opposition. The reason for this was, in great measure, the success of the West German economy. It was evident for all to see that the ruins had disappeared, the country was rebuilt, the standard of living was rising rapidly for the vast majority of the population, even for the millions of expellees and refugees. The market economy quite simply worked, so why change the political parties that had promoted it and put it into practice? The CDU/CSU used the example of the GDR, the 1953 uprising and the Hungarian revolution of 1956 to frighten the electorate away from 'socialism'. In the 1957 elections Adenauer went so far as to prophesy that the victory of the SPD would mean the end of Germany. The voters forgot the positive and considerable input that the SPD had made over the years, despite being in opposition, into the development of social policy in West Germany. The CDU/CSU won an absolute majority of 50.2 per cent. The SPD was forced to rethink its platform and develop a programme that would bring it votes and make it the governing party.

In the mid-1950s some sections of the party were considering how to appeal to a broader section of the population than its traditional working-class supporters and make the SPD into a *Volkspartei*, a catch-all party with general appeal (as the CDU/CSU had already become). From 1954 to 1958 a commission was created to work out a new programme for the party. The draft was put forward for discussion, and on 15 November 1959 a special party congress accepted the new programme (see text A, p.132–6).[9] What emerged marked a historic break with many of the traditions of German social democracy that had been cherished articles of faith for decades. The programme no longer aimed at wide-scale nationalization, but instead promised to protect and promote private ownership of the means of production. There was now no call for the working class to take over power or a resolve to end 'exploitation' – the favourite word of the Left throughout Europe. The SPD was to be not a 'party of the working class' but a 'party of the people'. Marxism was taken off the agenda and replaced by an 'ethical' position: namely, the party was to fight for freedom, justice and solidarity.

The changes in programme were followed in the next Bundestag election in 1961 by an increase in the SPD share of the vote to 36.2 per cent. The party decided to move further on to the ground already occupied by the Christian and Free Democrats. It also excluded the radical Sozialistischer Studentenbund, which was too embarrassingly left-wing, from the party. The SPD was rewarded in the 1965

Bundestag election by an increase to 39.3 per cent of the votes. It took part in negotiations with the CDU and CSU and at the end of 1966 joined a coalition with them. This was highly important, for it gave the SPD the opportunity of showing the electorate that it was capable of participating successfully in government, that it was responsible and that it could be trusted. What the public saw they evidently liked, for in the 1969 Bundestag election the SPD achieved 42.7 per cent of the votes and was at last able to take over the reins of government, constrained only by a small coalition party, the FDP. The SPD percentage rose still further to 45.8 per cent at the elections of 1972. The party really had become a *Volkspartei* and had gained the support of young people, office workers, people involved in the service industries and jobs in the new technologies, as well as of civil servants. At the same time, by keeping close links with the trade unions, the SPD maintained its credentials with the traditional working class. By 1972, the SPD had broken the 'automatic' link between the Catholic workers and the CDU/CSU, had won the backing of prominent authors and academics and was becoming increasingly attractive to women voters of all ages.

Over the years, the SPD/FDP government introduced reforms to education which led to the introduction of a limited number of comprehensive schools, increased provision for pre-school education, much greater access for young people to the universities, the setting up of new colleges and universities. Changes were made to taxation law and the legal protection of women and young people. The age at which young people could vote was lowered from twenty-one to eighteen. Changes were introduced to family law (including the area of divorce). The *Mitbestimmungsrecht* (Law on Co-determination) was passed in 1976 but did not meet all the demands made by the unions. Payments were increased for unemployment benefit, sick pay, child allowance and for the elderly. Improvements were made in the health service. This was financially possible because up to 1974 the economy was buoyant. Thereafter, and with the impact of the oil crisis and world-wide recession, the government had to slow down the introduction of social and legal measures requiring high financial outlay. This meant disappointment among members of the SPD and large sections of the electorate. The allegiance of the more recently recruited to the ranks of social democracy was put to the test. Many of the newly won intellectuals were moving on to the Greens and the women's groups.

Probably of more lasting implication than domestic policy was the

Ost- and *Deutschlandpolitik* of the SPD. In the 1950s the SPD set great store by building a democratic and social state in West Germany that could act as a model for East Germany and would allow, at some point in the future, the two states to join together again. It was for that reason that the leaders of the SPD were so opposed to the creation of a West German army, a rearming of the country and deeper integration with the West. They believed that such steps would make reunification of the country even more difficult. They also feared that the West was too much controlled by conservatives. It was, therefore, not surprising that the SPD was for a time against German membership of the Council of Europe, voted in the first Bundestag against the creation of a West German army and was against the Paris Agreements in 1955 which allowed the integration of the Federal Republic into NATO. The SPD was even involved in calling a protest meeting against NATO membership on 29 January 1955 in the Paulskirche in Frankfurt-am-Main (where the 1848 republic had been proclaimed). The party was active, too, against nuclear armaments and their stationing in Germany, and in 1958–9 worked out proposals for a nuclear-free zone in Germany and supported similar suggestions from the Polish foreign minister, Adam Rapacki.

During the period of the Grand Coalition Willy Brandt was foreign minister, and he used this time to build up his profile with foreign governments as a reliable and realistic statesman. Whilst now fully accepting integration with Western political, economic and defence institutions, Brandt spoke out for policies of *détente* and peace and helped bring his party to accept the necessity of creating normal relations with the Eastern bloc. Diplomatic relations were agreed with Romania on 31 January 1967.

Once the SPD took over in government, Brandt and his successors (Hans-Dietrich Genscher of the FDP as foreign minister and Helmut Schmidt as chancellor) played a key role in the East–West dialogue. On 18 October 1969 Brandt spoke for the first time in a government statement of 'two states in Germany', albeit states that would always have a special relationship. In November 1969 the Federal Republic signed the Non-Proliferation Treaty committing Germany to not acquiring her own nuclear weapons, a step that the Soviet Union had particularly wanted. In March 1970 Brandt visited the GDR for discussions in Erfurt with Willi Stoph, the chairman of the Council of Ministers. Brandt was deeply touched at the welcome he received from the East Germans on the streets. A reciprocal visit took place at Kassel in West Germany in May 1970. The symbolic significance of the two visits was high.

It was obvious that no real progress could be made in relations between the Federal Republic and the Eastern bloc or the GDR without improvements in relations with the Soviet Union herself. This became a major aim of Brandt's foreign policy. Negotiations with Moscow commenced in December 1969 and led, on 12 August 1970, to Brandt and Scheel signing the *Moskauer Vertrag* (Moscow Treaty). The two states agreed to use peaceful means in the resolution of disputes between them and renounce the threat or use of force. They accepted existing borders in Europe, a clause that was of fundamental importance for the improvement of relations between Germany and her eastern neighbours.

> Sie [Bundesrepublik und UdSSR] betrachten heute und künftig die Grenzen aller Staaten in Europa als unverletzlich, wie sie am Tage der Unterzeichnung dieses Vertrages verlaufen, einschließlich der Oder–Neiße Linie, die die Westgrenze der Volksrepublik Polen bildet, und der Grenze zwischen der Bundesrepublik Deutschland und der Deutschen Demokratischen Republik.[10]

Germany finally recognized internationally that she could not regain the territories lost to Poland, the Soviet Union and Czechoslovakia, and that she could make no territorial claims in future. The draft of the treaty was leaked in advance of its signing and caused a furore in the CDU and CSU, which saw it as a betrayal of German interests. The result was that the government was able to give a 'Letter on Germany Unity' to the Russians on the day that the treaty was signed, in which they made clear that the Federal Republic still had the right to pursue its aim of uniting the German people.

In parallel with the negotiations with the Soviet Union the Germans were also conducting talks in Warsaw, where the main difficulties centred on the recognition of the Oder–Neiße Line, the status of Germans still living in Poland and of those who wished to join their families in West Germany, as well as the development of economic relations. On 7 December Brandt and Scheel signed the *Warschauer Vertrag* (Warsaw Treaty), which was very similar to the one signed with Moscow.[11] Perhaps as important as the treaty was the action of Willy Brandt on that day. He laid a wreath at the monument for the Polish Jews who had been murdered by the nazis, and then knelt down in a genuinely and deeply symbolical gesture of sorrow and acceptance of German guilt.

The status of Berlin had next to be clarified, for without that the

Bundestag would refuse to ratify the Moscow Treaty. West Berlin had always been vulnerable to East German and Soviet pressure since the 1940s (the most obvious example being the Berlin Blockade of 1948-9), and the time was now ripe for ending uncertainties. On 3 September 1971 the *Viermächte Abkommen* (Four-Power Agreement) was signed, under which all sides undertook to make no unilateral changes to the situation of Berlin, and the Russians promised to maintain the transit routes open between West Berlin and the Federal Republic. Visits by West Berliners to East Berlin and the remainder of East Germany were to be made easier.[12]

The next and most difficult stage was to reach an agreement between the two Germanys. The result was the signing of the *Vertrag über die Grundlagen der Beziehungen der Bunderepublik Deutschland und der Deutschen Demokratischen Republik* (Basic Treaty) on 21 December 1972.[13] The aim of the treaty was to enable co-operation for the well-being of people in both states. The Federal Republic and the GDR promised to develop normal 'good neighbourly relations with each other on the basis of equality', to renounce the use of force and to use only peaceful methods for resolving their disagreements. Article 4 was of particular importance to the East Germans, for it stated that neither state could represent the other internationally or take actions in its name. In other words, the Federal Republic recognized the separate existence of the GDR and gave up the claim to represent all Germans. This, in turn, meant that the GDR could develop diplomatic relations with all the countries of the world and, importantly, could trade with them. This was also the prelude to both German states being accepted into the United Nations. The increase in prestige for the GDR, both internationally and in the eyes of many of her own citizens, was considerable. Permanent missions were to be set up by the Federal Republic in East Berlin and by the GDR in Bonn. The ratification of the Basic Treaty in the Bundestag created enormous discord, for many conservative members saw it as a betrayal of Germany, and particularly of people living in East Germany. Nevertheless this treaty led to a wave of further agreements between the two Germanys which made life easier for the East Germans and kept human contacts alive between East and West at a very important time.

Relationships with Eastern Europe were further improved by the Federal Republic signing a treaty with Czechoslovakia on 11 December 1973 (although it was not until December 1996 under a CDU/CSU/FDP government that the final seal was set on the unhappy legacy of the Second World War for German–Czech relations), by opening diplomatic relations with Bulgaria on 21 December 1973 and with Hungary on the same day. Also of considerable importance at this time was the support given by the Federal Republic to the development of the basis for the CSCE.

Despite supporting contacts between states across the East–West divide, the SPD was opposed to contacts at lower levels between social democrats and communists. In January 1960 the SPD leadership issued instructions that there should be no political or organizational contacts with communist bodies, particularly with the SED. In November 1970 it was decided that there could be no joint action with communists. In March 1971 SPD members were told that they had to have official SPD agreement before they could make any contacts with parties, organizations and institutions in Eastern bloc states. In 1977 the SPD also distanced itself from its own *Jungsozialisten*, who it felt were too radical and might give the party a bad public image.

The SPD leadership agreed with the NATO 'Twin-Track' decision on the stationing of new US nuclear weapons in Europe after 1979, linked with negotiations with the Soviet Union, but large numbers of party members and supporters did not. The latter became heavily involved in peace demonstrations and peace groups throughout West Germany. The party was also in difficulties at this time with its traditional allies, the trade unions, and was losing favour with the electorate since it could no longer afford the cost of further reforms and improvements to the social services, social security or education.

Once the SPD had returned to opposition after its defeat in the 1982 elections, its most urgent task was again to find consensus among its members and supporters on the questions of peace, security, economic and social policy. Now, too, with the advent of the Greens on the political scene, the SPD had to think seriously about environmental problems and policies to alleviate them. Under pressure from the regions and the special party congress in November 1983, the SPD changed course on the 'Twin-Track' decision, and in December voted against the stationing of American Pershing II and Cruise missiles in West Germany. It also decided on a new round of discussions with the SED which it hoped could lead to a pilot project that would, in turn, usher in a second phase of *détente*. The leading figure in this was Egon Bahr, an SPD member of the Bundestag subcommittee on disarmament and arms control. Bahr put forward the concept of 'common security', that security could be attained only by working with the enemy and not against him in the age of 'mutually assured destruction' through nuclear weapons. In 1985 the SPD and SED set up a joint working party to draft an agreement on the creation of a chemical- and nuclear-weapon-free zone, that would run through both Germanys and the Czechoslovak Republic. Other states in Central Europe could later join in.[14] The states concerned would rid their territories of chemical and nuclear weapons and open them to international verification and regular inspection. In this way a 300-kilometre corridor would be created in Central Europe, where one of the heaviest arms concentrations in the world was to be found and where there was a real danger of conflict. The SPD was seeking a new approach to the security problems that had bedevilled Europe for forty years, and above all the party wanted to create a new mentality with respect to peace and dialogue in Europe. Naturally, since the SPD lost the 1987 election and remained in opposition, the agreement that it reached with the SED was never implemented.

The summer and autumn of 1987 saw two new developments in the contacts between the two Germanys, one at government level when Erich Honecker made an official state visit to the Federal Republic and was cordially welcomed by Chancellor Kohl, and the other at the level of the SPD and the SED. On 27 August 1987 a document was published jointly by the two parties entitled 'Conflicting Ideologies and Common Security'. It was of importance because it was the first joint statement agreed by the German social democrats and communists in some seventy years. Whilst both parties stressed that there could be no ideological compromises made by either side, they envisaged peaceful competition in which each side would be judged on how it met the challenges of scientific and technological change, developed democracy and provided the best conditions for 'the development of humanity'. Surprisingly, the parties agreed that both systems (the market economy and communism) would continue to exist for a very long time and must coexist. 'No side must deny the other the right to exist'. Such words would have been unthinkable only a few years earlier.[15] The SPD came under considerable criticism in the Federal Republic for having lent its name to such a document. For the SPD itself it was, of course, an attempt to breathe new life into the East–West *détente* process when the risk of military confrontation was high.

The end of the 1980s saw the SPD rethinking how it was to recruit more members and win more voters. In 1987 party membership had reached its lowest point (910,000) since 1971. Above all, the number of young people had dropped from 92,000 in 1977 to 69,000 in 1980, and to only 30,741 in 1986. Whilst the SPD had been in government it had spent too little effort on its grass-roots organization, and this had now to be corrected by the formation of more local party groups. The party also had to increase the speed of its organizational reforms and improve the training of its paid officials. The other problem was how to explain its policies, how to engage in dialogue with the electorate and show that the SPD offered a valid alternative to the CDU/CSU.

In 1982 the SPD began working on a new basic party programme. Progress was slow and involved large numbers of party discussions, infighting between the various factions, two draft versions and a display of disarray at the five party congresses at which it was on the agenda. The new programme was finally launched in Berlin in 1989, thirty years after the famous Godesberg Programme. This time the effect was much more muted. The section dealing with the economy was comparatively weak, at a time when the economy and employment were about to become major issues again after reunification. There were no clear blueprints for how the party would deal with present or future economic problems. The so-called 'post-materialist' agenda aimed at the environment, women's rights and the developing world was not clearly different from policies espoused by the Greens. The programme was, in any case, overtaken by the events of reunification.

The SPD after 1990

The SPD took up a different position on unification from that of the CDU/CSU and FDP. This was partly due to the hope among many in the party that the East Germans who had accelerated the downfall of the SED and its system would be capable, if given time, of bringing about the reforms necessary to create social democracy. Many of the reforms that the SPD wanted in West Germany after 1945 were never fulfilled because, in the decisive years from 1945 to the early 1960s, the Western Allies, the Cold War and the conservative parties had all combined to block them. If a new form of democracy, linked with social justice and care for the environment, could evolve in East Germany, then there could be a revitalizing and reforming of the whole of Germany when unification ultimately came. Secondly, the party was realistic in its appraisal of the economic consequences of rapid reunification – far more realistic in fact than the governing coalition. Unfortunately for the SPD, people did not want to hear words of warning, but rather, when it was clear that rapid unification was going to come about, they wanted clear policies for what was to be done.

A major problem for the SPD was its position in East Germany. In contrast to the conservatives and liberals who had organizations, officials, members, newspapers and money from their activities as *Block* parties, the social democrats in East Germany started with nothing. The Sozialdemokratiche Partei in der DDR (SDP) was created at an illegal meeting at Schwante on 7 October 1989 (it was not to change to the form SPD until February 1990). Markus Meckel delivered a speech on behalf of an 'initiative group' in which he called for the reintroduction into East Germany of the values of social democracy that had been destroyed by the SED, the construction of democracy, pluralism, demilitarization – domestic and on the international level – and the introduction of the market and competition into the economy, though with state controls.[16] The growth of support for the new party was initially rapid so that by the end of 1989 there were some 25,000 members. Interestingly, most of its leaders and many of the members came from the Protestant church, where they had either been clergymen or had engaged in dissident activities under the umbrella of the Church. Despite this, one of the weaknesses of the party was to be factional infighting. The major areas of debate were unification and the economy. By February 1990 the East German SPD was clearly anxious to slow down the unification process as much as possible. Later the splits were over whether to participate in government in the last Volkskammer, and over the signing of the two *Staatsverträge* which led to unification.

The West German SPD helped their friends in the East by providing money and know-how for the election campaign. Prominent SPD politicians such as Willy Brandt and Helmut Schmidt made speeches at large gatherings in East Germany. Opinion polls in February 1989 predicted that the SPD would win the Volkskammer elections by gaining as much as 53 per cent of the vote. The results proved otherwise: the SPD achieved 21.9 per cent of the vote and the CDU 40.82 per cent. East Germans preferred to back the CDU on the basis that it had already proved that it could run the West German economy well. Why trust the untried SPD? Also the rapid unification advocated by the CDU was seen as the best way of ending political and economic chaos in the GDR. Since unification, the East German SPD has failed to improve its position despite the grave economic situation in the East. It is challenged on the Left by the PDS and the Bündnis 90/Greens. Those who voted for conservative parties, although disillusioned, have not moved over to the Left.

In West Germany the SPD continued to hope that they could win the first all-German elections, but it did not find the right message for the electorate, and it had leadership problems. In the elections the SPD had its worst result for three decades.

Since 1990 the SPD has continued to have problems with its leadership, image, organization, particularly in East Germany, and its policies. Despite this, the party made substantial gains at *Land* level and improved its position at the 1994 Bundestag elections. The heterogeneous nature of the SPD has enabled it to go into coalitions with the Greens and the FDP. In August 1996 the party emerged from its congress with greater self-confidence and a renewed vigour that augurs well for the 1998 elections.

Willy Brandt – a portrait

Willy Brandt was born on 18 December 1913 and christened Herbert Ernst Karl Frahm. At the age of 17 he joined the SPD but one year later, in 1931 he joined a splinter group, the Sozialistische Arbeiterpartei. When Hitler came to power in 1933 Brandt had to leave Germany. He moved to Norway, where he studied history. He became a journalist and, in particular, was known for his reporting of the Spanish civil war. In September 1938 he was stripped of his German citizenship by the nazis and became stateless. He was granted Norwegian citizenship in 1940 by the Norwegian government in exile (a fact that was to lead to his rejection as 'unpatriotic' by some on the German Right after 1945 and particularly so when he first stood for the chancellorship in 1961).[17] When the Germans occupied Norway in 1940 Brandt was forced to flee to Sweden. In 1945 he returned to Germany as a Scandinavian journalist and was press attaché at the Norwegian military mission in 1947. He gained German citizenship again but now took on the name Willy Brandt, which he had first used in March 1933 at an illegal meeting. In 1947 he rejoined the SPD and from 1949 sat in the Bundestag until in 1957 he became mayor of West Berlin, remaining in that office up to 1966. He stood twice as candidate for chancellor but was beaten by

Adenauer and Erhard successively. He returned to the Bundestag in 1966. In the Grand Coalition he was deputy chancellor and foreign minister, and in the years 1966–9 began to evolve his concept of *Ostpolitik*. After 1969 he was chancellor, and with his foreign minister, Walter Scheel of the FDP, was successful in bringing about dialogue and a rapid improvement in relations with the Eastern bloc. Brandt's efforts were recognized by the conferment of the Nobel Peace Prize in 1971. The next few years were to witness disagreements within the governing coalition. Yet it was finally the intrigues of the East German state security system that led to Brandt's resignation in May 1974. His personal assistant, Günter Guillaume, was exposed as a Stasi spy who had given high-quality intelligence information to East Berlin from 1972 to April 1974. Although Brandt personally had nothing to do with this, he felt himself responsible for the breach in security and left office. Brandt remained party chairman till 1987 and was made president of the Socialist International in 1976. He did excellent work as chairman of the international North–South Commission on poverty in the southern hemisphere. He was active in the unification process, and despite advancing years made speeches in many parts of the GDR in the run-up to the Volkskammer election of March 1990. He died on 8 October 1992.

Sources

Text A: 'Wirtschafts- und Sozialordnung', in *Grundsatzprogramm der Sozialdemokratischen Partei Deutschlands, beschlossen in Bad Godesberg vom 13.–15. November 1959*, 12–16

Stetiger Wirtschaftsaufschwung

Die zweite industrielle Revolution schafft Voraussetzungen, den allgemeinen Lebensstandard stärker als bisher zu erhöhen und die Not und das Elend zu beseitigen, die noch immer viele Menschen bedrücken.

Die Wirtschaftspolitik muß auf der Grundlage einer stabilen Währung die Vollbeschäftigung sichern, die volkswirtschaftliche Produktivität steigern und den allgemeinen Wohlstand erhöhen.

Um alle Menschen am steigenden Wohlstand zu beteiligen, muß die Wirtschaft den ständigen Strukturveränderungen planmäßig angepaßt werden, damit eine ausgeglichene Wirtschaftsentwicklung erreicht wird.

Eine solche Politik bedarf der volkswirtschaftlichen Gesamtrechnung und des Nationalbudgets. Das Nationalbudget wird vom Parlament beschlossen. Es ist verpflichtend für die Regierungspolitik, eine wichtige Grundlage für die autonome Notenbankpolitik und gibt Richtpunkte für die Wirtschaft, die das Recht zur freien Entscheidung behält.

Der moderne Staat beeinflußt die Wirtschaft stetig durch seine Entscheidungen über Steuern und Finanzen, über das Geld- und Kreditwesen, seine Zoll-, Handels-, Sozial- und Preispolitik, seine öffentlichen Aufträge sowie die Landwirtschafts- und Wohnbaupolitik. Mehr als ein Drittel des Sozialprodukts geht auf diese Weise durch die öffentliche Hand. Es ist also nicht die Frage, ob in der Wirtschaft Disposition und Planung zweckmäßig sind, sondern wer diese Disposition trifft und zu wessen Gunsten sie wirkt. Dieser Verantwortung für den Wirtschaftsablauf kann sich der Staat nicht entziehen. Er is verantwortlich für eine vorausschauende Konjunkturpolitik und soll sich im wesentlichen auf Methoden der mittelbaren Beeinflussung der Wirtschaft beschränken.

Freie Konsumwahl und freie Arbeitsplatzwahl sind entscheidende Grundlagen, freier Wettbewerb und freie Unternehmerinitiative sind wichtige Elemente sozialdemokratischer Wirtschaftspolitik. Die Autonomie der Arbeitnehmer- und Arbeitgeberverbände beim Abschluß von Tarifverträgen ist ein wesentlicher Bestandteil freiheitlicher Ordnung. Totalitäre Zwangswirtschaft zerstört die Freiheit. Deshalb bejaht die Sozialdemokratische Partei den freien Markt, wo immer wirklich Wettbewerb herrscht. Wo aber Märkte unter die Vorherrschaft von einzelnen oder von Gruppen geraten, bedarf es vielfältiger Maßnahmen, um die Freiheit in der Wirtschaft zu erhalten. Wettbewerb soweit wie möglich – Planung soweit wie nötig!

Eigentum und Macht

Ein wesentliches Kennzeichen der modernen Wirtschaft ist der ständig sich verstärkende Konzentrationsprozeß. Die Großunternehmen bestimmen nicht nur entscheidend die Entwicklung der Wirtschaft und des Lebensstandards, sie verändern auch die Struktur von Wirtschaft und Gesellschaft:

Wer in den Großorganisationen der Wirtschaft die Verfügung über Millionenwerte und über Zehntausende von Arbeitnehmern hat, der wirtschaftet nicht nur, er übt Herrschaftsmacht über Menschen aus; die Abhängigkeit der Arbeiter und Angestellten geht weit über das Ökonomische-Materielle hinaus.

Wo das Großunternehmen vorherrscht, gibt es keinen freien Wettbewerb. Wer nicht über gleiche Macht verfügt, hat nicht die gleiche Entfaltungsmöglichkeit, er ist mehr oder minder unfrei. Die schwächste Stellung in der Wirtschaft hat der Mensch als Verbraucher.

Mit ihrer durch Kartelle und Verbände noch gesteigerten Macht gewinnen die führenden Männer der Großwirtschaft einen Einfluß auf Staat und Politik, der mit demokratischen Grundsätzen nicht vereinbar ist. Sie usurpieren Staatsgewalt. Wirtschaftliche Macht wird zu politischer Macht.

Diese Entwicklung ist eine Herausforderung an alle, für die Freiheit und Menschenwürde, Gerechtigkeit und soziale Sicherheit die Grundlagen der menschlichen Gesellschaft sind.

Die Bändigung der Macht der Großwirtschaft ist darum zentrale Aufgabe einer freiheitlichen Wirtschaftspolitik. Staat und Gesellschaft dürfen nicht zur Beute mächtiger Interessengruppen werden.

Das private Eigentum an Produktionsmitteln hat Anspruch auf Schutz und Förderung, soweit es nicht den Aufbau einer gerechten Sozialordnung hindert. Leistungsfähige mittlere und kleine Unternehmen sind zu stärken, damit sie die wirtschaftliche Auseinandersetzung mit den Großunternehmen bestehen können.

Wettbewerb durch öffentliche Unternehmen ist ein entscheidendes Mittel zur Verhütung privater Marktbeherrschung. Durch solche Unternehmen soll den Interessen der Allgemeinheit Geltung verschafft werden. Sie werden dort zur Notwendigkeit, wo aus natürlichen oder technischen Gründen unerläßliche Leistungen für die Allgemeinheit nur unter Ausschluß eines Wettbewerbs wirtschaftlich vernünftig erbracht werden können.

Die Unternehmen der freien Gemeinwirtschaft, die sich am Bedarf und nicht am privaten Erwerbsstreben orientieren, wirken preisregulierend und helfen dem Verbraucher. Sie erfüllen eine wertvolle Funktion in der demokratischen Gesellschaft und haben Anspruch auf Förderung.

Eine weitgehende Publizität muß der Öffentlichkeit Einblick in die Machtstruktur der Wirtschaft und in die Wirtschaftsgebärung der Unternehmen verschaffen, damit die öffentliche Meinung gegen Machtmißbrauch mobilisiert werden kann.

Wirksame öffentliche Kontrolle muß Machtmißbrauch der Wirtschaft verhindern. Ihre wichtigsten Mittel sind Investitionskontrolle und Kontrolle marktbeherrschender Kräfte.

Gemeineigentum ist eine legitime Form der öffentlichen Kontrolle, auf die kein moderner Staat verzichtet. Sie dient der Bewahrung der Freiheit vor der Übermacht großer Wirtschaftsgebilde. In der Großwirtschaft ist die Verfügungsgewalt überwiegend Managern zugefallen, die ihrerseits anonymen Mächten dienen. Damit hat das Privateigentum an den Produktionsmitteln hier weitgehend seine Verfügungsgewalt verloren. Das zentrale Problem heißt heute: Wirtschaftliche Macht. Wo mit anderen Mitteln eine gesunde Ordnung der wirtschaftlichen Machtverhältnisse nicht gewährleistet werden kann, ist Gemeineigentum zweckmäßig und notwendig.

Jede Zusammenballung wirtschaftlicher Macht, auch die in Staatshand, birgt Gefahren in sich. Deshalb soll das Gemeineigentum nach den Grundsätzen der Selbstverwaltung und der Dezentralisierung geordnet werden. In seinen Verwaltungsorganen müssen die Interessen der Arbeiter und Angestellten ebenso wie das öffentliche Interesse und das der Verbracher vertreten sein. Nicht durch zentrale Bürokratie, sondern durch verantwortungsbewußtes Zusammenwirken aller Beteiligten wird der Gemeinschaft am besten gedient.

Einkommens- und Vermögensverteilung

Die Marktwirtschaft gewährleistet von sich aus keine gerechte Einkommens- und Vermögensverteilung. Dazu bedarf es einer zielbewußten Einkommens- und Vermögenspolitik.

Einkommen und Vermögen sind ungerecht verteilt. Das ist nicht nur die Folge massenhafter Vermögensvernichtung durch Krise, Krieg und Inflation, sondern im wesentlichen die Schuld einer Wirtschafts- und Steuerpolitik, die die Einkommens- und Vermögensbildung in wenigen Händen begünstigt und die bisher Vermögenslosen benachteiligt.

Die Sozialdemokratische Partei will Lebensbedingungen schaffen, unter denen alle Menschen in freier Entschließung aus steigendem Einkommen eigenes Vermögen bilden können. Das setzt eine stetige Erhöhung des Sozialproduktes bei gerechter Verteilung voraus.

Geeignete Maßnahmen sollen dafür sorgen, daß ein angemessener Anteil des ständigen Zuwachses an Betriebsvermögen der Großwirtschaft als Eigentum breit gestreut oder gemeinschaftlichen Zwecken dienstbar gemacht wird. Es ist ein Zeichen unserer Zeit, daß sich das private Wohlleben priviligierter Schichten schrankenlos entfaltet, während wichtige Gemeinschaftsaufgaben, vor allem Wissenschaft, Forschung und Erziehung vernachläßigt werden.

Vocabulary

die Voraussetzung (-en)	pre-condition
beseitigen	to remove
die Währung	currency
die Vollbeschäftigung	full employment
der Wohlstand	prosperity
ausgeglichen	balanced
bedürfen (plus genitive)	to require, necessitate
der Richtpunkt (-e)	co-ordinate(s)
der Auftrag (-"e)	order
der Wirtschaftsablauf	economic cycle
die Konsumwahl	consumer choice
der Wettbewerb	competition
die Zwangswirtschaft	command economy
der Verbraucher	consumer
die Zusammenballung	concentration
die Einkommens- und Vermögensverteilung	redistribution of income and property

Text B: 'Die Grundlagen unserer Politik', in *Grundsatzprogramm der Sozialdemokratischen Partei Deutschlands, December 1989*, 6–10

Das Godesberger Programm zog aus den geschichtlichen Erfahrungen neue Konsequenzen. Es verstand Demokratischen Sozialismus als Aufgabe, Freiheit, Gerechtigkeit und Solidarität durch Demokratisierung der Gesellschaft, durch soziale und wirtschaftliche Reform zu verwirklichen. Die Sozialdemokratische Partei stellte sich in Godesberg als das dar, was sie seit langem war: die linke Volkspartei. Sie wird es bleiben ...

Wir sind stolz darauf, in der Tradition einer Bewegung zu stehen, die niemals Krieg, Unterdrückung oder Gewaltherrschaft über unser Volk gebracht, sondern aus dem rechtlosen Proletariat selbstbewußte Staatsbürgerinnen und Staatsbürger gemacht hat.

Unsere geschichtlichen Wurzeln

... Der Demokratische Sozialismus in Europa hat seine geistigen Wurzeln im Christentum und in der humanistischen Philosophie, in der Aufklärung, in Marxscher Geschichts- und Gesellschaftslehre und in den Erfahrungen der Arbeiterbewegung. Die Ideen der Frauenbefreiung sind bereits im 19. Jahrhundert von der Arbeiterbewegung aufgenommen und weiterentwickelt worden. Wir haben mehr als 100 Jahre gebraucht, diese Ideen wirksam werden zu lassen. Wir begrüßen und achten persönliche Grundüberzeugungen und Glaubenshaltungen. Sie können niemals Parteibeschlüssen unterworfen sein.

Unser Bild vom Menschen

... Gemeinsam verstehen wir den Menschen als Vernunft- und Naturwesen, als Individual- und Gesellschaftswesen. Als Teil der Natur kann er nur in und mit der Natur leben. Seine Individualität entfaltet er nur in Gemeinschaft mit seinen Mitmenschen.

Der Mensch, weder zum Guten noch zum Bösen festgelegt, ist lernfähig und vernunftfähig. Daher ist Demokratie möglich. Er ist fehlbar, kann irren und in Unmenschlichkeit zurückfallen. Darum ist Demokratie nötig. Weil der Mensch offen ist und verschiedene Möglichkeiten in sich trägt, kommt es darauf an, in welchen Verhältnissen er lebt. Eine neue und bessere Ordnung, der Würde des Menschen verpflichtet, ist daher möglich und nötig zugleich.

Die Würde des Menschen verlangt, daß er sein Leben in Gemeinschaft mit anderen selbst bestimmen kann. Frauen und Männer sollen gleichberechtigt und solidarisch zusammenwirken. Alle sind für menschenwürdige Lebensbedingungen verantwortlich. Die Würde des Menschen ist unabhängig von seiner Leistung und Nützlichkeit.

Menschenrechte

... Wir sind den Menschenrechten verpflichtet. Staat und Wirtschaft sind für die Menschen und ihre Rechte da, nicht umgekehrt.

Volle Geltung der Menschenrechte verlangt gleichrangige Sicherung der Freiheitsrechte, der politischen Teilhaberechte und der sozialen Grundrechte. Sie können einander nicht ersetzen und dürfen nicht gegeneinander ausgespielt werden. Auch kollektive Rechte dienen der Entfaltung des Individuums.

Unser Verständnis von Politik

... Politik ist eine notwendige Dimension menschlichen Zusammenlebens. Sie beschränkt sich nicht auf Institutionen des Staates. Wo immer Information verbreitet oder vorenthalten, Bewußtsein oder Lebensverhältnisse verändert, Meinung gebildet, Wille geäußert, Macht ausgeübt oder Interessen vertreten werden, vollzieht sich Politik ...

Der demokratische Staat bezieht seine Inhalte von den gesellschaftlichen Kräften. Er ist nicht Selbstzweck, sondern Instrument zur Gestaltung von Gesellschaft. Politische Parteien sind Anreger und Mittler zugleich. Sie vermitteln zwischen Gesellschaft und Staat, indem sie gesellschaftliche Impulse und Erfordernisse aufgreifen und in Gesetzgebung und Regierungshandeln umsetzen. Sie müssen selbst Denkanstöße geben und Entscheidungsvorschläge zur Diskussion stellen ...

Der Bürgerdialog ist Ausdruck demokratischer Kultur. Er rückt ins Zentrum der Politik, wo – wie bei der Gestaltung der Technik – Entscheidungen zu treffen sind, die alle angehen und später nur schwer zu verändern sind.

Für den Bürgerdialog sind Meinungs- und Medienfreiheit unerläßlich. Alle Bürgerinnen und Bürger müssen das Recht und die Möglichkeit haben, zu Themen, die ihre oder ihrer Nachkommen Lebenschancen berühren, ihre Meinung zu erarbeiten und zu verbreiten. Staat, Wissenschaft und Medien müssen die Voraussetzungen zu einer fundierten Meinungsbildung und damit zu einer demokratischen Streitkultur schaffen.

Grundwerte des Demokratischen Sozialismus

Der Mensch ist als Einzelwesen zur **Freiheit** berufen und befähigt. Die Chance zur Entfaltung seiner Freiheit ist aber stets eine Leistung der Gesellschaft. Freiheit für wenige wäre Privileg ... Nur wer sich sozial ausreichend gesichert weiß, kann seine Chance zur Freiheit nutzen. Auch um der Freiheit willen, wollen wir gleiche Lebenschancen und umfassende soziale Sicherung ...

Gerechtigkeit gründet in der gleichen Würde aller Menschen. Gerechtigkeit erfordert mehr Gleichheit in der Verteilung von Einkommen, Eigentum und Macht, aber auch im Zugang zu Bildung, Ausbildung und Kultur ...

Gerechtigkeit, das Recht auf gleiche Lebenschancen, muß mit den

Mitteln staatlicher Macht angestrebt werden ...
Solidarität hat die Arbeiterbewegung im Kampf für Freiheit und Gleichheit geprägt und ermutigt. Ohne Solidarität gibt es keine menschliche Gesellschaft.
Solidarität ist zugleich Waffe der Schwachen im Kampf um ihr Recht ... Wer in Not gerät, muß sich auf die Solidarität der Gesellschaft verlassen können.
Solidarität gebietet auch, daß die Menschen in der Dritten Welt die Chance für ein menschenwürdiges Leben erhalten.

Vocabulary

verwirklichen	to realize, bring about
die Aufklärung	the Enlightenment
irren	to make a mistake, be wrong
Teilhaberechte (pl.)	right of participation
gegeneinander ausgespielt	played off against each other
sich beschränken auf	to be confined to

Text C: 'Zukunft sichern – Zusammenhalt stärken', *Beschluß des SPD-Präsidiums vom 25. April 1996, 6–8*

1.3 Arbeitnehmer am Privatkapital beteiligen

Seriösen Schätzungen zufolge verfügen derzeit ca. 3 Prozent der Bevölkerung über rund 80 Prozent des Produktivvermögens. Dies ist sozial ungerecht und verteilungspolitisch bedenklich. Die Schieflage bei der Vermögensverteilung hat sich infolge der Reallohnverluste der letzten Jahre verschärft. Die Beteiligung der Arbeitnehmer am Produktivkapital gewinnt als Flankierung der Lohnpolitik zur Sicherung der sozialen und demokratischen Stabilität unserer Gesellschaft zunehmend an Bedeutung. Das gilt für die neuen Länder, wo Betriebe mit hohen öffentlichen Hilfen gefördert werden ...

3.1 Reform der Einkommensbesteuerung

Das **Steuerrecht** muß **gerechter** und **einfacher** sein. Die Bundesregierung hat ihre eigene Zielsetzung – 'niedrigere Steuersätze und weniger Ausnahmen' – nachhaltig verfehlt. Stattdessen ist

die Belastung der Bürger mit der Lohnsteuer auf eine Rekordhöhe angestiegen; zudem wurden zahlreiche neue steuerliche Sondertatbestände geschaffen, die die Einkommensteuer immer komplizierter und für die Bürger undurchschaubarer gemacht haben ...
Das Existenzminimum darf nicht besteuert werden. Der steuerliche Grundfreibetrag ist entsprechend auszugestalten.
Vor allem der Eingangssatz muß gesenkt werden. Dabei wird ein Eingangssteuersatz von 20 Prozent angestrebt (bisher 25.9 Prozent). Durchschnittsverdiener und Leistungsträger der Gesellschaft wie Facharbeiter und Ingenieure sind im Durchschnitt stärker belastet als Spitzenverdiener. Dies muß sich ändern. Steuerschlupflöcher müssen geschlossen werden ...
Es ist unerträglich, den Bürgern weitere Leistungskürzungen und zusätzliche Belastungen zuzumuten, bevor nicht sämtliche Steuer- und Abgabenquellen, die dem Staat zustehen, vollständig ausgeschöpft sind. Dem Staat gehen jährlich Milliardenbeträge durch Steuerhinterziehung, Schattenwirtschaft und Vollzugsdefizite in der Finanzverwaltung verloren. Darüber hinaus führt Steuerhinterziehung zu Wettbewerbsverzerrungen und vernichtet Arbeitsplätze.
Vor diesem Hintergrund ist es dringend erforderlich, daß die Bundesregierung unverzüglich und gemeinsam mit den Ländern ein 'Aktionsprogramm gegen Wirtschaftskriminalität und Steuerhinterziehung' in die Wege leitet ...
Ein solches Aktionsprogramm muß wirksame Maßnahmen enthalten, um beispielsweise die Steuerhinterziehung in folgenden Bereichen zu bekämpfen: illegale Arbeitnehmerüberlassung, Schwarzgeschäfte, Vortäuschung von Beschäftigungsverhältnissen, Vertragsmanipulation, Kapitalflucht in Steueroasen, Gewinnverlagerungen ins Ausland, Scheinbetriebsausgaben, Scheinunternehmen, Schadensabwicklung im Versicherungsgewerbe, Einsatz von Arbeitnehmern für Privatzwecke ...
Mit einem Aktionsprogramm gegen Wirtschaftskriminalität und Steuerhinterziehung ließen sich in einem ersten Schritt Mehreinnahmen von etwa 10 Milliarden DM erzielen; davon würden allein 5 Milliarden DM auf wirksame Kontrollen im Zusammenhang mit der Besteuerung von Kapitaleinkünften entfallen.

Vocabulary

die Schätzung	estimate
der Reallohnverlust	drop in real income

das Steuerrecht	tax law
die Lohnsteuer	income tax (on earned income)
die Steuerschlupflöcher	tax loopholes
der Grundfreibetrag	basic tax allowance
der Eingangssatz	basic tax threshold
Durchschnittsverdiener	people on average income
die Spitzenverdiener	top wage-earners
die Steuerhinterziehung	tax evasion
Steueroasen	tax havens

Text D: Reden des Parteivorsitzenden Oskar Lafontaine, SPD-Parteitag, Mannheim, 14.–17. November 1995, 8–9

Die große Aufgabe nach der deutschen Einheit ist und bleibt die europäische Einigung. Ich wiederhole den Satz: Eine vordringliche und wichtige und große Aufgabe nach der deutschen Einheit bleibt die europäische Einigung. Dabei gilt vor allen Dingen auch, daß wir unbeschadet sachlicher Differenzen an der Freundschaft zu Frankreich festhalten. Sie ist konstituierend für die europäische Einigung.

Die ganze Weltgesellschaft entwickelt sich hin zur Integration. Was ich für die europäische Einigung gesagt habe, gilt im Grunde genommen auch für die Staaten Osteuropas. Es war kein falscher Ansatz, daß Michail Gorbatschow alle Anstrengungen unternommen hat, um die sowjetische Föderation zusammenzuhalten. Es ist eine Fehlentwicklung, wenn, wie in Jugoslawien, Teilstaaten auf völkischer Grundlage kreiert werden ...

Ich will nur sagen, warum wir nach der Entspannungspolitik Willy Brandts und nach dem KSZE-Prozeß, den Willy Brandt und Helmut Schmidt wesentlich mitgestaltet haben, in der besonderen Verpflichtung stehen, jetzt eine neue Sicherheitsarchitektur in Europa unter Einschluß der osteuropäischen Staaten und unter Einschluß Rußlands zu bewerkstelligen. Das ist die große Zukunftsaufgabe, der wir uns widmen müssen.

Wir haben nämlich alle eine moralische Verpflichtung dazu, das kann gar nicht oft genug gesagt werden. Wir haben eine moralische Verpflichtung dazu; denn die Freiheit der Ostdeutschen und die deutsche Einheit sind auch Ergebnis der Bemühungen der polnischen Solidarnosc, der Bürgerrechtler von Prag, des Gyula Horn, der die [ungarische] Grenze aufgemacht hat, und vor allen Dingen des

Michail Gorbatschow, der den letzten großen außenpolitischen Entwurf in dieser Welt vorgestellt hat.

Wir müssen bei der Außenpolitik stets auch unsere eigene Geschichte dieses Jahrhunderts reflektieren. Diese eigene Geschichte verpflichtet uns, dieses größere Deutschland, dazu, nachdem wir für zwei Weltkriege verantwortlich sind, Friedensmacht in dieser Welt zu werden und mit gutem Beispiel auch anderen Nationen voranzuschreiten ...

Ich bin stolz darauf, daß wir an mehreren Stellen mehr Verantwortung übernehmen als andere Staaten. Wir übernehmen Verantwortung, wenn es darum geht, diese Welt von der atomaren Bedrohung zu befreien. Es ist gut, das wir hier eine noch isolierte Position unter den großen Ländern haben. Wir wollen keine Nuklearwaffen, auch wenn andere sie haben.

Es ist gut, das wir zum Aufbau der osteuropäischen Staaten mehr geleistet haben als andere Staaten Europas, auch zum wirtschaftlichen Aufbau in Rußland. Wir haben dazu eine Verpflichtung. Ich bin stolz darauf, daß wir im Jugoslawien-Konflikt das Land sind, das mit 450,000 Flüchtlingen, die bei uns leben, mehr getan hat als alle anderen europäischen Staaten zusammen. Das heißt Friedensmacht Deutschland ...

Wir sind bereit, beim Aufbau und bei der Friedenssicherung zu helfen. Aber wir sind zurückhaltend, wenn es um militärische Kampfeinsätze geht. Und so soll es bleiben.

Vocabulary

vordringlich	pressing
sachlich	objective
bewerkstelligen	to bring about
die Verpflichtung	duty
die Solidarnosc	the Solidarity Movement
militärische Kampfeinsätze	battlefield intervention

Text E: *Reformen für Deutschland. Das Regierungsprogramm der SPD* (Bonn, 1996), 26–9

Wir werden die Möglichkeiten der Umweltpolitik dazu nutzen, umweltfreundliche Produkte und Produktionsverfahren durchzusetzen. Deshalb werden wir klare Regelungen für eine ökologische

Stoffwirtschaft aufstellen und Erzeugnisse fördern, deren Ausgangsstoffe in technische und biologische Kreisläufe zurückgeführt werden können. Dabei muß die Müllverbrennung auf ein Minimum beschränkt werden. Hierzu werden wir ein tatsächliches Kreislaufwirtschaftsgesetz vorlegen, das den Namen auch verdient, weil es nicht nur Abfallströme regelt, sondern auch Anforderungen an Stoffe und Produkte stellen soll. Wir werden die Verpackungsverordnung so überarbeiten, daß Mehrwegsysteme besser durchgesetzt werden können. Wir wollen die Abfallexporte konsequent unterbinden, weil im Grundsatz das Prinzip der nationalen Entsorgung gelten muß. Beschleunigen werden wir den ökologischen Wandel der Volkswirtschaft durch ein verbessertes Umwelthaftungsrecht, erweiterte Produkthaftung und Produktverantwortung sowie durch ökonomische. Anreize ... Wir werden ein Forschungs- und Entwicklungsinstitut für zukunftsfähige Produkte wie z. B. abbaubare, umweltverträgliche und wettbewerbsfähige Kunststoffe einrichten. Umweltbildung soll Bestandteil des Bildungs- und Wissenschaftssystems werden.

Mit einer ökologischen Steuerreform ... wollen wir gleichzeitig die Umwelt verbessern und die internationale Wettbewerbsfähigkeit der deutschen Wirtschaft dauerhaft stärken. Leitidee dieser Reform ist, einerseits die Arbeit zu entlasten und umweltverträgliches Verhalten zu fördern, andererseits den umweltschädlichen Energie- und Materialverbrauch in gleichem Umfang schrittweise auch durch Erhöhung der Preise einzuschränken ... Da globale Umweltprobleme nur durch internationale Anstrengungen gelöst werden können, wollen wir unsere Partner in der EU dafür gewinnen, ebenfalls eine ökologische Steuerreform durchzuführen ...

Wir halten an dem Ziel des Ausstiegs aus der Kernenergie fest, weil Reaktorkatastrophen nicht mit Sicherheit auszuschließen sind, die Entsorgung des Atommülls weltweit nicht gesichert ist und die Gefahr des internationalen Handels mit waffenfähigen Kernbrennstoffen wächst. Wir werden aus der Atomenergie aussteigen und das Atomgesetz durch ein Kernenergieabwicklungsgesetz ersetzen. Wir lehnen den Neu- oder Ersatzbau von Kernkraftwerken ebenso ab wie den Einstieg in eine neue Kernkraftwerksgeneration. Wir wollen das Problem der Entsorgung des radioaktiven Abfalls lösen. Dabei lehnen wir die Wiederaufarbeitung als zu gefährlich und zu teuer ab und treten für die direkte Endlagerung ein ...

Wir werden ein nationales Klimaschutzprogramm vorlegen. Unser Ziel ist, den CO_2-Ausstoß bis zum Jahr 2005 um mindestens ein

Viertel zu verringern. In einem ersten Schritt zu einer neuen, besseren Energieversorgung wollen wir regenerative Energieformen und rationellen Energieeinsatz voranbringen und dafür ein Investitionsprogramm aufstellen. Mit diesem Programm werden wir die Kraft-Wärme-Koppelung, die Sanierung und den Ausbau der Nah- und Fernwärme in Ost- und Westdeutschland sowie die Markteinführung erneuerbarer Energiequellen, insbesondere der Sonnenstrahlung, der Wind- und Wasserkraft und der Biomasse, fördern ... Die Solarzellen-Technologie werden wir durch ein 100 000-Dächer-Programm fördern. In der Forschungspolitik und in der Entwicklungshilfe werden wir den erneuerbaren Energien Priorität geben ...

Auch für eine ökologisch ausgerichtetete Wirtschaftsweise bleibt die sichere Versorgung mit Energie die wesentliche Voraussetzung für ein stetiges Wachstum. Deshalb setzen wir uns für einen dauerhaften Beitrag der heimischen Stein- und Braunkohle zur Energieversorgung ein. Wir dürfen nicht zulassen, daß unsere Abhängigkeit von importiertem Öl, Gas und Kohle zu groß wird. Deshalb verlangen wir einen effizienten und umweltverträglichen Einsatz der heimischen Steinkohle, für den die 1991 bei der Kohlerunde festgelegte Fördermenge über das Jahr 2000 hinaus finanziell abgesichert wird.

Vocabulary

die Produktionsverfahren	production processes
die Müllverbrennung	burning of rubbish, waste
die Verpackungsverordnung	regulations on packaging
das Mehrwegsystem	returnables system
unterbinden	prohibit
die Entsorgung	waste management
abbaubar	degradable
umweltverträglich	environmentally friendly
der Ausstoß	emission

Text F: Konstituierung des 12. Deutschen Bundestages im Reichstagsgebäude in Berlin. Ansprache von Alterspräsident Willy Brandt in Bundesministerium für Innerdeutsche Beziehungen, *Texte zur Deutschlandpolitik, Reihe III/Band 8b – 1990*, 887–9

Für uns in Deutschland geht es jetzt darum, mit welchem Inhalt wir das gemeinsame Gehäuse nicht nur materiell füllen.

Wir mit unseren Wahlkreisen und Landeslisten im Westen wollen, so hoffe ich, aufmerksam auf die Kolleginnen und Kollegen hören, die in den neuen Bundesländern gewählt worden sind. Noch wichtiger ist es, daß wir aufeinander hören mögen. Auch über dieses Hohe Haus hinaus mögen die Deutschen aus West und Ost unverkrampft aufeinander zugehen.

Sicherlich sind es wirtschaftliche Nöte und soziale Sorgen, die für viele im Vordergrund stehen und die die Gesetzgeber wie die Regierenden in der vor uns liegenden Zeit beschäftigen werden: Arbeitsplätze, Wohnungen, klare Eigentumsverhältnisse, Sicherheit im Gesundheits- und Bildungswesen, Erneuerung der Infastruktur und nicht zuletzt deutlich erkennbarer Abbau der Umweltlasten. Ich bin davon überzeugt: Alles dies ist zu schaffen.

Aber ich meine auch, wir schaffen es leichter, wenn wir auch die nichtmateriellen Faktoren wichtig genug nehmen. Der Ministerpräsident von Brandenburg [Manfred Stolpe, SPD] sprach dieser Tage von wundgescheuerten Seelen und davon, daß es das Selbstbewußtsein, das Selbstwertgefühl der Menschen zu festigen gelte. Ängste vor den Härten des Strukturwandels gehen um, und Demütigungen aus den Jahrzehnten der Diktatur wirken nach, und sei es nur das Empfinden, in das gemeinsame Haus weniger mit eingebracht zu haben.

Mauern in den Köpfen stehen manchmal länger als die, die aus Betonklötzen errichtet sind ...

Ich beschwöre unsere Landsleute: Möge das Gefühl, auf der falschen Seite der Geschichte gestanden zu haben, sich nicht in Mutlosigkeit oder gar Aggressivität entladen. Möge es in dem Gefühl aufgehoben sein, daß niemand zu spät kommt, wenn sich das Leben weitet.

Die rechtliche und möglichst gerechte Bereinigung dessen, was das alte Herrschaftssytem hinterließ, muß, meine ich, zügig vorankommen. Das heißt aus meiner Sicht und Erfahrung: Es ist so deutlich wie irgend möglich zwischen denen zu trennen, die sich so verhalten und so bereichert haben, daß sie vor den Kadi gehören, und vielen anderen, die politisch geirrt oder sich bloß durchgemogelt haben. Ihnen wird die Demokratie die Chance des Mittuns und der Bewährung nicht vorenthalten.

Die Maßstäbe des demokratischen Rechtsstaats lassen sich nun einmal an das Leben im diktatorischen Unrechtsstaates nicht anliegen, nicht an ein System, das von der kleinen Bestechung mindestens so lebte wie von der großen. Deshalb ist die moralische und juristiche Beurteilung von Verhalten und Fehlverhalten, von Falschspiel und Doppelspiel so sehr schwer.

Eines ist sicher: Zu Helden konnten auch im Staat der SED nur wenige geboren sein. Und das andere: Wer fühlt sich berufen, seines Bruders Richter zu sein?

Wir in der alten Bundesrepublik haben unsere Landsleute im Osten nicht aufgefordert, ihre Heimat zu verlassen; wir haben sie gebeten zu bleiben, so ging es.

Die gegensätzlichen Entwicklungen und die so unterschiedlichen Lebenswege zu überbrücken, wird uns für geraume Zeit Herausforderung bleiben.

Was die vor uns liegende und diesem Bundestag bevorstehende Diskussion um Ergänzungen des Grundgesetzes betrifft: Es hat sich für die alte Bundesrepublik voll bewahrt. Gleichwohl sollten wir nicht auf Erfahrungen verzichten, die die Landsleute im Osten für uns mit haben machen müssen ...

Im Westen – ich nehme den Faden noch einmal auf – brach hie und da eine Art Schuldvermutung gegenüber Landsleuten, die in der DDR zu leben hatten, hervor, als ob das Versagen des Systems den Menschen anzulasten sei. Das ist zutiefst ungerecht.

Aber man kann auch fragen: Woher sollte allen bei uns im Westen gleich bewußt gewesen sein, daß es nicht Verdienst, sondern Zufall gewesen ist, in die eine statt in die andere Ordnung hineingewachsen zu sein, und daß daraus das Gebot materieller Hilfe erwächst? Das muß ja nicht im Gegensatz zur Meinung anderer stehen, die frühzeitig um Klarheit bitten, wem was abverlangt werden wird.

Auch im eigenen Volk wollen Gerechtigkeit und Mitmenschlichkeit geweckt sein. Freilich, wenn man sich sicher fühlt, wie ich es tue, daß die Mehrheit der 'Wessis' zu helfen bereit ist, wird man auch manchen 'Ossis' von übertriebener Dünnhäutigkeit abraten dürfen.

Das sich vielerorts noch zeigende Verhältnis von oben und unten oder von Lehrern zu Belehrten wird sich, eher über kurz denn über lang, in eines von Gleichen zu Gleichen verwandeln. Wir tun uns alle miteinander keinen Gefallen, wenn wir den heute noch gegebenen Zustand, hier der Westen, dort der Osten fortschreiben wollten. Es wäre zudem realitätsfern.

Schon heute gibt es eine Fülle neuer Querverbindungen – zusätzlich zu den wiederbelebten – beides zu stärken und dabei die kulturelle Vielfalt nachhaltig zu fördern. Dies ist die eigentliche schöne Aufgabe, die wir vor uns haben.

Dazu gehört dann der Rat an die Landsleute: Scheut euch nicht, uns Abgeordnete – angefangen bei den Stadt- und Gemeinderäten – für die Vertretung eurer Interessen in Anspruch zu nehmen und zögert nicht, euch zur Wahrung eurer Rechte mit anderen so zusammenschließen, wie dies zum Sozialstaat gehört.

Ein in sich ruhendes gemeinschaftliches Selbswertgefühl erwächst nicht daraus, das wir von neuen Bundesbürgern erwarten, sie möchten möglichst widerspruchslos aufgehen im Land des großen Bruders. Ich bleibe bei meinem Rat, zusammenwachsen zu lassen, was zusammengehört, Abgeschlossen ist dieser Prozeß erst, wenn wir nicht mehr wissen, wer die neuen und wer die alten Bundesbürger sind.

Vocabulary

der Alterspräsident	the father of the house (parliamentary term)
aufeinander hören	to listen to each other
das Hohe Haus	i.e. Parliament
die Gesetzgeber	the lawmakers
Eigentumsverhältnisse	property relations (i.e. who owns what)
der Abbau der Umweltlasten	reduction of the strain on the environment
wundgescheuert	rubbed raw
das Selbstbewußtsein	self-confidence
das Selbstwertgefühl	feeling of self-esteem
die Demütigung	humiliation
der Strukturwandel	structural change
der Betonklotz (-klötze)	concrete blocks
zügig vorankommen	take place quickly
der Kadi	Muslim term for 'court'
durchmogeln	bluff their way through
die Bestechung	bribe

das Falschspiel	cheating
das Doppelspiel	double game
der Wessi, der Ossi	slang terms for West and East
(die Wessis, die Ossis)	Germans
die Querverbindung	connection, link

Questions on the Source Texts

Text A

1. In what ways does the state intervene in the economy?
2. What are the basic freedoms enshrined in SPD economic policy?
3. Why does the party accept the 'free market'? Where do its reservations lie?
4. To what degree does the traditional opposition of the SPD to the market show itself again in its views on 'property and power'?
5. What is the importance of competition in this context?
6. What are the 'positive aspects' of the entrepreneur?
7. Explain the importance of publicly owned property.
8. Examine the criticisms and the suggestions made on the distribution of wealth and income.

Text B

1. What does the SPD mean by describing itself as *die linke Volkspartei*?
2. To what extent do you think the SPD accords with the 'historic roots' that it describes here?
3. What basic views on the nature of human beings does the SPD hold?
4. What is the relationship between the individual and society?
5. How does the SPD define 'politics'?
6. What is the role of political parties according to the SPD?

Text C

1. Explain the following phrases:
   Arbeitnehmer am Produktivkapital beteiligen

'niedrigere Steuersätze und weniger Ausnahmen'
Vollzugsdefizite in der Finanzverwaltung

2. What policies does the SPD suggest for simplifying the tax system?
3. How would the SPD overcome tax evasion and increase the level of money coming in to the state?

Text D

1. Explain the following phrases:
   (die Freundschaft mit Frankreich) ist konstituierend für die europäische Einheit
   Die ganze Weltgesellschaft entwickelt sich hin zur Integration
   Teilstaaten auf völkischer Grundlage
2. Why should Germany support the integration of the East European states and Russia into a new 'security architecture'?
3. What examples are given of Germany taking on more responsibilities than other European countries?
4. What attitudes does Oskar Lafontaine express towards Germany as a military power?

Text E

1. Explain the following terms and phrases:
   deren Ausgangsstoffe in technische und biologische Kreisläufe zurückgeführt werden können
   die Abfallexporte unterbinden
2. What policies with respect to materials, production and the disposal of waste would the SPD pursue?
3. How does the party see environmental policy stimulating the German economy?
4. What is meant by an ecological tax reform? Would this be feasible?
5. What alternative sources of energy would the SPD develop?
6. Why does the SPD want to support the coal industry, given that the burning of fossil fuels damages the environment?

Text F

1. Explain the following terms and phrases:
   klare Eigentumsverhältnisse
   Schuldvermutung
   Land des großen Bruders
2. Compare and contrast the style of this passage with that of Helmut Kohl's on the eve of unification (pp. 72–5).
3. What criticisms does Brandt make of (a) the West Germans, (b) the East Germans?
4. What leads you to believe that Brandt understands the difficulties that the East Germans have experienced?
5. What is Brandt's opinion about the *Grundgesetz*?
6. What are his suggestions for bringing East and West Germans together?

Notes

1. Golo Mann, *Deutsche Geschichte des 19. und 20. Jahrhunderts* (Frankfurt-am-Main, Fischer Verlag, 1992), 193–250.
2. Bundessekretariat der Jungsozialisten (ed.), 'Offenes Antwortschreiben an das Zentralkomitee zur Berufung eines Allgemeinen Deutschen Arbeiterkongresses zu Leipzig von Ferdinand Lassalle', in *Programme der deutschen Sozialdemokratie* (Hanover, Verlag J. H. W. Dietz Nachf., 1963), 27–64.
3. 'Sozialistische Arbeiterpartei Deutschlands in Gotha beschlossenes Programm', in *Programme der deutschen Sozialdemokratie*, 73–5.
4. Vorstand der SPD, *Sozialdemokratie in Deutschland 1863–1988. Für Freiheit, Gerechtigkeit und Solidarität* (Bonn, 1986), 21–7.
5. Liebknecht became increasingly Marxist and revolutionary. See, for example, Karl Liebknecht, *Ausgewählte Reden und Schriften*, 1 (Frankfurt-am-Main and Vienna, Europäische Verlagsanstalt and Europa Verlag, 1969), 30–62 (anti-militarism), and 82–98 (against the existing state and judicial system).
6. Liebknecht and Luxemburg were murdered by army officers on 15 January 1919 in Berlin.
7. Heinrich Potthoff, *Die Sozialdemokratie von den Anfängen bis 1945* (Bonn-Bad Godesberg, Verlag Neue Gesellschaft, 1975), 109–45.
8. Susanne Miller, *Die SPD vor und nach Godesberg* (Bonn-Bad Godesberg, Verlag Neue Gesellschaft, 1974), 26–8.
9. Vorstand der SPD, *Grundsatzprogramm der Sozialdemokratischen Partei Deutschlands. Beschlossen in Bad Godesberg vom 13. bis 15. November 1959*.
10. Presse- und Informationsamt der Bundesregierung, *Dokumentation zur*

Entspannungspolitik der Bundesregierung (Bonn, 1976), 22–3.

11. 'Vertrag zwischen der Bundesrepublik Deutschland und der Volksrepublik Polen über die Grundlagen der Normalisierung ihrer gegenseitigen Beziehungen vom 7. Dezember 1970', in *Dokumentation zur Entspannungspolitik der Bundesregierung*, 32–5.

12. 'Viermächte-Abkommen über Berlin und die zwischen den zuständigen deutschen Behörden vereinbarten Regelungen', in *Dokumentation zur Entspannungspolitik der Bundesregierung*, 95–107.

13. 'Vertrag über die Grundlagen der Beziehungen zwischen der Bundesrepublik Deutschland und der Deutschen Demokratischen Republik vom 21. Dezember 1972', in *Dokumentation zur Entspannungspolitik der Bundesregierung*, 190–7.

14. G. E. Edwards, 'SPD–SED Initiatives for Chemical and Nuclear Weapon Free Zones in Central Europe', *Journal of Communist Studies*, 3, 2 (London, Frank Cass, 1987), 154–61.

15. G. E. Edwards, 'Further Developments in the East–West German Dialogue', *Journal of Communist Studies*, 4, 2 (London, Frank Cass, 1988), 217–23.

16. Zeno and Sabine Zimmerling, *Chronik DDR 1* (East Berlin, Verlag Tribüne, 1989), 78–88.

17. Barbara Marshall, *Willy Brandt* (London, Sphere Books, 1990), 44.

Bibliography

SPD

Publications in German

Bender, Peter, *Die Ostpolitik Willy Brandts oder Die Kunst des Selbstverständlichen* (Reinbek, Rowohlt, 1972).

Lösche, Peter and Franz Walter, *Die SPD – Klassenpartei – Volkspartei – Quotenpartei* (Darmstadt, Wissenschaftliche Buchgesellschaft, 1992).

Miller, Susanne and Heinrich Potthof, *Kleine Geschichte der SPD. Darstellung und Dokumentation 1848–1983* (Bonn, Verlag Neue Gesellschaft, 1985).

Osterroth, Franz and Dieter Schuster, *Chronik der deutschen Sozialdemokratie*, 3 vols. (West Berlin and Bonn, Verlag J. H. W. Dietz Nachf., 1975–6).

Rovan, Joseph, *Geschichte der deutschen Sozialdemokratie* (Frankfurt-am-Main, Fischer, 1988).

Schmidt, H. 'Die Sozialdemokratische Partei Deutschlands', in A. Mintzel and H. Oberreuter (eds.), *Parteien in der Bundesrepublik Deutschland* (Opladen, Leske + Budrich, 1992).

Publications in English

Braunthal, Gerard, *The German Social Democrats since 1969: A Party in Power and Opposition* (Boulder, Westview Press, 1994).

Fuhr, Eckhard, 'Zurück zur Mitte: Die SPD zu Beginn des Super-wahljahres 1994', in *Aus Politik und Zeitgeschichte*, 1/94 (Bonn, Bundeszentrale für politische Bildung), 8–11.

Hancock, M. Donald, 'The SPD Seeks a New Identity: Party Modernization and the Prospects in the 1990s', in Russell J. Dalton (ed.), *The New Germany Votes* (Providence and Oxford, Berg, 1993), 77–98.

Koelble, T. A., *The Left Unravelled: Social Democracy and the New Left Challenge in Britain and West Germany* (Durham, NC, Duke, University Press, 1991).

Silvia, Stephen J., '"Loosely Coupled Anarchy": The Fragmentation of the Left', in Stephan Padgett (ed.), *Parties and Party Systems in the New Germany* (Aldershot and Brookfield, Dartmouth, 1993).

Willy Brandt

Publications in German

Brandt, Willy, *Außenpolitik, Deutschlandpolitik, Europapolitik* (West Berlin, Berlin Verlag, 1968).

Brandt, Willy, *Erinnerungen* (Frankfurt and Zurich, Propyläen, 1989).

Hoffmann, G., *Willy Brandt. Porträt eines Aufklärers aus Deutschland* (Reinbek, Rororo, 1988).

Koch, G., *Willy Brandt. Eine politische Biographie* (Frankfurt, Ullstein, 1988).

Stern, Carola, *Willy Brandt in Selbstzeugnissen und Bilddokumenten* (Reinbek, Rororo, 1975).

Publications in English

Brandt, Willy, *A Peace Policy for Europe* (London, Weidenfeld & Nicolson, 1969).

Brandt, Willy, *People and Politics* (London, Collins, 1978).

Brandt, Willy, *World Armament and World Hunger: A Call for Action* (London, Gollancz, 1986).

Marshall, Barbara, *Willy Brandt* (London, Cardinal and Sphere Books, 1990).

Prittie, T., *Willy Brandt: Portrait of a Statesman* (London, Weidenfeld & Nicolson, 1974).

Further information may be obtained from:
SPD
Bundesgeschäftsstelle
Abt. Öffentlichkeitsarbeit
Erich-Ollenhauer-Haus
Ollenhauerstr. 1
D-53113 Bonn
Tel. (0228) 532-1
Fax (0228) 532-410

4. Die Grünen and Bündnis 90

A. Die Grünen

The Greens set themselves up as a party in 1980, as a coalition of various heterogeneous interests, and Bündnis 90 emerged in 1991 out of the civil movements that developed in the GDR in the 1980s and during 1990. The two parties joined together in 1994 as a result of the catastrophic downturn in the fortunes of the West German Greens, caused – in part – by their misjudging the question of German reunification in 1990.

Bündnis 90/Die Grünen is a young party and is supported mostly by voters under the age of forty-five. Women vote slightly more for the party than men do. The Bundestag election results in 1994 displayed the following pattern:

18–24-year-olds	14% (women: 15%)
25–34-year-olds	13% (women: 15%)
35–44-year-olds	12% (women: 14%)
45–59-year-olds	5% (women: 7%)
60 and above	2% (women: 2%)[1]

By the late 1970s the strength of the various protest movements had risen to many thousands of groups (exact figures are not available). One-third of these were involved in environmental issues and many of them had begun to form links within their region and with groups in other regions. They were committed to using extra-parliamentary activities for raising public awareness of environmental problems and putting the environment on the political map. At the end of 1977 and the beginning of 1978 local environmental groups put up candidates for local elections in Schleswig-Holstein, Lower Saxony and Bavaria. They passed the 5 per cent mark in two district elections in Schleswig-Holstein, which was important since it showed that voters could be won on an environmental ticket. This success gave the impetus for the various 'green' and 'alternative' groups to begin to work together, although they were by nature decentralist. The breadth and diversity of the ideology and politics of the various groups were clear, but they had enough in common to allow co-operation between them. Within their ranks there were committed Christians, humanists, feminists, environmentalists, liberals and Marxists of various hues.

The first step to the creation of a political party was taken on 17–18 March 1979 in Frankfurt-am-Main when an electoral alliance was formed under the name Sonstige Politische Vereinigung – Die Grünen (SPV – Die Grünen). Among the groups that came together were Aktionsgemeinschaft Unabhängiger Deutscher (AUD), which had been in existence since 1965, the Grüne Liste Umweltschutz (GLU), which had been formed in the early 1970s, and the Grüne Aktion Zukunft (GAZ), whose spiritual father was the former CDU member of the Bundestag, Herbert Gruhl. He was well known for his book *Ein Planet wird geplündert*. The SPV – Die Grünen called for a massive reduction in consumption as the only way to save the planet. At the European elections of June 1979 they received some 900,000 votes, and in the October of that year the Bremer Grüne Liste received 5.1 per cent of the votes and moved into the political arena at *Land* level in Bremen. The SPV – Die Grünen had 10,000 members by January 1980, and at their delegates' meeting that month in Karlsruhe it was accepted that other groups with a variety of agendas could join them so as to prevent the programme concentrating solely on ecology. There were thus three strands represented – the extra-parliamentary opposition with their ecological and pacifist agenda, city subcultures from the 'alternative scene' and the 'drop-outs', and finally the *Bürgerinitiativen* or citizen initiatives. In March 1982 the Greens entered a second *Land* Parliament (Baden-Württemberg) with 5.3 per cent of the votes.

By the spring of 1982 a manifesto had been worked out which was clearly anti-establishment and highly critical of the Federal Republic. It called for an end to short-term economic thinking and to the concept of economic growth. The industrial society – in East and West, in capitalism and communism – had reached a turning-point. New priorities needed to be set so that the environment could be protected for future generations, as well as for much more sparing use of natural resources. There should be an end to electricity generation using nuclear energy. The Greens wanted a reduction in the working week so as to create jobs for the unemployed and greater participation of the work-force in their place of employment. They wanted an extension of democracy across society so that people could be involved in town planning and transport policy. The *Berufsverbot* should be dropped and the right to demonstrate or call meetings fully implemented. A major plank in their policy was the gaining of equal rights for women and an end to discrimination against foreigners.

In their foreign policy the Greens called for world-wide arms reduction, rejected the stationing of Cruise and Pershing missiles in the Federal Republic and the production and storing of biological and chemical weapons. They wanted the staged abolition of NATO and the Warsaw Pact. They supported the independent peace groups that were starting to develop in a number of Eastern bloc countries, including the GDR, and aimed at creating an alliance with them that would transcend the blocs and eventually break them down.

At the Bundestag elections in October 1980 the Greens achieved only 1.5 per cent of the votes cast. Yet this was the period when millions of people were taking part in peace demonstrations and protests against nuclear weapons, and since the Greens were so involved in this they gained support from increasingly large numbers of West Germans. Two of the Greens, Petra Kelly and a former Bundeswehr general, Kurt Bastian, initiated the so-called 'Krefeld Appeal' in 1982 which demanded that American rockets should not be stationed in West Germany. This was signed by four million people. The Greens also issued their own 'Peace Manifesto' in October 1981 in which they attacked the nuclear policy of both the USA and the Soviet Union (for which they fell into disfavour with the Russian and East German leaders who had hoped that the Greens would make useful propaganda for them against the West).

By 1982 the Greens were achieving significant successes. They entered the *Land* parliaments in Lower Saxony (6.5 per cent), Hamburg (7.7 per cent), and Hesse (8.0 per cent). (At the same time the FDP failed to get into the parliaments in Hamburg and Hesse because they fell below 5 per cent.) Their membership had risen to about 25,000. The party programme for the Bundestag elections of 6 March 1983 called for the dismantling of nuclear power stations, the banning of herbicides and pesticides, the ending of night work, the discontinuing of television and radio advertising of tobacco and alcohol. Further, they wanted the sale of militaristic toys to be stopped. So as to help in the struggle for women's equality they proposed that both sexes should attend classes in domestic science and child-rearing. They wanted legislation to end discrimination against homosexuals. In the elections the Greens shot up to two million votes and gained twenty-seven members in Parliament. To the success at Bonn was soon added success in the elections to the European Parliament at Strasbourg – they achieved 8.2 per cent of the votes and seven seats. They were now able to put their views on the environment and other pressing issues on an even higher platform.

Since they came from outside the parliamentary tradition and had no experience of how the Bundestag worked, they were free of conventions. (Their very first appearance in the Bundestag shocked the politicians: they arrived in jeans and sandals, showered flowers around them and sang anti-war songs.) They disturbed the cosy consensus that existed between the established parties, questioned and criticized. In a very direct manner they voiced the matters that most affected the average voter – fear of unemployment, fear of war, destruction of the environment. It soon became clear that the Greens and the SPD had similar views on a number of issues – and were rivals in the struggle for votes – but that there was very much less common ground with the CDU/CSU or FDP. The Greens insisted on parity of men and women in their parliamentary group and in party offices.[2] They introduced a system of rotation of representatives – in the Bundestag and in most of the *Land* parliaments, their representatives resigned after two years and were replaced by others from the Green list. Parliamentarians were also expected to forgo much of their salary and plough it back into the party, since, apart from donations and state money to help fight the elections, the Greens had very few sources of income.

By the end of 1988 two broad groups began to emerge within the Greens – the *Realpolitiker* (Realos) and the *Fundamentalisten* (Fundis). The former believed that the market economy could be reformed and that they should work with the SPD to achieve this reform. This attitude found practical application when the Greens in Hesse formed a coalition with the SPD in the *Land* parliament between 1985 and 1987. The second group believed that the market economy could not be reformed and that the Greens should not be compromised by attempting to work within it, or with the SPD; they should stand by their principles as an opposition party providing a real alternative to the existing system. The *Fundis* represented a more 'green' and radical left-wing position. Nevertheless, and despite conflict and debate, consensus between the two groups was maintained.

In the Bundestag elections of 25 January 1987 the Greens increased their percentage of the votes to 8.3 per cent and had 3.1 million voters behind them. They had forty-two seats in the Bundestag. In the period between this and the previous election the population had been further sensitized to the precarious environmental situation by the melt-down of the reactor at Chernobyl in the Ukraine and the accident at the Sandoz chemical plant in Basle, which did serious damage to the Rhine. Instead of building on this further election success, however, the party degenerated in 1987 into a slanging match between the various factions. The reason for this was that the Greens had lost ground at a number of *Land* elections and there was disagreement within the party on how to recover lost ground and recruit new support. The serious weakening of the party contributed to the West German Greens losing their seats in the first all-German elections in December 1990, but it was the reaction of the party to the question of German reunification which above all caused its spectacular demise in 1990.

The Greens began well in 1989. They achieved one of their best results ever in the West Berlin elections – 11.8 per cent. With this they were able to go into coalition with the SPD. In the June European elections they were able to increase their share slightly to 8.4 per cent (in comparison with 8.2 per cent in 1984). They also increased their share of the vote slightly in the *Land* elections in North Rhine-Westphalia and Rhineland-Palatinate. Events in East Germany were soon to throw them off course. In contrast to the other parties in West Germany, the Greens, despite having so strongly supported human-rights and other dissident groups in the GDR, had seen positive aspects in East Germany itself, and in having a divided Germany. They wanted change in the GDR but did not want the East German state to cease to exist as a separate entity, so they came down against unification. They wanted East Germany to remain, since at least this part of Germany had 'escaped from capitalism'. They also did not believe that the Allies would allow German unification (this was a widely held view, not just among the Greens). They did not even accept the original plan put forward by Helmut Kohl in December 1989 for a confederation that would later lead to unification. At the same time more realistic Greens, as early as November 1989, seemed to understand that the GDR had little chance of surviving as an independent state and were highly depressed. Once Gorbachev had agreed with Helmut Kohl in February 1990 that the Soviet Union would not interfere if the Germans wished to unite, the hopes of the Greens that the GDR might survive were dashed. The party had to change direction shortly before the Volkskammer elections (although some individual members were still speaking out against unification weeks after the elections). The position adopted after it became clear that unification was inevitable was that the constitution should be rewritten to meet the needs of the new Germany, and that under no circumstances should the GDR join the Federal Republic under Article 23, since this would amount to nothing more than annexation (*Anschluß*). They also called for the demilitarization of reunified Germany. At their Dortmund conference in June 1990 they were still disagreeing on how unification should proceed and what the party should support or oppose. There was, however, agreement that the haste with which the unification process was being pushed through was leading to chaos, that the only solution lay in a gradual process of 'growing together', and that the treaty between the two states (*Staatsvertrag*) was unacceptable since it would lead directly to the 'annexation' of the GDR. By late summer they had clarified their position to a great extent and voted against the second *Staatsvertrag*, particularly on the question of ownership of property in the GDR (a problem which is still of considerable importance to many hundreds of thousands of East and West Germans).[3] They were also worried about abortion law after unification, since the GDR law was considerably more 'liberal' than that in West Germany. From the spring to the autumn, however, the Greens were unable to make any impact on the unification process or put forward strategies that would gain much support among the electorate. When they tried to return to their stronghold of the environment, for instance in opposing the transfer of the structure of the West German energy industry to East Germany, or the buying up of the GDR electricity distribution system by the West Germans, they gained little support or interest. The electorate was completely preoccupied with the bigger question of unification. In only one area were they successful: on the question of the electoral procedure to be used in the first all-German elections that were to take place in December 1990. They made an appeal to the Constitutional Court and it was upheld on 28 September. This meant that the 5 per cent hurdle was applied to the East and the West German electorates separately for that one election. The new small parties in East Germany would have had no chance of any representation in Bonn if they had had to reach 5 per cent of the national vote.

In the elections to the all-German Bundestag on 2 December 1990, the West German Greens gained 4.7 per cent of the vote, and no seats. The East German Greens and Bündnis 90 stood at 5.9 per cent and netted eight seats.

B. Bündnis 90

The possibility of dissent and opposition in East Germany between 1945 and 1989 had always been severely curtailed. Up to 1961 it had been limited in scope either by dissidents being forced to leave the country for West Germany (for example, many of the staff and students of the Humboldt University in East Berlin left for West Berlin in 1947–8, where they laid the foundations of the Free University) or in more extreme cases (such as Rudolf Herrnstadt, Wolfgang Harich, Walter Janka) were imprisoned as 'anti-socialists'. After the building of the Berlin Wall dissidents knew that they could not escape to West Berlin or West Germany if they overstepped the narrow limits of criticism or dissent that the SED tolerated. The whole history of the GDR was characterized by a series of 'hard lines' and 'thaws'. In contrast to other Eastern bloc countries such as Poland or Czechoslovakia, however, intellectuals in East Germany did not come out openly as a group and demand change or put forward alternatives. It was left to the grass-roots to do that in the 1980s, to some extent with the protection of the Churches.

There was only one niche in which opposition could be voiced and that was within the Church. The East German state followed the traditional Marxist line and tried over the decades to limit the influence of the Churches. (Most East German Christians were Protestants. Thus in the last official census in 1964 that gave details of religious affiliation, eleven of the seventeen million population registered as Christians, one million of whom were Catholics and most of the remainder were Protestants.)[4] In 1945 denominational schools were no longer allowed, by the early 1950s religious education had been completely removed from the schools, church newspapers and magazines could no longer be bought in shops or kiosks, and a series of secular ceremonies were set up by the state to mirror and compete with Christian baptism, confirmation, wedding and burial services. Yet in the 1960s the SED's attitudes towards the Churches changed somewhat, as it was perceived that the Churches had a number of useful roles to play in supporting state social service provision and on the international propaganda front. The Churches were prominent from the 1950s onwards in calling for disarmament, and officially they supported SED proposals for *détente*. The fact that there were reasonable working arrangements between Church and state meant that occasionally dissident views could be expressed within the Christian community without too dire consequences, and in the 1960s the occasional voice was raised against conscription or on the right to conscientious objection, and in 1978 some Christian parents did oppose the introduction of paramilitary training into the school curriculum. The situation changed at the end of the 1970s and during the 1980s under the impact of the new round in the arms race.

Officially, the GDR, in common with the rest of the Eastern bloc, had always regarded socialism as a 'peace-loving ideology' and capitalism as 'imperialist' and 'warmongering' since so much money could be made out of armaments and war. The SED thus encouraged the creation and activities of the Friedensrat der DDR (Peace Council) in making propaganda for peace, organizing demonstrations for peace or against the West and for collecting signatures (as, for example, in 1979 when it organized a petition in support of Soviet peace proposals and, allegedly, contacted some 96 per cent of the adult population). The SED also encouraged peace movements in the West, and particularly in West Germany, to protest against NATO's policies and the defence policy of their own state. At the end of the 1970s and in the 1980s, however, small groups of East Germans – mainly young people, many of whom were committed Christians and women – began to criticize not only the West for its part in the arms race but also the East, and even the SED. (At a later stage, as the SS 20s and American Pershing and Cruise missiles were removed, many of them turned their attention to the environment, where there were considerable problems of air and water pollution.) It was inevitable that they would come under the scrutiny of the Stasi and be persecuted for their actions. They tried turning to the West – to Greens, the SPD, accredited journalists and foreign embassies – to get their message broadcast (i.e. back to East Germany via West German television and radio) and, paradoxically, to give them some measure of protection against arrest and imprisonment. Their main source of support, however, was the Protestant church, for it had high standing in society and was the only organization that was not under the direct control of the SED. It had its own meeting places which could not be touched by the Stasi (even though there was harassment outside the churches and the Stasi infiltrated its ranks and the various meetings and demonstrations), it could produce leaflets for its own use and it could organize events. The protesters used the churches for their events and, if they were arrested, their supporters did their best to arrange for the Church to protest on their behalf or try to organize their release.

The importance of the peace and environmental groups was that, despite being weak, physically isolated (most of them were in East Berlin, Halle, Leipzig and Dresden) and very small in terms of membership, they formed a nucleus of activists who gained experience over a number of years of planning, organizing and engaging in political activity. It was not surprising that they played an active and important role in events from September 1989 to well into 1990. It was also not surprising that a number of the high-profile members elected to the Volkskammer in March 1990 came from the Protestant clergy, for instance Rainer Eppelmann (DA), Wolfgang Ullmann (DJ), Steffen Reiche (SPD), Friedrich Schorlemmer (DA and later SPD), Hans-Wilhelm Ebeling (DSU), Markus Meckel (SPD). Many others were committed Christians.

On 10 September 1989 the 'initiative' group, Bürgerbewegung Neues Forum (the most prominent signatories to the founding document were Bärbel Bohley, artist, and Professor Jens Reich, micro-biologist), came into existence and called for a dialogue between party and people, for the improvement of the range of goods in the shops, for the clean-up of the environment and the end of unlimited growth. They wanted legal recognition as an association under Article 29 of the constitution (this was refused on 15 September).[5] On 12 September the opposition group Bürgerbewegung Demokratie Jetzt (DJ) was formed, to be followed on 1 October by the Demokratischer Aufbruch (DA) and on 24 November by Die Grünen. In the coming weeks and months a number of other parties and organizations formed – Initiative Vereinigte Linke (VL), Grüne Partei Initiative Frieden und Menschenrechte (IFM), Grüne Liga, Bäuerlicher Unabhängiger Frauenverband. On 7 December the Churches invited their representatives, together with those of the Neues Forum, Demokratie Jetzt and the Greens to sit down at a 'Round Table' with the SED, LDPD, NDPD, DBD, CDU, VdgB and the FDGB in order to discuss how to overcome the crisis in the country. From then on the Runder Tisch was to play a continuous role in the political arena up to the elections in March 1990, and it was invited on 28 January to be involved in government. On 6 February Neues Forum, Demokratie Jetzt, and Initiative für Frieden und

Menschenrechte joined to form an electoral union, Bündnis 90. The Greens joined with the Unabhängiger Frauenverband on 14 February to form an electoral group. This meant that Bündnis 90, the Greens and the UFV had only a month to work out their campaign manifestos, organize their supporters, raise their funds and electioneer. It was a very difficult task, and it is not surprising that their success at the polls was limited. Bündnis 90 received 333,005 votes and the Greens and UFV 225,234.

After the elections there was disappointment and disillusionment in both alliances. These were the people who had struggled so hard against the SED, who had been tireless in their attempts to bring about reform and a new beginning since September 1989, and yet they had been effectively shut out of the process on 18 March. By the time the all-German elections took place in December Bündnis 90 and the Greens had agreed to join forces and stand as one party, separate from the West German Greens. The decision to stand separately from the West Germans was taken because they felt that their East German agenda had different priorities from those of their allies in the West. They were also allergic to receiving advice from West Germans – even their friends. The result of the election gave them only eight seats (6.05 per cent) and they had lost about fifteen thousand voters since March. More worryingly, the groups that made up the alliances lost members throughout 1990. Whereas some 200,000 people had signed the original founding document for the Neues Forum in 1989, by July 1990 the numbers may have been as low as 10,000–20,000, and one year later had dropped to only about 5,000. Demokratie Jetzt dropped from around 3,000–4,000 members in January 1990 to 836 by September and was to drop still further to 600 by June 1991. The IFM was down to only 200 members by that time.[6] Some members gave up their activities after it became clear that unification was going to take place, and a small number joined other parties. Many put their time and effort into tracking down the files that the Stasi had set up on them and then overcoming the shock and disappointment of realizing the extent to which they had been informed upon by their friends and others in the protest groups prior to 1989. The lack of members started to become a barrier to the expansion of parliamentary and other political activities. The Neues Forum also had a problem in that it was, from the outset, heterogeneous in its membership and policies and prone to splits and conflicts. A major area of debate lay in the definition of *Bürgerbewegung*. Was it a party or an association, should it have formal or informal structures? Should it participate in elections or work only at grass-roots level? Eventually Bündnis 90 worked out a basis for consensus but did not produce a programme in the conventional sense.

Bündnis 90 has emphasized in its parliamentary work the areas of environment, human rights, the development of democracy, and education. It has paid little attention to major areas of interest to the electorate, namely, employment, women's rights and social policy. This narrowness was – and remains – a problem. After the 1990 election it was clear that there would be no possibility of getting into the Bundestag except in conjunction with another party. The Greens could probably get into Parliament again, but only if Bündnis 90 did not split their vote. It was logical and, indeed, essential for the two parties to merge. After difficult negotiations during 1992–3, Bündnis 90 and the Greens merged to form one party. In the Bundestag elections in 1994 the new party gained forty-nine seats in Parliament and 7.3 per cent. In the European elections that year they polled 10.1 per cent of second votes and sent twelve members to sit in the European Parliament. They had good results in *Land* elections in 1995 (Berlin, 13.2 per cent; Bremen, 13.1 per cent; Hesse, 11.2 per cent; North Rhine-Westphalia, 10.0 per cent) and in 1996 (Baden-Württemberg, 12.1 per cent; Rhineland-Palatinate, 6.9 per cent; Schleswig-Holstein, 8.1 per cent). In West Germany the party's future once more looks assured, but it has not made up ground in East Germany since the early 1990s. A number of leading East German members defected in 1997 – mainly to the CDU.

Sources

Die Grünen

Text A: Bündnis 90/Die Grünen, *Politische Grundsätze* (Bonn, 1994), 13–17

Politik vor der Entscheidung

Der Epochenumbruch hat erst begonnen

Mit dem Fall der Mauer sind Politik und Geschichte erneut in Bewegung geraten. Die Überwindung einer über Jahrzehnte lähmenden Blockkonfrontation könnte enorme Möglichkeiten für eine fortschrittliche und lebensbejahende Entwicklung der Menschheit freisetzen. Die Gewißheit alter Feindbilder ist zerfallen. Neue werden aufgebaut. Lange erhobene Forderungen nach Auflösung der Militärblöcke, Abschaffung der ABC-Waffen, Abrüstung, Konversion der Rüstungsindustrie sowie Stopp des weltweiten Waffenhandels könnten jetzt erfüllt werden. Trotzdem müssen wir erkennen, daß das Ende des Kalten Krieges nicht der Anfang des ewigen Weltfriedens ist, sondern eher die Wiederbelebung ethnischer, nationaler und religiöser Rivalitäten und Konflikte ausgelöst hat. Die mit dem Golfkrieg deutlich gewordenen Ziele einer 'Neuen Weltordnung' weisen den Weg in zukünftige internationale Konflikte und Verteilungskriege, insbesondere der 1. gegen die 3. Welt. Es hat sich gezeigt, daß aus dem Gleichgewicht des Schreckens kein wirklicher Friede entstehen konnte. Wie eine stabile Friedensordnung jenseits des Ost-West-Gegensatzes aussehen kann, ist angesichts der Instabilitäten in Europa und anderen Erdteilen noch unklar.

Der Zusammenbruch des sozialistischen Systems hat den Ideenhaushalt des Westens gründlich erschüttert. Allzugern wurde verdrängt, daß die Beseitigung der totalitären Herrschaft nicht das Ergebnis eines Sieges des Westens über den Osten, nicht nur ein wirtschaftlicher Zusammenbruch war, sondern die Selbstbefreiung aktiver Menschen und die Lebensunfähigkeit einer Gesellschaftsordnung. Auch der Westen ist aufgefordert, seine aus dem kalten Krieg hervorgegangenen Strukturen zu überwinden. Doch die Unterschätzung eigener Probleme verstellt momentan die Bereitschaft, unverzüglich Veränderungen in Angriff zu nehmen. Noch ist die Ablösung der durch die Supermächte und die globale Systemkonkurrenz geprägten Weltordnung des 20. Jahrhunderts nicht abgeschlossen. Dem Zerfall der Sowjetunion muß der Rückzug der USA aus der Rolle des Weltpolizisten folgen. Noch fehlt es an geeigneten Instrumenten und Strukturen, diesen Prozeß zu begleiten. In ihrem derzeitigen Zustand sind die Vereinten Nationen weit davon entfernt, im Auftrag der Völkergemeinschaft eine friedliche und gerechte Weltordnung zu entwickeln und aufrechtzuhalten.

Auch Europa ist auf die neue Situation unzureichend vorbereitet. Die Wirtschaftskrise in Osteuropa und der brutale Bürgerkrieg im ehemaligen Jugoslawien zeigen ein politisches Europa, das unfähig ist, Konfliktlösungen zu entwickeln. Unterdrückung, Bevormundung und verordneter Internationalismus haben im Osten einen aggressiven Nationalismus hinterlassen. Im Westen gewinnen rechtsextreme und nationalistische Parteien zunehmend an Bedeutung. Der aufkeimende Nationalismus ist die große Herausforderung an ein demokratisches Europa. Wenn Gesamt-Europa sich nicht auf demokratische und faire Weise einigt, droht der Rückfall in alte Zerissenheit, in Hegemonialkonflikte und Völkerhaß. Wirtschaftliche Ausbeutung, soziale Not, Hunger, Bürgerkriege und ökologische Katastrophen haben weltweite Wanderungsbewegungen ausgelöst. Die reichen Industrieländer begegnen den Menschen, die um Aufnahme nachsuchen, mit zu wenig Solidarität. Es fehlt sowohl an der Bereitschaft, Flüchtlinge aufzunehmen, als auch daran, die Fluchtursachen wirksam zu bekämpfen. Die alten Ideologien sind brüchig geworden. Noch hat der Gewinn der Freiheit keine neuen Lebensperspektiven eröffnet. Visionslosigkeit und Handlungsunfähigkeit bedingen einander. In der gegenwärtigen Orientierungslosigkeit wachsen Ängste und Unsicherheiten und die Neigung, plumpen Versprechungen hinterherzulaufen. Ausländerhaß, Rassismus, Brandanschläge und rechtsextremer Terror vergiften das politische Klima, verletzen und töten Menschen ...

Ökologie in der Warteschleife

Im Verlauf weniger Jahrhunderte hat die von Europa ausgegangene ökonomische Unterwerfung der Erde unsere Welt an den Rand des ökologischen Kollaps geführt. Die immer schnellere und intensivere Ausbeutung der endlichen Ressourcen, die ungeheure Energieverschwendung und Müllproduktion durch die Industrieländer bedrohen mittlerweile das Überleben der menschlichen Zivilisation. Die Erdatmosphäre ist durch den Treibhauseffekt, die tägliche Freisetzung von Radioaktivität und die ungebremste Zerstörung der schützenden Ozonschicht akut gefährdet.

Der Glaube an grenzenloses Wachstum von Produktion und Konsum erweist sich als verhängnisvolle Gefahr. Schon heute sind viele Länder nicht mehr in der Lage, die Trinkwasserversorgung ihrer Einwohnerinnen und Einwohner sicherzustellen. Die Ernährung der wachsenden Weltbevölkerung ist vielerorts nicht gewährleistet. Die Armut, vor allem in den Staaten der Zweidrittel-Welt, trifft immer mehr Menschen. Gleichzeitig werden Unmengen an Kapital und Wissen für nutzlose Zwecke, vorrangig für die Entwicklung und Produktion neuer Waffen, eingesetzt.

Ökonomische, soziale und ökologische Probleme stehen in einem unlösbaren Zusammenhang. Ohne Bewältigung der ökologischen Probleme ist auch keine tragende Antwort auf die ökonomischen Fragen möglich. Der Ost-West Konflikt wird abgelöst von einer

Verschärfung der Nord-Süd-Gegensätze. Doch nur eine ökologische Solidargesellschaft wird in der Lage sein, die sich verschärfenden Verteilungskämpfe ohne Krieg und Massenvertreibung zu bewältigen.

Die kommenden Jahre werden unter dem Vorzeichen der globalen Umweltprobleme stehen. Die Erkenntnis, daß Umweltverschmutzung und -zerstörung vor Grenzen nicht Halt macht, wird die nationale und internationale Politik verändern. Ob es gelingt, das Überleben der menschlichen Zivilisation auf diesem Planeten zu bewahren, wird maßgeblich davon abhängen, inwieweit die Menschen bereit sind, aus dem Wissen über die weltweiten Zusammenhänge die notwendigen Konsequenzen für ihr Handeln zu ziehen.

Demokratie in der Krise

Die innere Verfaßtheit unserer Gesellschaft ist besorgniserregend. Verfassungsrecht und Verfassungswirklichkeit driften immer stärker auseinander. Die etablierten Parteien beginnen das Grundgesetz an die schlechte Wirklichkeit in der Bundesrepublik anzupassen. Die Bürgerinnen und Bürger spüren, daß es so wie bisher nicht weitergehen kann, während die etablierten Parteien diesen Anschein aufrechterhalten. Die aufziehende politische Krise ist eine Krise der Demokratie.

Die deutsche Vereinigung hat gezeigt, daß die westliche Parteiendemokratie den Anforderungen, die der weltgeschichtliche Umbruchsprozeß an sie stellt, in ihrer derzeitigen Form nicht gerecht wird. Die Bürgerinnen und Bürger fühlen sich weitgehend von der Politik entmündigt und erleben sie als geschlossenes System, in dem Taktik und Machtinteressen, nicht aber Problemlösungen und Konsensfindung vorherrschen. Das hat zu einem Glaubwürdigkeitsverlust geführt. Wahlenthaltung, Politik- und Parteiverdrossenheit sind die Folgen. Um dies zu überwinden, braucht die Politik einen Rückgewinn an Legitimation und konsensbildender Kraft. 'Wir sind das Volk' war der unmittelbare Ruf nach Demokratie im Herbst '89. Auch im Westen bestehen die Bürgerinnen und Bürger auf mehr Partizipation. Unsere Demokratie muß deswegen nicht nur repräsentativer, sondern zugleich auch direkter werden. Demokratie, Freiheit und Selbstbestimmung werden erst dann zu bestimmenden Werten, wenn wir sie handelnd erfüllen können.

Nachdem im Osten die soziale Lebens- und Erfahrungswelt zerschlagen wurde, sind die im Westen geprägten 'Werte der bürgerlichen Gesellschaft' kaum geeignet, den Menschen neue Maßstäbe für ihr Denken und Handeln zu geben. Unser Traum von einer gerechteren Gesellschaft bleibt bestehen.

Vocabulary

verstellen	to cloud
unverzüglich	without delay
die Völkergemeinschaft	community of nations
aufkeimend	nascent
fortschrittlich	progressive
Verteilungskämpfe	wars to divide up the world's resources
das Gleichgewicht des Schreckens	the balance of terror
die Visionslosigkeit	lack of vision
plump	crass
der Brandanschlag	arson
die Unterwerfung	subjugation
die Energieverschwendung	wasting of energy
die Müllproduktion	production of waste, rubbish
der Treibhauseffekt	greenhouse effect
spüren	to sense, feel
entmündigen	disenfranchise
der Glaubwürdigkeitsverlust	loss of credibility
die Wahlenthaltung	not going to the poll, people not voting
die Politikverdrossenheit	disillusionment with politics

Text B: 'Mit Ökosteuern umsteuern', in *Nur mit uns. Programm zur Bundestagswahl 1994* (Bonn), 11

Heute sagen viele Preise nicht die ökologische Wahrheit. Umweltzerstörende Produkte und Verfahren sind zu billig, weil noch nicht einmal die bekannten, durch sie verursachten ökologischen Folgekosten in ihren Preis eingehen. Zukunftsgefährdendes Wirtschaften und Verbrauchen wird damit begünstigt, zukunftsfähiges ökologisches Verhalten andererseits entmutigt. Dagegen wollen wir durch eine ökologische Steuerreform angehen: Wer die Umwelt schädigt, soll zahlen; wer sie bewahren hilft, soll gewinnen. Wir brauchen starke wirtschaftliche Steuerungsinstrumente, um Umweltschäden zu vermeiden und zu beseitigen. Das Aufkommen aus Umweltsteuern soll auch dazu verwendet werden, den ökologischen Umbau mitzufinanzieren.

Durch die verbrauchsabhängigen Ökosteuern und -abgaben soll umweltfreundliches Produzieren und Verbrauchen auch finanziell attraktiv werden. Wir wollen, daß Umweltverbrauch und Umweltschädigung zu einem wesentlichen Kostenfaktor in den betriebswirtschaftlichen Kalkulationen werden und ökologische Innovationen, die sich häufig schon heute rechnen, nicht länger blockiert werden. Damit gehen von Ökosteuern Impulse für neue Produkte, Produktionsweisen und Technologien aus, die wiederum neue Märkte eröffnen und Arbeitsplätze sichern und schaffen. Wir sind zugleich dafür, solche Betriebe, die in den ökologischen Umbau investieren, zu entlasten. Das kann durch entsprechende Abschreibungen, die steuermindernd sind, oder durch einen Ökobonus verwirklicht werden.

Vordringlich sind die Erhöhung der Mineralölsteuer, die Einführung einer Primärenergiesteuer, die Einführung von Abfallabgaben auf Landesebenen und eine Schwerverkehrsabgabe.

Vocabulary

umweltzerstörend	destroying the environment
die Folgekosten	resulting costs
entmutigen	to discourage
entlasten	to remove burdens
die Abschreibung	writing off (of debts)
steuermindernd	which reduce taxes (taxation)
vordringlich	imperative
die Mineralölsteuer	tax on petrol and diesel
die Primärenergiesteuer	tax on primary sources of energy

Text C: 'Arbeitszeitverkürzung und Lohnausgleich', in *Nur mit uns. Programm zur Bundestagswahl 1994* (Bonn), 15

Jede Arbeitszeitverkürzung der Vergangenheit wurde auch von den Beschäftigten durch teilweisen Verzicht auf Lohnzuwächse erkauft. Heute, mitten in der deutschen Einigungskrise und der Rezession im Westen, werden Arbeitszeitverkürzungen in großen Schritten auch erreichte Einkommen berühren. Ein voller Lohnausgleich für alle wird nicht erstritten werden. Doch die unteren Einkommen sind nicht weiter belastbar.

Eine gleichmäßigere Umverteilung von Erwerbsarbeit wird nur durchsetzbar sein, wenn ein sozial gestaffelter Lohnausgleich Einbußen bei den niedrigen Einkommen verhindert und wenn gleichzeitig den Besserverdienenden ein Mehr an Zeit auch ein Weniger an Geld wert ist. Arbeitszeitverkürzung muß einhergehen mit einer Wende zu einer neuen, solidarischen Lohn- und Gehaltspolitik, die zugleich mehr Verteilungsgerechtigkeit unter den abhängig Beschäftigten schafft.

Die Steuerpolitik hat dies unter anderem dadurch zu unterstützen, indem der Steuerfreibetrag auf Grundsicherungsniveau angehoben wird und das Ehegatten-Splitting durch einen verbesserten Kinderlastenausgleich – unter anderem mit einem deutlich erhöhten Kindergeld – ersetzt wird.

Bei ohnehin sinkenden Realeinkommen lassen sich Löhne und Gehälter nicht im gleichen Umfang kürzen wie die Arbeitszeit. Auch den Unternehmen – insbesondere in den rentabelsten und produktivsten Sektoren – muß ein kräftiger Beitrag zur Finanzierung der Umverteilung von Erwerbsarbeit abverlangt werden.

Wo die Kosten des sozial gestaffelten Lohnausgleichs nachweislich die Existenz von Betrieben oder Branchen gefährden, muß es möglich sein, im Einzelfall geeignete öffentliche Hilfen – auch in Form von Lohnkostensubventionierung – zu gewähren. Dies gilt insbesondere für Ostdeutschland.

Vocabulary

der Beschäftigte	
(die Beschäftigten)	employed person
der Verzicht	renunciation, giving up
der Lohnzuwachs	wage increase
gleichmäßigere	more equitable, more equal
die Umverteilung	redistribution
die Einbuße	loss
die Besserverdienenden	the higher earners
ein Mehr an Zeit	more time
ein Weniger an Geld	less money
einhergehen	to accompany

Text D: Bündnis 90/Die Grünen, *Ein Land Reformieren, 10 Reformprojekte und ein Finanzierungsvorschalg* (Bonn, 1994), 4

Wir wollen die Entwicklung in den Anwendungsgebieten der Gentechnologie umkehren. Anstatt immer weiter auf gentechnische Verfahren zu setzen, wollen wir alternative Forschungs- und Problemlösungsstrategien fördern: durch eine Umlenkung der Forschungsgelder, durch eine breite öffentliche Debatte, durch ein Gentechnikgesetz ausschließlich für den Schutz von Mensch und Umwelt. Wir wollen höhere Sicherheitsstandards, stärkere Öffentlichkeitsbeteiligung und eine umfassende Haftungsregelung. Wir lehnen die Freisetzung gentechnisch veränderter Organismen ab. Gentechnische Diskriminierung – z.B. im Arbeits- und Versicherungsbereich – wollen wir gesetzlich unterbinden. Embryonenforschung und Keimbahntherapie sollen verboten bleiben und die Patentierung von Lebewesen wollen wir verhindern. Wir wollen nicht alles umsetzen, nur weil es technisch machbar ist.

Vocabulary

die Anwendungsgebiete	the areas in which —— is to be used
das Verfahren	method
die Umlenkung	diversion
die Haftungsregelung	regulations on liability
die Keimbahntherapie	germ-line therapy
die Patentierung	patenting
technisch machbar	technically feasible

Text E: Bündnis 90/Die Grünen, *Nur mit uns. Programm zur Bundestagswahl 1994* (Bonn), 46–7

Emanzipierte Gesellschaft – feministische Politik

Ziel bündnisgrüner Frauenpolitik ist, das Selbstbestimmungsrecht von Frauen zu verwirklichen. Unsere Politik will die gesellschaftlichen Strukturen verändern, die sich einseitig an männlichen Werten orientieren und nach männlichen Mustern funktionieren. Arbeit von Frauen, die sie unbezahlt und jenseits von gesellschaftlicher Macht und Einflußnahme für die Familie und das soziale Gemeinwesen leisten, wird gesellschaftlich nicht angemessen anerkannt, gerade weil sie nur von Frauen ausgeübt wird.

Unsere Politik ist daher konsequent auf die Umverteilung von Arbeit, Einkommen, Status und Macht zwischen Frauen und Männern gerichtet. Wir setzten uns dafür ein, daß in allen gesellschaftlichen Bereichen traditionelle Vorstellungen von Männlichkeit und Weiblichkeit hinterfragt werden. Wir wollen, daß Frauen in allen öffentlichen Bereichen von Gesellschaft, Politik und Wirtschaft maßgeblich mitgestalten und daß Männer ihren Anteil an der Arbeit im privaten Bereich übernehmen ...

Ziel bündnisgrüner Politik ist die emanzipierte Gesellschaft. Deshalb ist unsere feministische Politik eng mit der Lösung ökologischer und sozialer Fragen verbunden und zielt auf die Veränderung der gesamten Gesellschaft ...

Ziel bündnisgrüner Frauenpolitik ist der Umbau des Erwerbssystems, um die vorhandenen Erwerbsarbeitsplätze zwischen Männern und Frauen gleichermaßen zu teilen und Frauen einen gleichberechtigten Zugang zum Erwerbsleben zu sichern.

Ein Antidiskriminierungs-Gesetz, das auch für die Privatwirtschaft klare Quotierungsregeln, verbindliche Frauenförderpläne und Maßnahmen zum Schutz vor sexueller Belästigung vorsieht, ist ein Mittel, um dieses Ziel zu erreichen. Wirtschaftspolitik und Wirtschaftsförderung müssen endlich Fraueninteressen berücksichtigen. Betriebe, die aktiv Frauen fördern, sind bei der Auftragsvergabe zu bevorzugen.

Vocabulary

das Selbstbestimmungsrecht	right to self-determination
das soziale Gemeinwesen	social community
hinterfragen	to question
maßgeblich	considerably
die Quotierungsregeln	quota regulations
sexuelle Belästigung	sexual harassment
die Auftragsvergabe	granting of contracts

Text F: Bündnis 90/Die Grünen, *Nur mit uns. Programm zur Bundestagswahl 1994* (Bonn), 55

Die Entmilitarisierung der Politik – dies bedeutet auch die Auflösung der NATO – und der Aufbau ziviler Strukturen sind Prozesse, die parallel laufen müssen. Abrüstung schafft neue Handlungsmöglichkeiten für zivile Konfliktlösungen: durch den Abbau von Feindbildern, durch die Umwidmung der Mittel und Ressourcen, durch einen neuen Zugang zur Konfliktlösung. Abrüstung muß gegen die militärischen Strukturen des Westens, insbesondere die NATO, durchgesetzt werden. Strukturen gemeinsamer Sicherheit müssen an die Stelle der Bündnisstrukturen treten und ermöglichen ihre Auflösung.

Europa braucht gerade jetzt einen neuen Anlauf zur Entmilitarisierung von Politik und Gesellschaft. Nicht ein neuer Euromilitarismus, wie ihn die christliberale Bundesregierung über die 'Gemeinsame Außen- und Sicherheitspolitik' der Maastrichter Verträge und der Westeuropäischen Union betreibt, sondern Abrüstung und zügige wirtschaftliche und politische Öffnung der Europäischen Union für alle Länder Mittel- und Osteuropas sind das Gebot der Stunde. Nicht der Ausbau von Militärbündnissen, sondern nur das Zusammenwirken von wirtschaftlicher und politischer Integration kann eine dauerhafte Perspektive des Friedens schaffen.

Unser Ziel ist ein ABC-Waffen-freies Europa. Wir treten darüber hinaus für eine weltweite Abrüstung und die Auflösung aller Armeen ein. Wir treten für koordinierte Rüstungskonversion und das konsequente Verbot aller Rüstungsexporte ein ...

Wir fordern den sofortigen Stopp aller militärischen Großprojekte, insbesondere des Baus von Jäger 90/Europafighter 2000 und des Panzerabwehrhubschraubers PAH 2. Eine Beteiligung der Bundeswehr an UNO-Blauhelmmissionen lehnen wir weiterhin ab. Alle Planungen, die Bundeswehr an schnellen Eingreiftruppen zu beteiligen, sind zu beenden.

Vocabulary

die Auflösung	dissolution
die Konfliktlösung	conflict resolution
die Abrüstung	disarmament
schnelle Eingreiftruppen	rapid-response troops

Questions on the Source Texts

Text A

1. Explain the following words and phrases:

der Epochenumbruch hat erst begonnen
Die Überwindung einer über Jahrzehnte lähmenden Blockkon-
   frontation
Neue (Feindbilder) werden aufgebaut
der Golfkrieg
Gleichgewicht des Schreckens
verordneter Internationalismus im Osten
endliche Ressourcen
der Treibhauseffekt
Zerstörung der schützenden Ozonschicht
der Glaube an grenzenloses Wachstum
Zweidrittel-Welt

2. What changes did the party hope for after the collapse of communism?
3. What dangers have arisen instead?
4. If the party's wish that the USA gives up its so-called role of world policeman were fulfilled, what might be the implications?
5. What does the party have to say about Europe's political role and the dangers which confront her?
6. Do you think that it is a fair assessment to say that Europe is historically responsible for the world now being on the edge of an ecological collapse?
7. Explain the six factors mentioned here that are contributing to the pending ecological disaster.
8. What problems are confronting the Third World?
9. What chance does the party see for changes in the field of international politics?
10. From your general knowledge of the Federal Republic do you think the party overestimates the 'drifting apart' of the constitution and the real situation in the country?
11. What is suggested to overcome the 'crisis of democracy' in Germany?

Text B

1. Explain the following terms and expressions:
   ein sozialgestaffelter Lohnausgleich
   Ehegatten-Splitting
2. What has been the problem in shortening working time in the past, and if working time is to be reduced, how is it to be

'allocated' and who is going to pay for the reduction?
3. What changes to the tax system does the party suggest?
4. In what other way would the state intervene in the process of reallocating work?

Text C

1. Explain the following terms and expressions:
    mit Ökosteuern umsteuern
    ökologische Folgekosten
    Abschreibungen
    Primärenergiesteuer
2. Outline the party's basic principles on taxing environmental pollution.
3. To what extent do you think they could be implemented and what would be the economic and social consequences?

Text D

1. In advocating a turn away from further usage of gene technology, what does the party suggest as an alternative?
2. What aspects would their law on gene technology cover?
3. In what areas do the Greens see dangers in using gene technology?

Text E

1. Explain the following terms:
    emanzipierte Gesellschaft
    Selbstbestimmungsrecht von Frauen
    männliche Werte, männliche Muster
2. What does the party say is wrong with the present relationship between men and women?
3. How do they envisage changing the situation?
4. What would be the results of setting quotas for the employment of women?

Text F

1. Explain the following terms and expressions:
   die Entmilitarisierung der Politik
   zivile Konfliktlösung
   Abbau von Feindbildern
   ABC-Waffen
   Rüstungskonversion
   UNO-Blauhelmmissionen
2. To what extent is demilitarization in Europe a realistic possibility?
3. Why is the party opposed to the German involvement in United Nations missions?
4. Do you perceive any feminist attitudes in the party's pacifism?

Sources

Bündnis 90

Text A: Reinhard Schult, 'Offen für alle – das "Neue Forum"', in Hubertus Knabe (ed.), *Aufbruch in eine andere DDR* (Reinbek, Rowohlt Taschenbuch Verlag, 1989), 168–70

Programmatische Grundsätze

Im Aufruf des NEUEN FORUM ist das Wort Sozialismus nicht zu finden. Einige der Mitglieder haben dies kritisiert. Viele möchten ausdrücklich keine kapitalistische Gesellschaft. Wir haben bewußt auf alle ideologischen Begriffe verzichtet, denn heute kann niemand mehr die Frage beantworten, was denn eigentlich Sozialismus, was denn links sei. Es gehört mit zu den Verbrechen des Stalinismus, der sogenannten linken Bewegung die Sprache genommen zu haben. Eine Aufarbeitung der Geschichte dieser Bewegung verfehlt aber ihr Ziel, wenn sie sich nur den Verbrechen der Stalinzeit und der nachfolgenden Stagnation zuwendet, ohne sich gründlich mit den Problemen der Grundlagen ihrer Theorie auseinanderzusetzen.

Die Gründungsmitglieder des NEUEN FORUM waren sich einig, daß die Ökologie beim wirtschaftlichen Umbau Vorrang haben soll. Keinesfalls darf die Folge von Reformen eine soziale Verelendung größerer Teile der Bevölkerung sein. Darüber hinaus wurden von uns

Teile der Subventionspolitik kritisiert, die zur Verschwendung führen. Wie der wirtschaftliche Umbau konkret aussehen soll, darüber gehen die Meinungen weit auseinander. Unsere erste Aufgabe besteht darin, den Ist-Stand der Gesellschaft zusammenzutragen. Dies wird nicht einfach sein, da vieles an Daten und Statistiken über die wirtschaftliche, finanzielle und soziale Situation entweder unter Verschluß stand, mitunter verklausuliert veröffentlicht oder kurzerhand gefälscht wurde (so beispielsweise die Bevölkerungsstatistik in den letzten beiden Jahren). Jetzt kommen scheibchenweise die benötigten Fakten ans Licht.

Spürbar ist für alle DDR-Bürger die permanente Mangelsituation, außerhalb Ost-Berlins noch weitaus stärker. Ob es nun lange Wartezeiten bei vielen Dienstleistungen, ein stets mangelhaftes Obst-, Gemüse- und Bekleidungsangebot oder die zu geringe Zahl von Gaststättenplätzen sind – der Zeitaufwand für die Organisation des täglichen Lebens ist beträchtlich.

Keine Wiedervereinigung

Die Wiedervereinigung ist für uns kein Thema. Wir finden dieses CDU-Gedudel von den Schwestern und Brüdern im Osten nervend und widerlich. Als Verursacher von zwei Weltkriegen sollten die Deutschen die nationale Trommel in der Rumpelkammer stehenlassen, die Nachkriegsgrenzen endlich anerkennen und den Heimatvertriebenverbänden den Status der Gemeinnützigkeit entziehen, damit dieses künstliche Trachtengetümmel endlich aufhört. Es gibt kein Schlesien, Ostpreußen und Pommern mehr – und sollte es auch nicht mehr geben. Deutsche – wenn sie bereit sind, Lehren aus der Vergangenheit zu ziehen – müßten sich als Weltbürger begreifen und solidarisch mit allen Verfolgten auf dieser Welt sein. Einerseits jubelt die Bundesregierung über jeden Deutschen, der aus dem Osten oder aus der DDR kommt, andererseits werden Flüchtlinge aus dem Libanon oder aus Ceylon, die nur das nackte Leben retten konnten, wieder zurück in den sicheren Tod geschickt. Auch die DDR hat hier reichlich umzudenken. Ein Asylrecht existiert in unserer jetzigen Verfassung nicht einmal.

Wir wollen also keinen Anschluß etwa als zwölftes Bundesland. Wir wollen Veränderungen jetzt und nicht erst warten, bis die DDR-Stalinisten das Land so weit abgewirtschaftet haben, wie das die ungarische Partei mit ihrem Land getan hat. Die Ungarn haben nicht mehr viele Alternativen, da sie bereits in der finanziellen

Abhängigkeit der Banken stecken. Denn was für einen realen Zuwachs an Freiheit bringt es, wenn Menschen zwei Jobs brauchen, um Geld für das Lebensnotwendige zusammenzubekommen; oder wenn ein Drittel der Bevölkerung unter dem Existenzminimum leben muß? Es ist keine Alternative, wenn die politische Diktatur der Bürokraten durch die ökonomische ersetzt wird. Wir hoffen, daß es in der DDR nicht so weit kommt, daß uns das Messer an der Kehle sitzt, wie den Polen und Ungarn.

Hier fängt auch der Dissenz mit den anderen neuen Parteien wie SDP und 'Demokratischer Aufbruch' an. Es gibt keine einheitliche Opposition in der DDR. Herr Schnur, Vorsitzender des Demokratischen Aufbruch, hat schon die Konföderation mit der Bundesrepublik im Kopf und schlägt Richard von Weizsäcker als gemeinsamen Staatspräsidenten vor. Das ist eine Politik des Ausverkaufs der DDR, die wir auf keinen Fall mittragen.

Unsere Forderungen waren bisher in erster Linie politischer Natur:
- Reform des Versammlungs-, Demonstrations- und Vereinigungsrechts.
- Medienreform, eigene Zeitung.
- Offenlegung und Abbau aller Vergünstigungen und Privilegien.
- Kontrolle von Polizei- und Sicherheitsorganen.
- Trennung von Partei und Staat.
- Reform der Armee.
- Reform der Volksbildung.
- Offenlegung von Wirtschafts- und Sozialdaten.
- Reform des Wahlrechts.
- Freizügigkeit.
- Reform des Strafrechts.
- Rehabilitierung aller politisch Verfolgten usw.

Eine weitere unserer Forderungen ist die nach freien und geheimen Wahlen. Vor diesen Wahlen wollen wir aber schon jetzt politische Veränderungen und Absicherungen, die einen Rückfall in den Stalinismus unmöglich machen. Es ist uns lieber, die SED beschließt selbst, die Kampfgruppen aufzulösen, als daß solche Entscheidungen auf den Tag nach der Wahl verschoben werden. Von daher sind freie Wahlen nicht unsere Hauptforderung. Wir können auch nicht wünschen, daß sie in den nächsten Wochen oder Monaten stattfinden, da die Opposition sich erst im organisatorischen Aufbau befindet und die SED und die Blockparteien da einen immensen Vorlauf haben. Und der SED-beherrschte Staatsapparat wäre nach solchen Wahlen auch nicht verschwunden. Aus diesen Gründen favorisiert das NEUE FORUM im Gegensatz zu den anderen neuen Parteien und Gruppierungen Kommunalwahlen anstelle sofortiger Volkskammerwahlen. So kann die Gesellschaft von unten verändert werden, und neue Strukturen können wachsen. Wir wollen reale Verantwortung übernehmen und eine Kontrollfunktion ausüben, wir streben nicht nach Herrschaft und Macht.

Grundsätzlich unterscheidet sich das NEUE FORUM von allen anderen Parteien und Gruppierungen durch seinen basisdemokratischen Ansatz. Wir wollen nicht, daß die alten Bonzen durch neue abgelöst werden, sondern, daß der mündige Mensch sein Leben selbstbestimmt in die Hand nehmen kann.

Vocabulary

ausdrücklich	specifically
die Aufarbeitung	reappraisal
verfehlen	miss, fail to achieve
auseinandersetzen	examine critically
sich einig sein	to be in agreement
die Verelendung	impoverishment
darüber hinaus	additionally
die Verschwendung	waste
scheibchenweise	little by little
Dienstleistungen	services
das Gedudel (slang)	claptrap
der Status der Gemeinnützigkeit	charitable status
der Aufbruch	renewal
der Ausverkauf	sell-out, sell-off
die Absicherung	guarantee
die Kommunalwahlen	local elections
die Bonzen (slang)	party hacks

Note. Richard von Weizsäcker was president of the Federal Republic from 1984 to 1993.

Text B: Detlef Pollack, 'Was ist aus den Bürgerbewegungen und Oppositionsgruppen der DDR geworden?', in *Aus Politik und Zeitgeschichte* (Bonn), 29 September 1995, 34

In der Öffentlichkeit werden die Vertreter der ostdeutschen Bürgerbewegungen nicht selten als Verlierer der Wende dargestellt, die sich

angesichts des dramatischen Niedergangs ihrer Bewegung resigniert
in die Schmollecke zurückgezogen haben und bis heute ihren illu-
sionären Vorstellungen von einem dritten Weg zwischen Sozialismus
und Kapitalismus anhängen. In den Jahren seit der Wiedervereinigung vollzogen sich innerhalb der Bürgerbewegungen und
alternativen Gruppierungen Ostdeutschlands jedoch gravierende
Wandlungsprozesse, in deren Ergebnis es zu einer starken Differen-
zierung in den politischen Haltungen ihrer Vertreterinnen und
Vertreter gekommen ist. Natürlich halten manche von ihnen nach wie
vor an alten Idealen – an den Ideen von einer gerechten, solidarischen und egalitären Gesellschaft – fest und haben, wenn sie in
der Öffentlichkeit auftreten – und sie treten oft auf – nichts anderes
zu tun, als uns ihre Unzufriedenheit mit dem Rechtsstaat, der parlamentarischen Demokratie oder der Aufarbeitung der
DDR-Vergangenheit mitzuteilen. Die Mehrheit der Bürgerrechtler –
und ihre Vertreter kommen in der Öffentlichkeit nicht so oft zu Wort
– bejaht aber längst die parlamentarische Demokratie, auch wenn sie
ihre Ideale nicht vergessen hat und manches an dieser Demokratie
für verbesserungswürdig hält. Andere kritisieren inzwischen sogar
das moralisierende Politikverständnis von einigen ihrer einstigen
Mitstreiter und sind mittlerweile zu kämpferischen Verfechtern der
Parteiendemokratie geworden.

Freilich fiel den Vertretern der Bürgerbewegungen und Opposi-
tionsgruppen die Umstellung auf die neuen Gesellschaftsverhältnisse
so schwer wie kaum einer zweiten Gruppe von DDR-Bürgern,
ausgenommen vielleicht die regimetreuen Aktivisten. Dies hat vor
allem zwei Gründe: *Erstens*: Mit der Vereinigung ist den Bürger-
rechtlern der Gegenstand ihrer politischen Aktivitäten abhanden
gekommen: die DDR. Sie wollten die DDR ja nicht abschaffen,
sondern reformieren. Genauso wie die Funktionsträger des Systems
hatten sie die DDR zu ihrem Lebensthema gemacht und mußten nach
deren Untergang wie diese mit ihrem Verlust fertigwerden. Politische
Ziele, für deren Realisierung sie sich jahrelang eingesetzt hatten,
waren mit einem Schlag erfüllt. Damit verloren sie nicht nur ihre
politische Funktion, sondern auch ihre politische Ausnahmestellung.
Zweitens: die Öffnung der Berliner Mauer und der einsetzende Vereinigungsprozeß bedeuteten für alle ostdeutsche Akteure eine
Einschränkung ihrer zuvor gewonnen Handlungsmöglichkeiten.
Angesichts ihres seit Jahren gegen die Bevormundungsversuche des
DDR-Systems behaupteten Selbstbestimmungsanspruches waren die
Bürgerbewegungen von der im Vereinigungsprozeß einsetzenden

Eigendynamik besonders stark betroffen. Viele von ihnen rieben sich daran, daß dieser Prozeß über ihre Köpfe hinwegging und eine andere als die von ihnen intendierte Richtung nahm.

Vocabulary

in der Öffentlichkeit	in public, publicly
in die Schmollecke zurückziehen	to go into the corner and sulk
gravierend	serious
festhalten an + dative	cling to, stick by
nach wie vor	as before, as earlier
die Aufarbeitung	coming to terms with
der Bürgerrechtler	civil-rights activist
mittlerweile	in the meantime
regimetreu	loyal to the regime
mit einem Schlag	suddenly

Questions on the Source Texts

Text A

1. Explain the following terms:
   der Stalinismus
   der Ist-Stand der Gesellschaft
   das Asylrecht
   der Anschluß
   das Existenzminimum
   basisdemokratisch
   der mündige Mensch
2. Why did NEUES FORUM not wish to use the word 'socialism' in its political programme?
3. Why do you think that NEUES FORUM laid such emphasis on the environment?
4. What factors made life difficult for East German citizens?
5. Why did the NEUES FORUM reject unification with the Federal Republic?
6. What opinion is voiced with respect to Poland and Hungary?
7. What reforms are demanded?
8. What reasons are given for putting off national elections and carrying out local elections first?

Text B

1. Explain the following terms:
   Bürgerbewegung
   die Wende
   Bürgerrechtler
   regimetreue Aktivisten
   Funktionsträger des Systems
   Selbstbestimmungsanpruch
   Eigendynamik
2. Why have the East German civil groups and movements been called the *Verlierer der Wende*?
3. What changes have taken place in these groups and movements since unification and what attitudes do they now have?
4. Why does the author maintain that they have been as deeply affected by unification as former SED supporters?

Notes

1. Bündnis 90/Die Grünen, *Die Politische Alternative. Von A bis Z.* (Bonn, 1996).
2. Gerard Braunthal, *Parties and Politics in Modern Germany* (Boulder, Westview Press, 1996), 93.
3. The problem of who owns land and property in East Germany has slowed down investment and economic development considerably.
4. John Sandford, *The Sword and the Ploughshare: Autonomous Peace Initiatives in East Germany* (London, Merlin Press, 1983), 13.
5. Zeno and Sabine Zimmerling, *Chronik der DDR 1* (East Berlin, Verlag Tribüne, 1989), 33–5.
6. Jan Wielgohs, Marianne Schulz and Helmut Müller-Engbergs, *Bündnis 90* (Berlin, GSFP, 1992), 20–1.

Bibliography

Die Grünen

Publications in German

Bündnis 90/Die Grünen, *Politische Grundsätze* (Bonn, 1996).
Fücks, R. (ed.), *Sind die Grünen noch zu retten?* (Reinbek, Rowohlt, 1991).

Kleinert, Hubert, *Aufstieg und Fall der Grünen. Analyse einer alternativen Partei* (Bonn, Verlag J. H. W. Dietz Nachf., 1992).

Kluge, Thomas (ed.), *Grüne Politik* (Frankfurt-am-Main, Fischer Verlag, 1984).

Langner, Manfred (ed.), *Die Grünen auf dem Prüfstand. Analyse einer Partei* (Bergisch Gladbach, Bastei-Lubbe, 1987).

Müller-Rommel, Ferdinand, *Grüne Parteien in Westeuropa* (Opladen, Westdeutscher Verlag, 1993).

Raschke, Joachim, *Krise der Grünen. Bilanz und Neubeginn* (Marburg, Schüren, 1991).

Raschke, Joachim, *Die Grünen. Wie sie wurden, was sie sind* (Cologne, Bund-Verlag, 1993).

Publications in English

Frankland, E. Gene and Donald Schoonmaker, *Between Protest and Power: The Green Party in Germany* (Boulder, Westview Press, 1992).

Kolinski, Eva (ed.), *The Greens in West Germany* (Oxford, Berg, 1989).

Poguntke, Thomas, *Alternative Politics: The German Green Party* (Edinburgh, Edinburgh University Press, 1993).

Scharf, Thomas, *The German Greens: Challenging the Consensus* (Oxford and Providence, Berg, 1994).

Schoonmaker, Donald and E. Gene Frankland, 'Disunited Greens in a United Germany: The All-German Election of December 1990 and Its Aftermath', in Russell J. Dalton (ed.), *The New Germany Votes*, 135–62.

Wiesenthal, Helmut, *Realism in German Politics: Social Movements and Ecological Reform in Germany* (Manchester, Manchester University Press, 1993).

Bündnis 90 and opposition groups in East Germany

Publications in German

Büscher, Wolfgang, Peter Wensierski and Klaus Wolschner, *Friedensbewegung in der DDR. Texte 1978–1982* (Hattingen, edition transit, 1982).

Deutschland Archiv (ed.), *Umweltprobleme und Umweltbewußtsein in der DDR* (Cologne, Verlag Politik und Wissenschaft, 1985).

Haufe, Gerda and Karl Bruckmeier (eds.), *Die Bürgerbewegungen in der DDR und in den ostdeutschen Bundesländern* (Opladen, Westdeutscher Verlag, 1993).

Müller-Engbergs, Helmut (ed.), *Was wollen die Bürgerbewegungen?* (Berlin, AV-Verlag Franz Fischer, 1994).

Müller-Engbergs, Helmut, Marianne Schulz and Jan Wielgohs, *Von der Illegalität ins Parlament. Werdegang und Konzept der neuen Bürgerbewegungen* (Berlin, Ch. Links Verlag, 1993).

Pollack, Detlef (ed.), *Die Legimität der Freiheit. Politisch alternative Gruppen in der DDR unter dem Dach der Kirche* (Frankfurt, Berlin, New York and Paris, Verlag Peter Lang, 1990).

Probst, Lothar, *Ostdeutsche Bürgerbewegungen und Perspektive der Demokratie. Entstehung, Bedeutung, Zukunft* (Cologne, Bund Verlag, 1993).

Rüddenklau, Wolfgang, *Störenfried. ddr-Opposition 1986–1989* (Berlin, Basis-Druck, 1992).

Thaysen, Uwe, *Der Runde Tisch oder: wo blieb das Volk?* (Opladen, Westdeutscher Verlag, 1990).

Wielgohs, Jan, 'Auflösung und Transformation der ostdeutschen Bürgerbewegung', in *Deutschland Archiv*, 26 (Cologne, Verlag Wissenschafft und Politik), 426–34.

Wielgohs, Jan and Marianne Schulz, 'Von der illegalen Opposition in die legale Marginalität', *Berliner Journal für Soziologie*, 1 (1991), 385–91.

Wielgohs, Jan, Marianne Schulz and Helmut Müller-Engbergs, *Bündnis 90. Entstehung, Entwicklung, Perspektiven*, Sonderausgabe der Berliner Debatte INITIAL (Berlin, 1992).

Publications in English

Torpey, John, 'Two Movements, not a Revolution: Exodus and Opposition in the East German Transformation 1989–90', *German Politics and Society*, 26 (1992), 21–42.

Further information may be obtained from:
Bündnis 90/Die Grünen
Bundesgeschäftsstelle
Baunscheidtstraße 1a
D 53 113 Bonn
Tel. (0228) 9166-0
Fax (0228) 9166-199

5. Sozialistische Einheitspartei Deutschlands (SED)

Despite the fact that Marx and Engels, the ideological founders of twentieth-century communism, had been German and were, in part, a product of German culture and the German education system, communism in Germany did not have its own political party until 1 January 1919 when the KPD was formed. During the 1920s and early 1930s the KPD and SPD fought each other for ideological reasons, as well as to win the working-class electorate. This struggle was at times as bitter as each party's fight against the nazis and helped, in part, the nazis' take-over of power. The polarization of the electorate into far right and far left out of despair at the powerlessness of the mainstream parties led to five million votes being cast for Ernst Thälmann, general secretary of the KPD, and eleven million votes for Hitler in 1932.

After Hitler became chancellor on 30 January 1933, one of the first steps taken by the nazis was the banning of the KPD, the sequestration of party assets and the imprisonment of KPD leaders in the first of the concentration camps that were built by the nazis. Many of those who were not imprisoned fled abroad or stayed on in Germany and carried on limited resistance to the nazis. The nazi period left an indelible mark on the psychology of the communists and was one of the factors that drove SED policy after 1945. Of the communists who left Germany, it was natural that some chose to go into exile in the Soviet Union, which had been their model and ideal, but in fact many of them were persecuted there, and some were killed.

Nevertheless the Politburo of the KPD continued to function in Moscow and on 16 June 1943 decided to create the Nationalkomitee 'Freies Deutschland', which came into being on 12–13 July 1943[1] and had the function of bringing together, under the leadership of the communists Walter Ulbricht, Wilhelm Pieck, Anton Ackermann, Johannes R. Becher – amongst others – KPD and other German *émigrés* in the Soviet Union with German prisoners of war to form an anti-Hitler coalition in preparation for the ending of the war. The NKFD wanted to form a strong, democratic state apparatus and government as soon as possible after Germany's surrender, to try and punish war criminals and former nazis and improve social conditions in all spheres of life.[2] As the war came to an end the Russians flew in NKFD groups under Walter Ulbricht, to the areas of Germany under Soviet control. These groups immediately began to organize the German population and to act as a bridge between the Germans and the Soviet army, so that Soviet orders to alleviate the worst practical problems and begin denazification were put into practice. As soon as the Soviet Military Administration permitted the formation of German political parties, the KPD was legalized (11 June 1945).

The Russians had a number of scenarios with regard to Germany. Ideally, they would have liked to have a socialist or communist united Germany that was positive towards them. A second possibility was a reunited Germany that was militarily neutral and which would never again invade the Soviet Union or pose a military threat to her. A third scenario was a divided Germany with one part of it under Soviet control, in which a model for socialism or communism on the Soviet pattern could be created. This model might one day be exported to West Germany or be the foundation for a reunified Germany. Through circumstances the Russians were forced into implementing the third scenario in their zone and later in the GDR.

Communism was a system that was built to fit in with an ideology – the ideology of Marx and Engels, with additions from the theories and practice of Lenin and Stalin. It was the planned application of theories on economics and politics.

Marxist ideology is based on aspects of the philosophy of Hegel,[3] on a system of political economy, a theory of the state and on the role of revolution in social development.[4] Marx started from the premise that people have to have the material means to support themselves before all else, and that consequently all human relations are determined by the production of the means to support life and by the exchange of the goods produced. According to Marx and Engels, the economic structure forms the basis or substructure of all human life, while laws, ethics, culture and other social institutions form the superstructure (*Überbau*) and are determined by the nature of the economic base. The history of mankind was interpreted as a history of the struggle between different social classes for the control of the 'means of production', wealth and power. History was divided into a number of phases. Primitive society was communist, with all things jointly owned. It was followed by slave society, feudal society and capitalism. In each case a minority owned, respectively, people, land, property, and (later) factories or firms. The catalyst for change had been new means of production (for example, as a result of the introduction of new technology) and revolution. At the time that Marx and Engels were writing, industrialization was changing the way of life of millions of people most radically, and both Marx and Engels recognized that the capitalist economic system was the most advanced the world had seen up to that time.[5] Yet they criticized that system for its crass social inequalities, its hypocrisy (especially in family and sexual matters) and its inability to regulate production so as not to have recurrent bouts of over-production leading to the destruction of the market and to economic recession and unemployment. They believed that the two classes that industrialization and capitalism had produced, the 'bourgeoisie' and the 'proletariat' (i.e. industrial working class), would be engaged in a struggle that would lead to the disappearance of capitalism and the introduction of socialism, a system where all the means of production would be in the hands of the state, the working class would be in power, and laws, culture and social institutions would become 'socialist'. The final stage of human history would be communism where there would be a classless, non-antagonistic society in which the distribution of social wealth would be on the basis of 'each according to his needs'. These ideas and attempts to implement them were to rock the twentieth century and impinge directly on the lives of at least one-third of the world's population.

In East Germany it was the KPD and, later, the SED that sought to implement Marxism by destroying the old economic and social order and replacing it with the 'dictatorship of the proletariat' (as exercised by the party). The communists assumed political power, nationalized industry and commerce and took control of agriculture. They also made all institutions such as education and the legal system 'socialist'. They destroyed the economic and social status of the middle class and its values. They created a security system to defend the changes that they had brought about. All this was done in a number of stages.

In the *Land* and province elections in the Soviet zone from 4 to 16

July 1945, the KPD, SPD and CDU/LDPD each gained about one-third of the votes and initially worked well together in tackling the immense problems that confronted them. In the ensuing months the KPD had considerable advantages over the other parties, for it had direct access to the Soviet army and enjoyed its support. The KPD could not supplant the SPD as the most popular party in the zone, however, and until that happened the communists could not gain the political and administrative control that they needed to introduce a communist system. The KPD thus suggested to the SPD that the two parties should unite in order to prevent the Left ever again being split and allowing fascism to return to power. This proposal was rejected by very many in the SPD, but some of the leaders supported the merger, which then went ahead on 21–2 April 1946, when the SED was created. When the SED stood in the only free elections to be held in East Germany between 1946 and 1989 it received only 50 per cent of the votes, and the SPD, which also stood as an independent party in East Berlin, was its main rival. The influence of the SPD had to be countered if the SED had any hope of pushing through its policies. Within the SED itself a battle was fought over the next two years to remove the influence of the former members of the SPD, and in many cases to drive them out of the party, and even the country.[6]

In 1946 the SED set up the 'anti-fascist democratic bloc' consisting of the existing parties and the so-called mass organizations created to integrate and mobilize large sections of the population: the work-force (Freier Deutscher Gewerkschaftsbund or FDGB, created 9–11 February 1945); the intellectuals ('Kulturbund' für die Demokratische Erneuerung Deutschlands or KB, founded 4 July 1945); youth (Freie Deutsche Jugend, founded 7 March 1946); and women (Demokratischer Frauenbund Deutschlands or DFD, founded 9 March 1947). These organizations were created and led by the SED and its members who had predominantly come from the communist rather than the SPD wing of the party. (They were what Lenin described as the 'transmission belts of the party'.) The SED, with its helpers in the mass organizations, was able to describe all its measures as 'anti-fascist' and 'democratic', so that opposition to them could be branded as 'neo-fascist' or 'anti-democratic'. The SED monopoly on power strengthened consistently up to 1949. The party had effectively taken over the press and radio. Its members ran the Authors' Union (Schriftstellerverband), the Artists' Union (Künstlerverband) and the Kulturbund. Many university professors and lecturers became party members, and those who disagreed with the SED were forced out of their posts and in some cases had to flee to West Germany.

The voting system was reduced to a mere formality, far removed from the practice in Western democracies. Candidates were put up by the parties and the mass organizations. They introduced themselves at public meetings and answered the occasional question. In theory, if voters put up a petition against a particular candidate an alternative had to be found, but in fact this never happened. The names of the candidates were then put on the National Front list. In advance of the elections, *Wahlhelfer*, particularly from the SED, went around the community propagating SED ideas and policies and on the day of the election they 'reminded' voters of their duty to vote, visiting them at work or at home. The vote itself was cast for the whole National Front list. Theoretically, a voter could go into the voting booth and cross out the name of one or more candidates. In fact, however, the vast majority did not use the booth, but simply dropped the whole list, without amendments, into the voting box. Some did so out of fear of future discrimination, others felt that voting secretly was pointless anyway since National Front candidates would be declared as having gained 99 per cent of the votes, however many people voted against them.

The political system was operated on the principle of 'democratic socialism', that is, policies and suggestions emanating from above were passed down the hierarchy for discussion, were endorsed and then passed back up the ladder for legislation. 'Discussion' often did take place at the lower levels, but it was long-winded and often meaningless since it was not aimed at modifying or overturning what had already been decided at the higher level.

The SED exercised complete control over all aspects of the economy. In 1946 heavy industry, mineral resources, banks and insurance institutions had been nationalized without compensation. In the 1950s medium-sized businesses were converted into semi-state enterprises, with the state making major investments in them and then taking up 51 per cent of the shares. In 1972 the last 5,500 independent firms and 6,000 semi-state enterprises were nationalized. Many of their owners were made into managing directors and compensated. In 1948 shops, hotels and restaurants were taken into the *Handelsorganisation* (HO – trade organization) which was in turn under the control of the SED and the state. Retailing co-operatives (*Konsum*) which were a feature of German life up to 1933 were allowed to re-establish themselves after 1945 and gained a large membership (4.5 million in 1989), but they were indirectly under the control of the SED and certainly were not allowed to compete with or be more successful than the HO.

As far as agriculture was concerned, two main developments ultimately brought this important sector under state control. Firstly, land reform (*Bodenreform*) in 1945–6 did not just affect former nazi supporters or the Junker, since the size of holding at which land was expropriated was 100 hectares (250 acres) and above. One-third of this land was put into state-owned model farms (*Volkseigene Güter*, VEG) on the Soviet kolkhoz method, and the remainder was distributed to farm-workers, farmers with less than 10 hectares (25 acres) and refugees.[7] The size of the holdings so created was not economically viable in the longer term, for either the individual farmer or the state, so the second major development was the creation of the Landwirtschaftliche Produktionsgenossenschaften between 1952 and 1960 into which farmers, including those who had benefited from the land reform, were either induced or coerced. By 1962 over 90 per cent of the land was either in VEG or LPG ownership, and it was thus easy to integrate agriculture into the state economic planning system.

Part of the profits created within the economy were distributed across society through subsidies for all essentials such as housing, basic foodstuffs, children's clothing, gas, electricity and public transport, through high subsidies to crèches and kindergarten, and to the arts and sport, as well as through social-policy measures. The subsidies were, however, too generous for what the economy could afford.

The State Planning Commission (*Staatliche Plankommission*) was created to plan and control the whole economy. Planning generally was for a five-year period, but annual targets were also set. The economic plan had the force of law, and attempts to change it, for example at factory level, could lead to charges of economic sabotage. The Planning Commission was made up of SED members, worked under the control of the Council of Ministers, and in the 1980s particularly under Günter Mittag. The SED was in total control of the economy but also treated state money and properties to a great extent as its own. The manner and degree to which the party and its leaders used state funds for their own ends became known in late 1989 and 1990. It was one of the reasons for many members leaving the SED in disgust, as it had always been assumed that the leaders of the party had enjoyed few privileges and were honest.

In the areas of education and science, the SED exercised a mono-poly of power and control. All schools had been under state control since 1946 and used the same curriculum and textbooks throughout the Republic. Textbooks, in particular in history, civics (*Staatsbür-gerkunde*), literature, Russian, English and geography, gave a Marxist interpretation. Crèches and kindergarten, with the exception of those owned by the Churches, operated to curricula and norms set by the relevant ministry in Berlin. Many university professors and lecturers, and many of the 20,000 staff of the Academy of Sciences (the most important and prestigious research body in the GDR), were members of the SED and subject to its directives and discipline.

The mass media were totally under the control of the SED. Amongst other things, nothing that was critical of the party and its policies, of the Soviet Union or of other states in the communist bloc was permitted. Furthermore, constant anti-Western propaganda was demanded of the media, and the image of a hostile West German state was created. Every word to be published was scrutinized, every word broadcast was carefully weighed. Words with a political conno-tation, such as 'democracy', 'peace', 'freedom' and 'justice', were given the SED's political slant. The media ended up using repetitive slogans which had little meaning.

The SED itself set up a party structure parallel to that of the state. It was organized at national, *Bezirk, Kreis* and town or village level. It was also organized at the place of work (*Betriebsparteiorganisa-tion*) and in the community (*Wohnbezirksorganisation*). This meant a very large party apparatus. The party had some 2.3 million members (16–17 per cent of the adult population), and absolute loyalty was demanded of them (see text A, pp.194–5). The party could – and did – intervene even in the private lives of its members, for instance in preventing a marriage or demanding the break-up of a relationship.

On 8 February 1950 the *Ministerium für Staatssicherheit* (MfS or Stasi) was created and was later to regard itself as the 'sword and shield' of the SED. It fulfilled the roles of a political police that watched over dissidents or critics of the regime, a body that coun-tered Western intelligence activities within the GDR and organized East German intelligence work abroad, particularly in the Federal Republic.[8] The Stasi was also responsible for creating and maintain-ing an atmosphere of suspicion that was like a canker in East German society as the basic element of trust between people that makes them happy and at ease was destroyed. Ulbricht and later Honecker were clearly in charge of the state, including the state security system, and responsibility for allowing it to become an instrument of repression of the East German population, as well as of dissident opposition, lay with the general secretary of the SED and the higher echelons of the party. At the same time, even leading members of the SED could not be sure whether they were being spied upon by state security.[9] The SED created an instrument that ultimately caused uncertainty and to some extent even fear in its own ranks (see text C, p.198). The world of the SED, the Stasi and the GDR was highly reminiscent of the world of Franz Kafka.[10]

In short, the SED was directly or indirectly, through its members in influential positions, in control of and responsible for every aspect of life in East Germany – political, economic, social and cultural. This was to prove part of the reason for its downfall in 1989. Everything that was wrong in East Germany could be – and was – attributed to the SED and its leaders. The leaders themselves were totally out of touch with the population and had no idea how to deal with the crisis that faced them in the summer and autumn of 1989 (see text B, pp.196–7). Furthermore, as legal and effective opposition was forbidden, there were no alternative party or political leaders with the experience to lead the GDR in 1990 or negotiate on equal terms with West German politicians during the crucial period from October 1989 to October 1990.

Erich Honecker – a portrait

Erich Honecker was born into a working-class family on 25 August 1912 in Neunkirchen in the Saarland. He was one of six children and grew up in a strongly politicized household. Shortly before his tenth birthday he joined the local communist children's group. After attending the *Volksschule* he trained as a roofer. In 1926 he joined the Kommunistische Jugendverband (KJVD) and held a number of offices. In 1929 he became a member of the KPD and was sent by the party to attend the Lenin College, Moscow, in 1930–1. Honecker was deeply impressed by the Soviet Union and developed a strong loyalty towards the Soviet communists. On his return to Germany he again became active in the KJVD and the KPD, and after the nazis came to power he continued illegal communist activities.[11] He was arrested by the Gestapo in December 1935 in Berlin and sentenced to ten years' hard labour in June 1937. He managed to escape from prison in Berlin on 6 March 1945 but could find no safe hide-out and returned to prison in mid-April. There is no account in his auto-biography[12] of any questions asked by the prison authorities, and he received no punishment. After the end of hostilities he took an active part in KPD work and became chairman of the FDJ on its formation in 1946. He remained in that office until 1955. From 1958 he was a member of the Politburo of the Central Committee of the SED. In 1971 he replaced Walter Ulbricht as first secretary of the SED and chairman of the National Defence Council. In 1976 he became general secretary of the Central Committee and chairman of the Council of State.

In his early years as head of the party and the state, Honecker took a somewhat more tolerant line than Ulbricht with respect to the intellectuals in the GDR, promising, for instance, a 'literature without taboos', but in 1976 the singer and writer Wolf Biermann was refused re-entry to the GDR after a concert in Cologne, and intellectuals who protested on his behalf were discriminated against and, in some cases, forced to leave for West Germany. Protests against the stationing of new Soviet rockets in East Germany and pollution of the environment were also suppressed under Honecker. In his foreign policy, however, and in his relations with West Germany he had a number of successes, such as in his dealings with Franz Josef Strauß on West German loans, negotiations with the SPD on peace policies and his official visit to the Federal Republic in 1987, where he was in every respect treated as a head of state by the CDU.

As time went on, however, Honecker became more and more inflexible. He refused to introduce *perestroika* and *glasnost*, as Mikhail Gorbachev was doing in the Soviet Union, and argued that all necessary reforms had already been carried out in the GDR. On 18 October 1989 Honecker was forced out of office. On 29 January 1990 he was arrested and subsequently spent 169 days on remand up to 13 January 1993. In the intervening period he had spent time in a Soviet military hospital in East Germany being treated for cancer, and had sought refuge in the Soviet Union, only to be returned by the Russians to Germany to stand trial. Finally, Honecker was released and went into exile in Chile where he died on 29 May 1994. He remained a communist to the end, refusing to admit the mistakes made by the regime that he had headed, placing the blame for everything that had gone wrong on the 'capitalist system' and clinging tenaciously to the idea that one day 'socialism' would still triumph (see text D, pp.199–200).

Sources

Text A: *Statut der Sozialistischen Einheitspartei Deutschlands, einstimmig eingenommen auf dem IX. Parteitag der SED*, Berlin, 18–22 May 1976

Die Parteimitglieder, ihre Pflichten und Rechte

(1) Mitglied der Sozialistischen Einheitspartei Deutschlands zu sein ist eine große Ehre. Die Zugehörigkeit zur Sozialistischen Einheitspartei Deutschlands erlegt jedem Kommunisten hohe Verpflichtungen auf ...

(2) Das Parteimitglied ist verpflichtet:

    (a) die Einheit und Reinheit der Partei als die wichtigste Voraussetzung ihrer Kraft und Stärke stets zu wahren und sie in jeder Weise zu schützen; am Leben der Partei und regelmäßig an den *Mitgliederversammlungen* teilzunehmen;

    (b) aktiv die Parteibeschlüsse zu verwirklichen, unablässig die Deutsche Demokratische Republik allseitig zu stärken, für ein hohes Entwicklungstempo der sozialistischen Produktion, die Erhöhung der Effektivität, den wissenschaftlich-technischen Fortschritt und das Wachstum der Arbeitsproduktivität zu wirken; eine vorbildliche sozialistische Einstellung zur Arbeit zu beweisen, Bahnbrecher des Neuen zu sein ... und vorbildlich die gesellschaftlichen Pflichten zu erfüllen;

    (c) Verbundenheit mit den Massen unaufhörlich zu festigen, ihnen den Sinn der Politik und der Beschlüsse der Partei zu erläutern, sie von der Richtigkeit der Politik der Partei zu überzeugen, sie für deren Durchführung zu gewinnen und von den Massen zu lernen ... Jedes Parteimitglied tritt ein für die unverbrüchliche Freundschaft, Zusammenarbeit und das brüderliche Bündnis mit der Sowjetunion, für den engen Zusammenschluß der Länder der sozialistischen Gemeinschaft. Jedes Parteimitglied führt den kompromißlosen Kampf gegen alle Erscheinungen des Antikommunismus, Antisowjetismus, Nationalismus und Rassismus ...

    (d) ständig an der Hebung seines politischen Bewußtseins, an der Aneignung des Marxismus-Leninismus zu arbeiten und die marxistisch-leninistische Weltanschauung zu verbreiten;

die Normen der sozialistischen Moral und Ethik einzuhalten und die gesellschaftlichen Interessen über die persönlichen zu stellen ...

(j) Partei- und Staatsgeheimnisse zu wahren, in allen Fragen politische Wachsamkeit zu üben und sich stets bewußt zu sein, daß Wachsamkeit der Parteimitglieder auf jedem Gebiet und in jeder Lage notwendig ist ...

(7) Parteimitglieder oder Kandidaten, die die Verbindung zur Partei verloren oder nicht den Willen haben, den mit der Mitgliedschaft in der Partei verbundenen Pflichten nachzukommen, können nach Beschluß der Mitgliederversammlung der Grundorganisation und Bestätigung durch die Kreisleitung als Mitglied oder als Kandidat der Partei gestrichen werden.

(8) Wer gegen die Einheit und Reinheit der Partei verstößt, ihre Beschlüsse nicht erfüllt, die innerparteiliche Demokratie nicht achtet, die Partei- und Staatsdisziplin verletzt oder seine Mitgliedschaft und ihm übertragene Funktionen mißbraucht, im öffentlichen und persönlichen Leben sich eines Parteimitgliedes nicht würdig zeigt, ist von der Grundorganisation oder einem höheren Parteiorgan zur Verantwortung zu ziehen.

Je nach Art des Vergehens können folgende Parteistrafen beschlossen werden:

(a) die Rüge

(b) die strenge Rüge

(c) Ausschluß aus der Partei

(9) Der Ausschluß aus der Partei ist die höchste Parteistrafe.

Vocabulary

die Verpflichtung	obligation
wahren	to maintain
die Mitgliederversammlung	party meeting
unablässig	unswervingly
der Fortschritt	progress
vorbildlich	exemplary
die Einstellung	attitude of mind
der Bahnbrecher	trailblazer
unaufhörlich	tirelessly
unverbrüchlich	unbreakable, indissoluble
die Kreisleitung	district party leadership
die Rüge	reprimand

**Text B: 'Sitzung des SED-Politbüros am 29. August 1989',
G.-R. Stephan (ed.), *Vorwärts Immer, Rückwärts Nimmer!*
(Dietz Verlag, Berlin, 1994, 98–103)**

Genosse Dohlus

In den Betrieben gibt es große Aktivitäten zur Auswertung der 7.
und 8. ZK-Tagung. Es geht um die Sicherung der Planerfüllung.

Genosse Sindermann

In erster Linie müssen wir den Stoß gegen den Feind führen
–   Grenzen von 1937
–   Obhutspflicht für alle Deutschen
–   Aufrüstung
–   Neonazismus
–   Antikommunismus
–   Druck auf sozialistische Staaten ...
    Die guten Kommunisten brauchen unsere Unterstützung. Es gibt
verschiedene sozialistische Konzeptionen. Wir haben die unsere, und
sie ist erfolgreich. Wir halten daran fest. Manchmal gibt es bei uns
eine regelrechte Versorgungspsychose. Warum die Menschen
abhauen, diese Frage wage ich hier nicht so schnell zu beantworten.
Auch hier gibt es eine Psychose, das sind doch verwirrte Leute. Sie
gehen dem Gegner ins Netz und dienen dem Rechtsruck in der BRD,
sogar dem Neonazismus. Das müssen wir angreifen. Man sollte eine
Parteiinformation herausgeben.

Genosse Axen

Diese Diskussion ist gut ... Die Gegenattacke des Gegners richtet
sich besonders gegen die DDR. Zum ersten Mal in der Geschichte
gibt es aber auch Schwankungen in der KPdSU, auch darauf setzt der
Gegner im Kampf gegen die DDR.
    Das erste ist, die DDR weiter zu stärken und den XII. Parteitag
vorzubereiten.
    Zweitens müssen wir sagen, daß die Attacke des Gegners – mit
seinem stärksten Medium, dem Fernsehen – Wirkung hat. Wir
müssen den Feind angreifen und entlarven: Aufrüstungspolitik –
Ausbeutung – Neonazismus.

Genosse Tisch

Was sich in der Sowjetunion entwickelt, wirkt auf unsere Menschen. Früher hatten wir nur den Frontalangriff in deutscher Sprache von vorn, jetzt entwickelt er sich im Rücken an allen Ecken und Kanten ... Wir müssen auch unser Geschichtsbild besser vermitteln, besonders den jungen Leuten. Dem Frontalangriff begegnen wir am besten, wenn wir die DDR stärken. Die Wachsamkeit wird unterschätzt, und es gibt auch Sabotage in der Versorgung. Die Versorgungsdiskussion wird z.T. bis zur Psychose geführt. 3.5 Millionen DDR-Bürger waren im Westen. Sie kommen mit dem Bild von der BRD als Überflußgesellschaft zurück. Sie sehen die Arbeitslosen und Obdachlosen usw. nicht. Wir müssen mit ihnen reden. Das Vertrauen zur Parteiführung muß gestärkt werden.

Genosse Stoph

Die Öffentlichkeitsarbeit muß vielseitiger werden. Wenn Leute weglaufen, müssen wir das untersuchen – Mangel in der Erziehung, Mangel im Staatsapparat, mit denen wir Leute verärgern.

Wir müssen unseren Menschen besser begreiflich machen, was Kapitalismus ist.

Wir haben mit Polen, Ungarn usw. Verträge über Zusammenarbeit und gegenseitigen Beistand, und es gibt keinen Grund davon abzuweichen. Im Gegenteil: Wir müssen Einfluß nehmen ... Wir können uns die führenden Leute in diesen Ländern nicht aussuchen. Wir müssen die Zusammenarbeit maximal stärken. Ich will die Grundfrage stellen: Wie will die DDR sich weiterentwickeln, wenn nicht in Zusammenarbeit mit den sozialistischen Ländern? Doch nicht mit der BRD! Wir haben keinen Grund, pessimistisch zu sein.

Vocabulary

der Stoß	thrust
die Obhutspflicht	duty of care
die Aufrüstung	rearmament
verwirrt	confused
der Rechtsruck	swing to the right
entlarven	unmask
die Überflußgesellschaft	society swimming in milk and honey

die Obdachlosen	homeless
die Öffentlichkeitsarbeit	public relations work

Text C: Frank Sieren and Ludwig Koehne (eds.), *Günter Schabowski, Das Politbüro. Eine Befragung* (Reinbek, Rowohlt Taschenbuch Verlag, 1991), 24–5

Honecker war kein Ideologe, er hat sich der Ideologie bedient. Stalin war Ideologe. Er hat selbst Ideologie fabriziert, was ihm den Machterhalt erleichtert hat. Honecker hantierte mit eher simplen Formeln. Macht ist immer mit Ideologie verknüpft ... Aber ihn kennzeichnete eine unbeirrbare Überzeugtheit von der Berechtigung der Sache, die er verfocht. Ferner war ein übersteigertes Selbstbewußtsein ein Element seines Machtinstinktes. Das entwickelte sich in einer merkwürdigen Beziehung zu denen, die anfänglich mit ihm kooperiert hatten, dann mehr und mehr zu seinen Jüngern geworden waren und mit ihm schließlich nur noch nach dem Mund redeten. Die zurückhaltendste Art des Auftretens dieser Jüngerschaft war noch zu schweigen ...

Eine wichtige Taktik, mit der Honecker seine Macht behauptete, war die Isolierung der einzelnen Politbüromitglieder. Das schlimmste Vergehen war Fraktionsbildung. Diesem Gesetz haben wir uns alle unterworfen ...

Wir haben uns zwar alle unsere Spielräume verschafft, ich zum Beispiel in der Berliner Parteiorganisation. Aber eine Gruppe oder nur zwei Mitglieder, die enge Diskussionen prinzipieller oder gar existentieller Art geführt hätten, hat es im Politbüro nicht gegeben. Niemand konnte sicher sein, ob eine Offenbarung von bestimmten Vorstellungen oder Zweifeln gegenüber einem Politbürokollegen nicht an die falsche Adresse geriet. Honecker war in dieser Richtung ein großer Stratege. Schon wenn zwei oder drei besonders harmonierten, war das ein Verdachtsmoment. Er hat dann meist den einen gegen den anderen ausgespielt, den einen kritisiert, den anderen gelobt ...

Wir waren alle isoliert. Das war die Situation. Honecker hockte nur mit Mittag[13] und – seltener – mit Mielke[14] zusammen. Ich kann mir jedoch nicht vorstellen, daß sie uneingeschränkt Bescheid wußten. Die Entscheidungsgewalt hat Honecker kaum an Mittag abgetreten. Honecker war ein selbstbewußter Mann, der allerdings vor lauter Selbstbewußtsein bald den gleichen Fehler wie Ulbricht[15] beging: er wähnte sich in allen Fragen kompetent. Auf dem Bau wußte er Bescheid, weil er Dachdecker gelernt hatte, in die Landwirtschaft hatte er auch schon mal hineingerochen. Als Superwirtschaftswissenschaftler fühlte er sich zwar gerade nicht, aber er achtete immer darauf, daß die letzte Entscheidung in diesem Bereich bei ihm lag.

Aber sein eigentliches Strategiefeld war die Kaderpolitik. Er traf größtenteils einsame Entscheidungen. Dazu mußte er den Apparat genau kennen. Er war ein Mann des Apparats.

Text D: Erich Honecker, *Moabiter Notizen. Letztes schriftliches Zeugnis* (Berlin, edition ost, 1994), 10

Der Untergang der DDR hat mich hart getroffen, aber er hat mir und nicht wenigen Kampfgefährten nicht den Glauben an den Sozialismus als der einzigen Alternative für eine menschliche, eine gerechte Gesellschaft genommen. Die Kommunisten gehören, seit es den Kapitalismus gibt, zu den Verfolgten dieser Erde; aber sie gehören nicht zu den Zukunftslosen.

Was wir gemeinsam mit den Parteien der Ost-CDU und LDPD, von denen sich diverse Vertreter schnell in die neuen Regierungsbänke drängten, in mehr als 40 Jahren unter schwierigen Bedingungen auf deutschem Boden für ein Leben im Sozialismus geleistet haben, war nicht umsonst, es wird in die Zukunft wirken. Ich denke dabei an die sozialistischen Produktionsverhältnisse, an solche Verhältnisse, die allen Arbeit bieten und zugleich soziale Sicherheit, bezahlbare Wohnungen, Kinderkrippen, Kindergärten, Jugendclubs und ein niveauvolles geistiges und kulturelles Leben.

Es wird eine Gesellschaft sein, die für alle, für Arbeiter und Bauern, für Wissenschaftler, Techniker, Lehrer, Künstler, für Frauen, die Jugend, die Alten, eine lebenswerte Perspektive hat.

Der Niedergang des Kapitalismus, der, an seinen Grenzen angelangt, heute verschämt als Marktwirtschaft bezeichnet wird, und der Aufbruch in eine neue Gesellschaft ist nicht aufzuhalten. Diese Gewissheit bleibt – trotz der Niederlage, die wir erlitten haben durch Fehler und Mängel, die nicht zu sein brauchten, trotz allem Verrat, der an Schändlichkeit nicht übertroffen werden kann ...

Der Hauptwiderspruch der kapitalistischen Gesellschaft, der Widerspruch zwischen gesellschaftlicher Arbeit und privater Aneignung, existiert und bleibt bestehen, so sehr der Kapitalismus sich im Laufe seiner Entwicklung auch zu wandeln vermag. Erst wenn dieser

Widerspruch aufgehoben wird, wenn nicht mehr der Profit die Welt regiert, erst dann werden die Bedingungen geschaffen, damit der Einzelne ein menschenwürdiges Leben führen kann. Die vielzitierte Selbstverwirklichung kann gewiß nicht darin bestehen, daß mit der Entwicklung und Anwendung von Hochtechnologien künftig nur noch 20 oder 10 Prozent der Menschen einen Arbeitsplatz finden. Eine neue Gesellschaft muß unter Berücksichtigung aller technologischen und anderen Bedingungen für jedes ihrer Mitglieder einen Platz, in erster Linie einen Arbeitsplatz finden. Der Kapitalismus kann das nicht, das ist heute klarer als je zuvor. Die Möglichkeiten der kapitalistischen Gesellschaft sind dort erreicht, wo die Jagd nach Profit dem Grenzen setzt. Es sind also tiefliegende, zwingende gesellschaftliche Gründe, die es erfordern, den Weg freizukämpfen für eine gesellschaftliche Alternative, für eine sozialistische Gesellschaft, wie immer sie auch strukturiert und konkret ausgestaltet sein mag. Deshalb beurteile ich aus historischer Sicht die Dinge nicht so pessimistisch, wie dies aus verständlichen Gründen viele nach der 'Wende' von 1989 taten. Die soziale Frage wird auch in Zukunft Kern der gesellschaftlichen Auseinandersetzung in allen kapitalistischen Ländern sein.

Auch jene, die ihre Kraft für das Zustandekommen der 'Wende' einsetzten, die noch heute glauben oder zumindest behaupten, sie wollten damit einen verbesserten Sozialismus, eine bessere DDR bewirken, müssen heute bitteren Realitäten ins Auge sehen. Wir wollten alle einen noch besseren Sozialismus. Das Erreichte hat uns nie genügt. Aber all die kleinen 'Reformer' haben den Sozialismus preisgegeben, indem sie auf den 'großen Reformer' hörten, der es im Laufe von sechs Jahren fertigbrachte, seine Partei, die KPdSU, deren Generalsekretär er war, zu entwaffnen und die UdSSR in ihren Untergang zu führen.

Die Opferung der DDR auf dem Altar des von Gorbatschow so eifrig verfochtenen 'europäischen Hauses' ist für mich, wie für viele andere, das Schmerzlichste in meinem Leben. Wie man heute erkennen muß, war dies nur möglich wegen der durch Tradition und Disziplin geprägten Haltung gegenüber Moskau, selbst dann, als man dort nicht mehr bereit war, den Sozialismus zu verteidigen. Und schließlich war das nur möglich, weil Teile unserer Partei an der Beseitigung des Sozialismus objektiv mitgewirkt haben, darunter sogar einige bewußte Verräter, die sich heute damit brüsten, durch ihre jahrelangen Kontakte zur BRD den Weg für die Annexion der DDR mitgebahnt zu haben.

Vocabulary

niveauvoll	high-class
lebenswert	worth living
verschämt	coy
die Schändlichkeit	disgracefulness, shamefulness
der Hauptwiderspruch	main contradiction
die Selbstverwirklichung	self-fulfilment
das Zustandekommen	bringing about
sich brüsten	boast, brag

Questions on the Texts

Text A

1. Comment on the following phrases:
   Reinheit der Partei
   der wissenschaftlich-technische Fortschritt
   Rassismus
   innerparteiliche Demokratie
   Grundorganisation
2. In what ways does the party member fulfil a propaganda role?
3. What can lead to a member or a candidate being disciplined?
4. To what did the concept of *politische Wachsamkeit* lead?

Text B

1. Explain and comment on the following phrases:
   Grenzen von 1937
   Obhutspflicht für alle Deutschen
   Neonazismus
   Versorgungspsychose
   Ausbeutung
   Überflußgesellschaft
   Öffentlichkeitsarbeit
   Kapitalismus
2. What does this text tell you about how the Politburo members interpreted the events in the summer and autumn of 1989?

3. To what extent were they wrong?

Text C

1. What methods did Honecker employ to keep himself in power in the SED?
2. How did the members of the Politburo react to Honecker?
3. What sort of man was Honecker, according to Schabowski?
4. What was the atmosphere in the Politburo?
5. What do you understand by *Er war ein Mann des Apparates*?

Text D

1. Explain the following phrases:
    diverse Vertreter in die neuen Regierungsbänke drängten
    sozialistische Produktionsweise
    der Widerspruch zwischen gesellschaftlicher Arbeit und privater Aneignung
    die soziale Frage
    der große Reformer
    das europäische Haus
2. To what extent do you think Honecker's view that 'socialism' will still influence the future holds?
3. What reasons does Honecker give for the 'inevitable' collapse of the market economy?
4. What does he have to say about the dissidents who helped to bring down the communist system?
5. Examine what he says about his attitudes towards the Soviet Union and Gorbachev.
6. How does he view his own party's contribution to bringing about reunification?

Notes

1. William L. Shirer, *The Rise and Fall of the Third Reich* (London, Pan Books, 1964), 197–202.
2. 'Manifest des Nationalkomitees "Freies Deutschland" an die Wehrmacht und an das deutsche Volk', *Freies Deutschland*, 19 July 1943.
3. Hegel was an early nineteenth-century German philosopher.

4. R. N. Carew Hunt, *The Theory and Practice of Communism* (London/ Harmondsworth, Penguin, 1966).
5. Karl Marx and Friedrich Engels, *The Communist Manifesto* (Harmondsworth, Penguin Books, 1968), 84–6.
6. Gert Gruner and Manfred Wilke (eds.), *Sozialdemokraten im Kampf um die Freiheit* (Munich and Stuttgart, Piper, 1986).
7. Up to 1949 refugees from Germany's former Eastern Provinces (Silesia, East Prussia, Pomerania, Danzig) made up 25 per cent of the East German population, and very many of them had found refuge in the countryside.
8. For a general description of the activities of the Stasi and its relationship with the SED see Manfred Schell and Werner Kalinka, *Stasi und kein Ende. Die Personen und die Fakten* (Frankfurt-am-Main and Berlin, Ullstein and Die Welt, 1991).
9. See Günter Schabowski, *Das Politbüro* (text C, p.198–9).
10. It is not surprising that the major works of Kafka such as *Der Prozeß* and *Das Schloß* were banned by the SED – an East German reader could have drawn parallels with Kafka's world.
11. Allegations have been made that Honecker betrayed other communists during the period, but proof has not been found.
12. Erich Honecker, *Aus meinem Leben* (East Berlin, Dietz Verlag, 1980), 106–8.
13. Günter Mittag was a member of the Politburo and Central Committee secretary for the economy.
14. Erich Mielke was the minister for state security, an army general and a member of the Politburo.
15. Walter Ulbricht was a leading figure in the KPD and SED (for instance, general secretary of the SED) who was Stalinist and 'hard-line'.

Bibliography

Publications in German

Benser, Günter, Gert Dietrich, Sonja Eichhofer and Gerhard Naumann, *Dokumente zur Geschichte der SED, 2, 1945–71* (East Berlin, Dietz Verlag, 1986).

Honecker, Erich, *Aus meinem Leben* (East Berlin, Dietz Verlag, 1980; English edition: Oxford, Pergamon Press, 1980).

Honecker, Erich, *Moabiter Notizen* (Berlin, edition ost, 1994).

Hölder, Egon, *Im Trabi durch die Zeit – 40 Jahre Leben in der DDR* (Stuttgart, Metzler Poeschel, 1992).

Kenntemich, Wolfgang, Manfred Durniok and Thomas Karlauf, *Das war die DDR. Eine Geschichte des anderen Deutschland* (Berlin, Rowohlt, 1993).

Kobert, Heide and Anke Rasch (eds.), *Der Fischer Weltalmanach. Sonderband DDR* (Frankfurt-am-Main, Fischer Taschenbuch, 1990).
Schabowski, Günter, *Das Politbüro* (Reinbek, Rowohlt, 1991).
Schneider, Eberhard, *Die DDR. Politik, Wirtschaft, Gesellschaft* (Stuttgart, Verlag Bonn aktuell, 1976).
Thomas, Rüdiger, *Modell DDR. Die kalkulierte Emanzipation* (Munich, Hanser Verlag, 1975).

Publications in English

Childs, David (ed.), *Honecker's Germany* (London, Allen & Unwin, 1985).
Dennis, Mike, *German Democratic Republic: Politics, Economy and Society* (London and New York, Pinter, 1988).
Edwards, G. E., *GDR Society and Social Institutions* (London, Macmillan, and New York, St Martin's Press, 1985).
McCauley, Martin, *The German Democratic Republic since 1945* (London, Macmillan, 1983).
Scharf, Bradley C., *Politics and Change in East Germany: An Evaluation of Socialist Democracy* (Boulder, Westview Press, and London, Pinter, 1984).

6. Partei des Demokratischen Sozialismus (PDS)

In three short months after Honecker's departure from office to the formation of the Partei des Demokratischen Sozialismus (PDS), the power, bureaucracy and base of the SED collapsed. In October and November 1989 the leaders of the SED, both the old and those who were hurriedly called in to replace them, showed clearly that they had no idea how to stabilize the situation. The demands from grass-roots party members for immediate changes, the huge loss of members – 200,000 by late November 1989 and 900,000 by early January 1990 – coupled with a massive drop in morale, all showed a party in terminal crisis.[1] From the two special SED conferences in December (8-9 and 16-17 of the month) onwards, the call was increasingly for a new name for the party (the name SED-PDS was adopted on 19 December) or the dissolution of the SED and the formation of a new party. The further renaming of the party as the PDS was accepted on 4 February and confirmed at the next party conference. By then it was increasingly clear that unification with West Germany was becoming inevitable – the only questions were when it would take place, and how anything could be saved from the GDR and introduced into the new Germany. For the PDS there had to be a new beginning.

At the PDS party congress (24-5 February) it was obvious that much of the old ballast had been thrown out and that large numbers of young people and women were making their mark. There was a feeling of optimism and self-confidence among the delegates. This was, in part, personified by the party chairman, Gregor Gysi (elected to the post in December 1989), a highly articulate solicitor by profession. The PDS was to fight the Volkskammer election as the party that would represent the interests of the East German people in the processes of German and European integration. It would be a 'pro-GDR' party and do its best to maintain an independent GDR for the immediate future, although the principle of German unity had now been accepted. The PDS would stand for democracy, social justice and the rule of law. It would fight to maintain existing social security provisions and to protect the rights of children and young people. It supported the maintenance of a co-operative sector in the economy.

The party programme proclaimed that Marxism was no longer its only ideological base, there was no aspiration to a 'leading role', and the party no longer sought to appeal to only one social class. It saw itself as an opposition party standing to the left of the SPD. Whilst accepting the market economy, the PDS still expressed the view that capitalism, although economically efficient, could not solve the problems of peace, disarmament and the environment.[2]

The Volkskammer elections brought the PDS a good result – 16.4 per cent, 1,892,381 votes and sixty-six of the 400 seats. However, the emotion of the rapid move to national unity in the coming months operated against the PDS. The party, as a minority political force, was able to 'save' none of the aspects of the GDR system – such as a job for everyone who wanted one – in the new united country. The PDS was, in any case, largely ostracized by the other parties in the Volkskammer and by the West German parties. By the summer of 1990 it was looking for allies among the various disparate communist and Marxist parties and groups in West Germany, but with little success. The Linke Liste/PDS was created in August but consisted of small West German groups plus some of the former DKP. The election congress in September showed clear differences in positions between the East and the West German participants, particularly on economic and social policies.

The all-German Bundestag elections of December 1990 brought a further decrease in PDS fortunes – 11.1 per cent of votes in East Germany and 0.3 per cent in the West. This still meant seventeen PDS members in the Bundestag, since the party had passed the 5 per cent threshold in East Germany. The PDS still had a firm core of voters in East Germany, some 285,000 members (December 1990), as well as a strong party organization there. The next year saw disagreements between those who wanted reform and those who still resisted it, between those who wanted the PDS to be a party and those who wanted it to develop as a grass-roots, extra-parliamentary movement. The party was full of contradictions. It was also slow to examine the SED past, and particularly the relationship between the

SED and the Stasi. Revelations about some PDS members having worked for the Stasi also increased the negative image of the party. Financial difficulties added to these problems. The *Treuhand* took control of 140 million DM that the PDS had brought in between October 1989 and 1992, as well as the 14 million DM received by the party for its election costs, and PDS assets were temporarily frozen (until August 1992).[3]

Part of the reason for the *Treuhand* action was that the PDS was involved in financial scandals in its attempts to hold on to money that had been in the hands of the SED. In January 1990 the SED/PDS gave over into public ownership eleven newspapers, twenty-one printing houses, the advertisement firm DEWAG, Intertext (the translation service) and Genex, a firm that had concentrated on raising hard currency for the GDR. The party also relinquished its guest-houses and convalescent homes to the government, and gave some of its buildings for the use of other parties. It gave 250 million DM to the Humboldt University, Berlin (though the payment was prohibited by the Berlin *Landgericht* until 7 July 1994).[4] On 31 May 1990 the Volkskammer decided to investigate the finances of all parties and former mass organizations. The PDS set up a working party to 'save' its property, which showed how seriously concerned the party was that it was going to be killed off politically by being starved of funds for its activities. Three PDS members – Karl-Heinz Kaufmann, Pohl and Wolfgang Langnitschke – attempted to divert millions of DM from the PDS to bank accounts in Germany, Norway and Russia. They were caught, tried in court and given suspended sentences. By 1990 PDS admitted that it had already lent 214 million DM to newly founded firms, many of them controlled by its members.[5] The PDS stated that it had helped to set up the firms so as to give employment to those who had previously worked in firms owned by the SED, and claimed that the support was legitimate. In 1990 an attempt was made by Langnitschke to deposit over fourteen million DM in a bank in Luxemburg. The media and the other political parties were able to make considerable capital out of the financial affairs of the PDS, but in the last few years matters seem to have been cleared up and the PDS remains on a good financial footing.

The high levels of unemployment and increasing disappointment among East Germans at the inability of the West German political and economic systems to solve their problems led to a reversal of fortunes for the PDS. In the Berlin election in June 1992, for instance, it was able to gain 29.7 per cent of votes in East Berlin.

The PDS projected itself as the party that represented and fought for the interests of the East Germans, the only party that, most importantly, accepted and symbolized an East German identity.

That sense of identity has not diminished significantly since unification. In representative surveys carried out in East Germany in 1992 and 1995 (1992 figures in brackets), 19.2 per cent of respondents felt themselves to be European (24.8 per cent), 53.4 per cent German (48.2 per cent), 17.8 per cent *Bundesbürger* (13 per cent), 41.2 per cent as East German (34.7 per cent), 36.1 per cent as former GDR citizens (40 per cent) and 41.8 as Berliners or Brandenburgers etc. (43.1 per cent).[6] Interestingly, 54.3 per cent of the 18–34-year-olds felt themselves to be East German, 29 per cent as former GDR citizens and only 15.4 per cent as *Bundesbürger*. The highest percentage (21.1) that identified with the Federal Republic were the over-60-year-olds. As Heiner Moellemann expresses it, 'The collapse of an unjust and ineffective system for the first time allowed the East Germans to be unequivocally proud of what they had achieved in that very system.'[7] Since West German politicians have tended to ignore or deny a specific East German identity, it is not surprising that the PDS has gained support among many East Germans. Similarly, the constant description by West German politicians of the GDR as an *Unrechtsstaat* and the refusal to accept anything done by that state as 'positive' do not fit with the opinions voiced by East Germans in the 'ident '95' survey. For instance, in answer to the question 'How do you evaluate the GDR today?' 74.8 per cent agreed with the statement 'DDR war vor allem der Versuch, eine gerechtere Gesellschaft zu gestalten'; 78.7 per cent agreed that 'DDR hatte negative und positive Seiten'; 42.8 per cent said yes to: 'DDR verkörperte Leistungen der Bürger', 42.8 per cent disagreed that 'DDR war vor allem ein Unrechtsstaat', 18.2 per cent said it was, and 33.9 per cent partly agreed with the statement.[8] There is thus a tendency for East Germans to be alienated by West Germans who have never lived in the GDR but who express opinions that do not coincide with their own or with their experience there. Furthermore, in answer to the question put in the 'ident '93' survey. 'Wie soll in Deutschland mit der Geschichte der DDR umgegangen werden?', 76.5 per cent answered yes to 'die Geschichte der DDR ist Teil meines Lebens, sie darf nicht verdrängt werden', and 88 per cent agreed that 'die Geschichte der DDR muß wie die Geschichte der BRD als Bestandteil der deutschen Geschichte behandelt werden.'[9] The West Germans have tried to remove the traces of the GDR and wipe out the experiences of two generations as quickly as possible. This is not making them popular in East Germany. The PDS does the exact opposite and correspondingly garners support, for people do not easily accept their own identity being questioned. It is essential for the West German parties to realize that they have paid far too little attention to the East Germans' psychology and identity. They must change their attitudes if they want to weaken the influence of the PDS.

A further reason for the success of the PDS is that it has supported, and in return received support from, a large number of groups that sprang up to represent various sections of the East German population, from the unemployed to the elderly, from tenants to former academics or army officers. In other words, the PDS has cultivated contacts with those who had lost out during reunification. The PDS has also strengthened its work at local-government level and developed its image as the party of action. In December 1993 it reached 21 per cent of the vote in the *Land* elections in Brandenburg, and was thus in good form for the *Superwahljahr* of 1994 (so-called because elections took place that year for the Bundestag, the European Parliament and a number of the *Land* parliaments). It had a new programme (although factional disputes were to break out again as soon as the Bundestag elections were over) and a new chairman, Lothar Bisky. The PDS entered the Bundestag elections with so-called *offene Listen*, that is, it put people on its ticket who were not party members but who came from among the cultural or scientific community. (An example was Stefan Heym, who had been a dissident during the SED period; although clearly strongly left-wing, he had not joined the PDS.)

The results in 1994 were good for the PDS – 21 per cent in East Germany and 4.7 per cent nationally in the European elections, nearly 20 per cent in the *Land* elections in Saxony-Anhalt, and thirty parliamentarians in the Bundestag elections. The latter was the result of the PDS gaining four direct seats, for although the party won 19.8 per cent of the votes in East Germany, it reached only 4.4 per cent nation-wide. In East Berlin it gained 34.7 per cent and in Mecklenburg-Pomerania 23.6 per cent.

Despite these electoral successes and the high level of activity at local level in East Germany, the PDS has many problems. The first concerns its programme and ideology. So much that is said and written is still conventional left-wing and partly Marxist in tone. The PDS is addressing two disparate electorates in East and West

Germany. By supporting and accepting the far-left splinter groups in West Germany, the party alienates West Germans who have for decades equated such groups with extremism and viewed them as a threat to democracy and to the Federal Republic itself. The PDS has gained very few votes by trying to expand to be an all-German party. Similarly, by accepting the group known as the Kommunistische Plattform and tolerating extremist groups, the party has laid itself open to criticisms of not having broken with the SED past, and of not disowning extremism. This makes it much easier for conservatives to call for the whole PDS to be scrutinized by the *Verfassungsschutz*. (For example, the demand has been made by Secretary of State Kuno Böse (CDU) that the whole of the Berlin PDS should be kept under intelligence surveillance.)[10] Party leaders such as Lothar Bisky are aware of the need to expose the mistakes of the SED and to learn from them, but admit that there are people in the party who are reluctant to do this: 'Es darf aber auch nicht verschwiegen werden, daß es Kreise gibt, in denen es kaum eigene Anstrengungen auf diesem Gebiet gibt.'[11] The author Stephan Hermlin was even more direct in his criticism in 1995: 'Es gibt eine Vergangenheit, von der manche nicht loskommen. Es gibt ein Scheitern, dessen verdiente Endgültigkeit sie nicht begreifen wollen.'[12] Secondly, the PDS does not seem to have understood the market economy and how it functions. Some of its demands have no chance of being implemented in the present-day world, especially with the great economic power concentrated in the hands of the multinationals and the rapidly increasing globalization of the world economy. Thirdly, with respect to PDS disarmament policies, too many major states have an interest in the maintenance of NATO for its disbandment to be a serious possibility, and Germany is a far too important military partner for North America and Western Europe to accept a neutral Germany.

The PDS also has a problem with the age structure of its membership. It is an ageing party and must recruit more young members. In December 1993 only 5 per cent of the members were under thirty, while 50 per cent were pensioners and a further 12 per cent were in early retirement.[13] Interestingly, 45 per cent were women and 12 per cent were unemployed.

It is clear that in the 1998 Bundestag elections the CDU, CSU and FDP, in particular, will mount a strong campaign against the PDS. It is also clear that the SPD and Bündnis 90/Die Grünen will not enter coalition agreements at Bundestag level with the PDS. Unless the PDS is banned (which is unlikely, given that millions of people are voting for the party, that in all its official statements it makes sure that it stays within the constitution, and that a party driven underground is much more dangerous to a state than is the use of the democratic process to oppose it), it is likely to return to the Bundestag after the next elections.

Sources

Text A: PDS, 'Programm der Partei des Demokratischen Sozialismus', *Disput*, 3/4 (Berlin, 1993), 38–9

Das Scheitern des sozialistischen Versuchs

Der Sozialismusversuch in der DDR hat die Lebensgeschichte der Menschen im Osten Deutschlands entscheidend geprägt. Zu ihren Erfahrungen zählen die Beseitigung von Arbeitslosigkeit, weitgehende Überwindung von Armut, ein umfassendes soziales Sicherheitssystem, bedeutende Elemente sozialer Gerechtigkeit, insbesondere ein hohes Maß an sozialer Chancengleichheit im Bildungs- und Gesundheitswesen sowie in der Kultur, neue Rechte für Frauen und Jugendliche. Die DDR war ein Staat, der konsequent mit dem deutschen Großmachtchauvinismus gebrochen hatte. Jedoch war auch die DDR-Gesellschaft nicht in der Lage, einen wirksamen Beitrag zum Ausbruch aus der bedrohlichen globalen Entwicklungslogik zu leisten. Und es ist deutlich geworden, daß ein Sozialismusversuch, der nicht von der großen Mehrheit des Volkes erkämpft, entwickelt und getragen wird, der nicht die Selbstbefreiung des Menschen gewährleistet, früher oder später scheitern muß.

Der Weg im Osten wie im Westen war zunächst vom Willen und Einfluß der jeweiligen Siegermacht und vom Kalten Krieg bestimmt. Ostdeutschland entwickelte sich unter anhaltend ungünstigen äußeren Wirtschaftsbedingungen, litt unter dem Aderlaß von 96 Prozent der Reparationen für ganz Deutschland und der Spaltung des gesamtdeutschen Wirtschaftssystems. Die Embargopolitik der westlichen Länder und dadurch begünstigte Autarkiebestrebungen schlossen die DDR weitgehend von der internationalen Arbeitsteilung außerhalb des RGW aus. Auch innerhalb des RGW wurde keine effektive Arbeitsteilung verwirklicht. Die DDR war einer Bedrohungs- und Konfrontationspolitik ausgesetzt. Die Beteiligung an dem von den

kapitalistischen Ländern ausgehenden Wettrüsten verzehrte einen
beträchtlichen Teil ihrer Wirtschaftskraft und beschleunigte den
Niedergang.

Das Scheitern des sozialistischen Versuchs in der DDR ist ursäch-
lich mit dem Scheitern des Modells der Sowjetunion verbunden ...
Wesentlichen Anteil hatte die UdSSR an der Niederschlagung des
deutschen Faschismus. Von Anfang an wurde der Versuch, eine
sozialistische Ordnung zu schaffen, aber dadurch beeinträchtigt, daß
er am Rande und außerhalb der entwickelteren kapitalistischen
Industrieländer erfolgte, in einem sozial, ökonomisch, politisch und
kulturell zurückgebliebenen Land, ständig bedroht von einer kapitalistischen Umwelt. Bis zur Unkenntlichkeit entstellt wurde das, was
als Aufbau des Sozialismus gedacht war, durch Willkür, Grausamkeit
und Bürokratie erfüllte Herrschaft des Stalinismus.

Der Sozialismus in Osteuropa und in der DDR war nicht von vorn-
herein zum Scheitern verurteilt. Sein Zusammenbruch war eine
notwendige Folge seiner zunehmenden Unfähigkeit, das Eigentum an
den Produktionsmitteln in einer für die Produzenten spürbaren Weise
zu vergesellschaften. Alle Versuche zur Erneuerung und Rettung des
Sozialismus wurden letztlich blockiert. Es gelang nicht, die erforder-
liche ökonomische Effektivität zu erreichen und sie mit
wirtschaftlicher und politischer Demokratie sowie konsequenter
ökologischer Orientierung zu verbinden. Die verabsolutierte Entge-
gensetzung von Plan und Markt führte zum Fehlen von
Selbstregulierungsmechanismen in der Wirtschaft und zur Totalpla-
nung. Bürokratische Verstaatlichung beherrschte das gesellschaftliche
Leben. Trotz bedeutender Schritte zur Gleichberechtigung und
ökonomischen Unabhängigkeit der Frau wurde auch das Patriarchat
nicht ernsthaft erschüttert.

Die traditionelle Gewaltenteilung wurde abgelehnt, der Sinn
demokratischer Wahlsysteme mißachtet; Mitbestimmungs- und
Mitentscheidungsrechte wurden deklariert, aber zu selten realisiert.
Es kam zu einer falschen, in großem Maße von Mißtrauen gegen die
Bevölkerung des eigenen Landes erfüllten Sicherheitspolitik. Hinzu
traten Bevormundung der Rechtssprechung, Verletzungen der Freiheit von Wissenschaft und Kultur, Mediengängelei. Eine
überzeugende alternative gesellschaftliche Produktions- und
Lebensweise mit dem Ziel solidarischer Individualitätsentfaltung und
im Einklang mit der Natur wurde nicht geschaffen.

Immer deutlicher wurde: eine demokratische sozialistische
Gesellschaft, nicht bestimmt vom Profitprinzip, kann nur auf den

gemeinsamen Anstrengungen unterschiedlicher sozialer und politischer Kräfte basieren, oder sie muß untergehen. Sie braucht die Austragung der realen Widersprüche, Kompromiß und Konsens, Toleranz und demokratische Offenheit in einem pluralistischen Prozeß politischer Willensbildung. Wir brauchen neue Zugänge zu Theorie und Praxis des Sozialismus.

Vocabulary

anhaltend	continuing
der Aderlaß	blood-letting
das Wettrüsten	arms race
verzehren	to consume
ursächlich	originally
beeinträchtigen	to spoil, detract from, harm, impair
zurückgeblieben	backward
vergesellschaften	to socialize

Text B: PDS, 'Programm der Partei des Demokratischen Sozialismus', *Disput*, 3/4 (Berlin, 1993), 42

Das System der gesellschaftlichen Arbeit verändern
Wir betrachten das Recht auf Arbeit, die soziale, humane und ökologische Umgestaltung des gesellschaftlichen Arbeitssystems wie auch das Recht auf soziale Grundsicherung als Schlüsselfragen sozialistischer Politik.

Daher fordern wir:
- eine auf Vollbeschäftigung gerichtete Wirtschaftspolitik;
- gerechte Verteilung der bezahlten Arbeit; Verkürzung der Wochen- und Lebensarbeitszeit auch auf dem Wege von bezahlter Weiterbildung und Bildungsurlaub, damit die Massenarbeitslosigkeit überwunden und die Beschäftigungspolitik nicht selbst zur Triebkraft einer zerstörerischen Produktionsausweitung wird; Durchsetzung der 35–Stunden-Woche mit dem Ziel einer weiteren Senkung auf 30 Wochenstunden.
- gesellschaftliche Anerkennung und materielle Vergütung von Kindererziehung, Alten- und Krankenpflege und anderen sozialen Tätigkeiten, die außerhalb der Erwerbsarbeit geleistet werden;
- Schaffung von Arbeitsplätzen durch öffentliche Investitions- und

Beschäftigungsprogramme und Ausweitung der Beschäftigungsmöglichkeiten im sozialen und kulturellen Bereich sowie für die Erhaltung und Wiederherstellung der natürlichen Umwelt;
- Möglichkeiten für die Beschäftigten, ihre Arbeitsplätze souverän zu gestalten; vor allem sind für die bessere Vereinbarkeit von Beruf und Familie für Frauen und Männer, insbesondere für Alleinerziehende, entsprechende Arbeitszeitregelungen erforderlich; Abbau von Sonn- und Feiertagsarbeit; Einschränkung des Mehrschichtbetriebes und der Nachtarbeit;
- wesentlich erweiterte Mitbestimmung der Beschäftigten am Arbeitsplatz, in den Betrieben und Unternehmen;
- Beschäftigten, Kommunen und anderen gesellschaftlichen Kräften sind bedeutend mehr Mitbestimmungsmöglichkeiten und -rechte über die Produktion, ihre soziale und ökologische Verträglichkeit sowie ihre gebrauchswertmäßigen Ergebnisse einzuräumen;
- Einspruchsrechte bei Produktionsverfahren und Stoffen, die ökologische Risiken für die Betroffenen und die Umwelt mit sich bringen;
- die Verbesserung des betrieblichen Gesundheitsschutzes und die Ausweitung der Liste anerkannter Berufskrankheiten;
- eine einkommens- und gewinnabhängige Arbeitsmarktabgabe zur Finanzierung aktiver Arbeitsmarktpolitik.
- Um diese Forderungen durchzusetzen, sind der DGB und die Einzelgewerkschaften als einheitliche und autonome Gewerkschaften sowie starke Betriebs- und Personalräte unverzichtbar.

Text C: Gregor Gysi, *Ingolstädter Manifest – Wir – mitten in Europa. Plädoyer für einen neuen Gesellschaftsvertrag* (Berlin, Wahlbüro der PDS, 1994), 7–8, 11–12

Die bislang letzte große Stunde der Politik in der Bundesrepublik war 1989/90. Es war die blinde Politik des Anschlusses um jeden Preis. Es war der Versuch der Nichtveränderung der BRD. Es war Nichtpolitik. Sie hat einen Großteil jener Chancen zerstört, die wieder einmal durch und für Menschen in Deutschland entstanden waren ... Die politischen Institutionen Deutschlands scheinen nur noch zur Verwaltung des Gegebenen und zur Veränderung zuungunsten der Schwächeren und auf Kosten von Zukunft geeignet zu sein. Dazu gibt es aber Alternativen. Sie wurden 1989 diskutiert und seitdem totgeschwiegen. Lassen Sie uns darüber wieder sprechen.

Die Dritte Stimme

Bei Wahlen können die Stimmen nur für Personen und Parteien abgegeben werden. Wieso nicht auch für nichtstaatliche Organisationen mit einzelnen Sachthemen wie Umweltschutz, Feminismus, Dritte-Welt-Problemen, Altersfürsorge, Drogenschutz, usw. Wieso sollten wir nicht durch eine dritte Stimme, daß ihnen und eben nicht den staatlichen Bürokratien Gelder zur Verfügung gestellt werden, um einen Beitrag zur Lösung jener Probleme zu leisten, die uns am wichtigsten scheinen. Je mehr Stimmen solche Organisationen auf sich vereinigen können, desto mehr Geld müßte ihnen aus dem Bundeshaushalt bzw. den Länderhaushalten zur Verfügung gestellt werden. Anstatt über Benzin-, Alkohol-, und Tabaksteuern Gelder in anonyme Fonds abzuziehen, auf die wir keinen Einfluß haben, deren Verwalter uns niemals Rechenschaft ablegen, sollten wir zunächst einmal fünf Prozent der öffentlichen Haushalte per Dritte Stimme verteilen – direkt durch uns bestimmt und uns gegenüber abrechenbar. Ein Stück mehr Souveränität hätten wir gewonnen. Wir, die eigentlich Betroffenen, würden einige Entscheidungen wieder selbst fällen. Ein Stück Zukunft läge in unseren eigenen Händen. Eine Reihe von Problemen könnten endlich ohne Vater Staat gelöst werden.

Die zweite Kammer

Die Parteien und Bürokratien entscheiden zu oft unser Schicksal. Der einzige Weg, der dann Betroffenen bleibt, ist der Gerichtsweg. Das ist eine Waffe der Schwachen, aber oft auch eine schwache Waffe, denn Recht haben und Recht bekommen, ist häufig zweierlei und muß allzu oft durch hohe finanzielle Vorleistungen zusammengeführt werden. Und die Waffe des Rechts ist defensiv. Wir aber brauchen die direkte politische Mitbestimmung durch die sozialen Kräfte dieser Gesellschaft und vor allem durch jene, die sich sonst nicht Gehör verschaffen können. Neben dem Bundestag der Parteien sollte es eine Bundeskammer der sozialen Bewegungen geben, in die hinein Interessenverbände gewählt werden: Gewerkschaften und Unternehmer, Umwelt- und Mieterverbände, Initiativen von Menschen mit Behinderungen, Interessenvertreter ausländischer Bürgerinnen und Bürger, Organisationen der Arbeitslosen und Frauenbewegungen, Verbände der Schwulen, Amnesty International, die Volkssolidarität oder Greenpeace. Sie sollten das Recht auf die

Vorbereitung und das Einbringen eigener Gesetze, auf die Diskussion von Gesetzen des Bundestages und deren zeitweilige Zurückweisung bei Entscheidungen haben, die tief in das Leben von Betroffenen eingreifen. Einige Teile der Haushaltsentscheidungen müßten an diese Kammer abgegeben werden.

Bis zur Angleichung der Lebensverhältnisse in Ost und West sollen die Ostdeutschen eine eigene Kammer wählen können, die mit Initiativ- und Einspruchsrechten gegen die Benachteiligungen Ostdeutscher wirksam werden sollte ...

Kapitalressourcen für den sozialökonomischen Umbau

Über 700 Mrd. DM haben deutsche Unternehmen als liquides Kapital ohne feste Anlage. Es lohnt sich offensichtlich zur Zeit nicht, sie in die Produktion zu investieren. Allein von 1990 bis 1992 wurden von Unternehmen und Handelsketten der alten Bundesländer rund 40 Mrd. DM zusätzliche Gewinne in den neuen Bundesländern gemacht. Auf das Neunfache, auf über 200 Mrd. DM gestiegen sind in den vergangenen zwei Jahrzehnten die arbeitsunabhängigen Einkommen aus Vermögen in der Bundesrepublik. Weltweit werden täglich fast 1 Billion Dollar an Devisen gekauft und verkauft. Würde auf diese internationalen Umsätze von Finanzkapital eine Umsatzsteuer von einem Zehntel Prozent erhoben, so wären dies jährlich schon eine halbe Billion Deutscher Mark, die ihrer parasitären und weltwirtschaftlich bedrohlichen Verwendung entzogen wären. Eine Kürzung der weltweiten Rüstung auf die Hälfte würde etwa eine dreiviertel Billion DM freisetzen.

Die Kapitalressourcen sind also da. Sie müssen nur erschlossen werden. Und sie sind für die Schaffung einer Nachfrage zu nutzen, die dieses Kapital in neue Richtungen lenkt. Durchsetzung einer naturerhaltenden Produktions- und Lebensweise, Verwandlung von Elendsregionen der Erde in lebenswerte Landschaften, wo Menschen unsere Produkte brauchen und wir ihre, Ausbau verbindender Infrastrukturen zwischen Ost und West, Nord und Süd, ein Leben ohne soziale Angst braucht Kapital, verantwortungsfähiges Unternehmertum, vor allem aber unsere eigene Arbeit.

Den Markt gestalten

Eine globale ökologische und soziale Revolution steht ins Haus. Sie verlangt bewußtes Eingreifen in völlig neuen Größenordnungen. Sie muß den Markt gestalten, bevor er sich durch ein spontanes Weiter-So selbst zerstört hat. Wir sind weder so blind, daß wir den Markt beseitigen wollen noch so pessimistisch, daß wir nicht glauben würden, ihn gestalten zu können.

Das Ende der Nachkriegsschönwetterperiode in der Wirtschaft, die Zivilisationskrise, die Unterentwicklung im Süden und die Transformationskrisen fordern den Wandel in der Regulation von Markt, Staat und Zivilgesellschaft heraus. Der Markt soll wesentliche Regulierungsfunktionen behalten. Die Nationalstaaten sollen ihre sozialen Standards in der Europäischen Union gegen Ausgleichstendenzen nach unten verteidigen können ...

Sich der Welt öffnen und Welt sein

Westeuropa muß seine Märkte für Ost und Süd öffnen. Dies ist schmerzhaft, da vieles anderswo billiger hergestellt wird. Es zwingt uns aber auch, die eigenen Stärken auszubauen und nicht weiter unsere Schwächen zu subventionieren. Die Chancen sind größer als die Gefahren.

Zugleich müssen wir die regionalen Märkte stärken – die eigenen und die in Osteuropa und Rußland, in Asien, Afrika und Lateinamerika. Der ökologische zerstörerische Transport von allen Alltagsdingen, die um die Ecke wachsen können, ist durch internationale Energie- und Rohstoffsteuern zu begrenzen. Verkehrsverminderung und -vermeidung sind notwendig und möglich. Die internationale Arbeitsteilung muß ökologisch und sozial sein. Sie soll Selbständigkeit und nicht Ausbeutung befördern.

Text D: PDS, 'Veränderungen von unten. Sozial und solidarisch, demokratisch und antimilitaristisch', *Disput,* **2 (Berlin, 1996), 29–30**

Demokratisierung und Entmilitarisierung der Europa- und Außenpolitik

Die PDS ist eine antimilitaristische Partei, die auch pazifistischen Traditionen und Bestrebungen Rückhalt und Unterstützung gewährt. Als Verfechterin antikapitalistischer Alternativen und sozialer Leitbilder und Utopien bewährt sich ihr demokratischer Charakter zuerst und vor allem in der bedingungslosen Gegnerschaft zur Militarisierung der internationalen Beziehungen. Widerstand gegen Aufrüstung und Krieg, gegen die Anwendung von Gewalt zur Lösung zwischen-staatlicher Konflikte, ist unsere internationalistische Aufgabe. Niemand hat das Recht, andere zum Töten in die Welt zu schicken. Wir tragen dazu bei, die Basis für aktive Friedensarbeit zu vergrößern. Wir intensivieren den Dialog, die Zusammenarbeit und den gemeinsamen Widerstand mit anderen Friedenskräften, um politische Mehrheiten für die Durchsetzung einer alternativen Außenpolitik, für Gewaltverzicht und für eine Zivilisierung der internationalen Beziehungen zu gewinnen. Wir lehnen militaristische Konfliktlösungen grundsätzlich ab. Das gilt auch allen Bestrebungen im Rahmen der UNO, regionale Auseinandersetzungen und einzelne innerstaatliche Konflikte mit militärischen Mitteln bewältigen zu wollen, anstatt die jeweils vorhandenen Möglichkeiten der Kriegsverhütung und der politischen, nichtmilitärischen Problem- und Konfliktlösung zu nutzen. Insbesondere lehnen wir auch nach den verhängnisvollen Entscheidungen von Bundestagsmehrheiten am 30. Juni und 6. Dezember 1995 die Einbeziehung der Bundeswehr in alle über den verfassungsmäßig begrenzten Verteidigungsfall hinausgehenden Militäraktionen ab. Wir widersetzen uns der Instrumentalisierung der NATO für großmachtpolitische Bestrebungen und fordern die Auflösung dieses Militärpakts. Die PDS wendet sich daher gegen die eingeleitete Umstrukturierung und Umrüstung der Bundeswehr zu einer weltweit aktionsfähigen Streitmacht. Wir unterstützen die Bewegung zur Verweigerung von Wehr- und Ersatzdiensten und alle Initiativen für radikale Abrüstung, Rüstungsexportverbot und Konversion der Rüstungsindustrie. Die PDS fordert die Abschaffung der Wehrpflicht.

Der unwiderrufliche Verzicht Deutschlands auf atomare Bewaffnung, auf jede Verfügungsgewalt über diese im Rahmen bestehender Mitgliedschaft Deutschlands in den militärischen Bündnissen NATO und WEU sowie die ABC-Waffenfreiheit seines gesamten Territoriums gehören ins Grundgesetz. Analoge Verpflichtungen sind im Vertrag über die Europäische Union festzuschreiben. Deutschland sollte der erste Kriegsdienstverweigerer unter den Staaten sein. Die PDS wendet sich strikt gegen die beständige Modernisierung von Waffensystemen, einschließlich der Beteiligung an der Forschung und dem Aufbau einer WEU-Weltraumrüstung. Sie wendet sich gegen Entwicklung, Produktion und Export von Minen und Minenabwurfsystemen.

Die PDS setzt sich für eine demokratische Reform der UNO, für weltweite kooperative, nichtmilitärische Sicherheitssysteme und für die weitere Entwicklung der OSZE als zentrale Säule einer gesamteuropäischen Sicherheitsarchitektur ein. Da die PDS für die Auflösung von militärischen Blöcken wie der NATO eintritt, sieht sie auch keinen Zugewinn an Sicherheit durch eine Ausdehnung der NATO nach Osten. Im Gegenteil, eine solche Ostausdehnung würde Rußland und vielleicht andere Staaten Osteuropas in eine gefährliche Isolierung treiben, die dort Bedrohungsängste auslösen muß.

In der Europapolitik geht die PDS von einem gesamteuropäischen Ansatz aus. Sie lehnt eine erneute West-Ost-Spaltung Europas ab, ebenso die Vorstellung von einem Kerneuropa oder von der hegemonialen Rolle eines Staates oder einer Gruppe von Staaten.

Die PDS erarbeitet Alternativen zum Maastrichter Konzept der Wirtschafts- und Währungsunion und zu der mit Maastricht II verbundenen Absicht, durch die geplante Integration der WEU in die EU, eine selbständig kriegsführungsfähige europäische Armee aufzubauen und damit den bisherigen zivilen Charakter des westeuropäischen Integrationsprozesses aufzugeben.

Die PDS unterbreitet Vorschläge zur Demokratisierung der Europäischen Union. Sie setzt sich für eine Erweiterung der EU nach Osten und Süden und eine dafür notwendige Umgestaltung der EU ein. Wir sehen dies auch als eine Voraussetzung dafür, die politischen, ökonomischen und geistig-kulturellen Potenzen in Europa für die Lösung der neuen Herausforderungen dieser einen Welt einzusetzen. Alternativvorschläge sind zur Innen- und Rechtspolitik sowie zur Reform der EU-Agrarpolitik zu entwickeln.

Die PDS setzt sich mit den Konvergenzkriterien und finanzpolitischen Maßnahmen zur Einführung einer gemeinsamen europäischen Währung sowie ihren sozialen und gesellschaftlichen Auswirkungen auseinander. Sie setzt sich dafür ein, daß die im Maastrichter Vertrag vereinbarte Wirtschafts- und Währungsunion mit der Herstellung einer Sozialunion verbunden wird. Die Einführung der gemeinsamen europäischen Währung in die Bundesrepublik darf nicht, wie vorgesehen, nur von Regierung und Parlament entschieden werden. Dieser Schritt bedarf der Legitimation durch den Volksentscheid.

Questions on the Source Texts

Text A

1. Explain the following words and expressions:

Großmachtchauvinismus
aus der bedrohlichen globalen Entwicklungslogik
Embargopolitik der westlichen Länder
Autarkiebestrebungen
internationale Arbeitsteilung
in einem sozial, ökonomisch, politisch und kulturell zurückge-
    bliebenen Land
Eigentum an den Produktionsmitteln
Patriarchat
traditionelle Gewaltenteilung
Stalinismus

2. What are the reasons given by the PDS for the collapse of communism?
3. Pick out the words and phrases that show this is a clearly left-wing text.
4. Do you think that the assessment of the Soviet Union shows a change of attitude from that of the SED?
5. According to the PDS, what political, economic and social elements are a prerequisite for a 'democratic socialist society not based on profit'?

Text B

1. What steps does the PDS suggest should be undertaken to reduce unemployment?
2. What forms of unpaid work are there and how should they be recognized by society?
3. What does the PDS say about *Mitbestimmung*?
4. What other policies with respect to the workplace does the party suggest?

Text C

1. What is Gysi's tone in the first paragraph? Is there any justification in what he says or is it purely propaganda?
2. Do you find merit in the idea of the *Dritte Stimme*?
3. What do you think of the suggestion that a third chamber should be set up? How could this possibly fit in with the traditional role of the politicians in the Bundestag and Bundesrat?

4. Examine the ideas in the section *Kapitalressourcen für den sozialökonomischen Umbau.* To what extent are they Marxist? To what extent could they be attractive to the market economy?
5. Examine the argument that Gysi uses for opening European markets to competition from the East and South.
6. What does he say about the transport of goods world-wide?

Text D

1. Comment on the phrase, *Niemand hat das Recht, andere zum Töten in die Welt zu schicken.* How realistic is its application in the present world?
2. What does the PDS have to say about the Bundeswehr and its engagement in UN activities?
3. What attitude does the party adopt towards NATO?
4. What alternative non-military and anti-military policies does the PDS wish to implement?
5. Examine the party's statements on Maastricht, European integration and the single European currency.

Notes

1. At the end of February the PDS had only between 650,000 and 700,000 members; Heinrich Bortfeldt, *Von der SED zur PDS: Wandlung zur Demokratie?* (Bonn and Berlin, Bouvier, 1991), 74–150.
2. Ibid., 177–84.
3. Thomas Falkner and Dietmar Huber, *Aufschwung PDS* (Munich, Knauer, 1994), 148.
4. Ibid., 137.
5. Ibid., 142.
6. The 'ident '95' survey was carried out by Gesellschaftswissenschaftliches Forum, and covered 3,200 individuals or households. It was one in a series of surveys that have been carried out each year since 1990. Three responses could be given. See Sozialwissenschaftliches Forschungszentrum (ed.), 'Identitätswandel in den neuen Bundesländern', *Sozialreport*, 1 (Berlin, 1996), 4.
7. Heiner Meulemann, 'Value Changes in Germany after Unification: 1990–95', *German Politics*, 1 (London, Frank Cass, 1997), 135.
8. SFZ, 'Identitätswandel in den neuen Bundesländern', 9.
9. Gunnar Winkler (ed.), *Sozialreport 1995* (Berlin, SFZ, 1995).
10. 'Neue Debatte um Überwachung der PDS', *Berliner Zeitung*, 30 December 1996, 17.

11. Lothar Biskey, 'PDS '95: Solidarisch. Alternativ. Bundesweit', 4. Parteitag der PDS/1. Tagung, *Disput*, 3/4 (Berlin, 1995), 5.
12. Stephan Hermlin, 'Ein Pseudosozialismus scheiterte', *Disput*, 3/4 (Berlin, 1995), 9.
13. Martin Harnack, 'Nachfolge und völliger Bruch mit der SED', *Pressedienst PDS*, 2 December (Berlin, 1994), 2.

Bibliography

Sources in German

Baumann, Eleonore et al., *Der Fischer Weltalmanach. Sonderband DDR* (Frankfurt, Fischer Taschenbuch Verlag, 1990).

Behrend, Manfred and Helmut Meier (eds.), *Der schwere Weg der Erneuerung. Von der SED zur PDS* (Berlin, Dietz Verlag, 1991).

Bortfeldt, Heinrich, *Von der SED zur PDS: Wandlung zur Demokratie?* (Bonn and Berlin, Bouvier, 1992).

Falkner, Thomas and Dietmar Huber, *Aufschwung PDS. Rote Socken – zurück zur Macht* (Munich, Knauer, 1994).

Gysi, Gregor (ed.), *Wir brauchen einen dritten Weg* (Hamburg, Konkret Literatur Verlag, 1990).

Klein, Markus and Claudio Caballero, 'Rückwärtsgewandt in die Zukunft. Die Wähler der PDS bei der Bundestagswahl 1994', *Politische Vierteljahresschrift*, 3 (1996), 229–47.

Modrow, Hans, *Aufbruch und Ende* (Hamburg, Konkret Literatur Verlag, 1991).

Moreau, Patrick, *PDS. Anatomie einer postkommunistischen Partei* (Bonn and Berlin, Bouvier Verlag, 1992).

Moreau, Patrick and Jürgen P. Lang, *Was will die PDS?* (Frankfurt-am-Main and Berlin, Ullstein, 1994).

Moreau, Patrick and Jürgen P. Lang, 'Aufbruch zu neuen Ufern? Zustand und Perspektiven der PDS', *Aus Politik und Zeitgeschichte*, 2 (February 1996), 54–61.

Neugebauer, Gero and Richard Stöss, *Die PDS. Geschichte. Organisation. Wähler Konkurrenten* (Opladen, Leske + Budrich, 1996).

Schabowski, Günter, *Der Absturz* (Berlin, Rowohlt, 1991).

Schabowski, Günter, *Das Politbüro. Das Ende eines Mythos* (Reinbek, Rowohlt, 1990).

Zimmerling, Zeno and Sabine, *Neue Chronik der DDR, Folge 1, 2, 3, 4–5, 6* (Berlin, Tribüne Verlag, 1989–90).

Sources in English

Bastian, Jens, 'The *Enfant Terrible* of German Politics: The PDS between GDR Nostalgia and Democratic Socialism', in *Superwahljahr: The German Elections in 1994* (London, Frank Cass, 1995), 95–110.

Betz, Hans-Georg and Helga A. Welsh, 'The PDS in the New Party System', *German Politics*, 4 (London, Frank Cass, 1995), 92–111.

Lees, Charles, 'Bringing the PDS into the Coalition Equation', *German Politics*, 4 (London, Frank Cass, 1995), 150–4.

Phillips, Ann L., 'Socialism with a New Face? The PDS in Search of Reform', *East European Politics and Societies*, 8, 3 (1994), 495–530.

Further information may be obtained from:
PDS
Bundesgeschäftsstelle
D–10178 Berlin
Karl-Liebknecht-Haus
Kleine Alexanderstr. 28
Tel. (030) 24009–0
Fax (030) 2814169

7. The far right – right-wing extremism

Although right-wing extremism has been largely held in check in Germany, East and West, since 1945 and is not represented by a large political party, an overview of German political parties requires some examination of the far right.

Germans distinguish between the terms *Rechtsextremismus and Rechtsradikalismus*. The former term is used to describe the political stance of organizations or persons who systematically act against the basic principles of the *Grundgesetz*, who are hostile to foreigners, strongly nationalistic and authoritarian. They do not advocate the use of force but are prepared to justify it when it is used. *Rechtsradikalismus* covers organizations and individuals who criticize aspects of the *Grundgesetz* from a right-wing perspective but who do not reject it.[1] Both right-wing radicalism and right-wing extremism have existed in West Germany since 1945 and have also become evident in East Germany since reunification.

Despite the fact that the nazis and their party had been banned after 1945, it was an illusion to believe that all former convinced and dedicated nazis would be transformed overnight into democrats. Over the years a number of attempts were made to form neo-fascist parties in West Germany. In 1946 the Deutsche Rechts-Partei (DRP) was created and was banned in 1952 after adopting an increasingly extremist stance. In October 1949 the *Sozialistische Reichspartei* (SRP) was formed by some of the former and more extreme DRP members. Some of the leaders were former high-ranking nazis, and members were recruited from people who had been in the nazi party. The party was banned in October 1952 for, among other things, its championing of the Third Reich and of Adolf Hitler. At that point it had 20,000 members, most of whom transferred to the Deutsche

Reichspartei (again, DRP), which in the 1953 Bundestag elections received 295,739 votes (1.1 per cent), in 1957 gathered 308,564 votes (1.0 per cent) but dropped to 262,977 (0.8 per cent) in the election in 1961.[2]

By the early 1960s, despite a recession (which normally helps extremist parties) the far right was making little progress. The decision was taken to try to unite the disparate groups into one 'union of all national democratic forces'. On 28 November the National Demokratische Partei (NPD) was formed at Hanover under the leadership of Adolf von Thadden (the Deutsche Reichspartei was dissolved a year later). Within two years the party had organizations in 70 per cent of urban and rural districts. It was the first post-war party to appeal successfully to latent authoritarian and anti-liberal sentiments. The programme was anti-American and anti-Soviet, required the withdrawal of all foreign forces from Germany and called for the unification of the German people. It was against foreign influences and 'gegen den Ungeist des Materialismus und seiner kulturfeindlichen Folgen'. It alleged that people were the 'victims of consumer propaganda'. The programme rejected German guilt in respect of the two world wars and called for Germans to be given work in preference to foreigners. It also covered all aspects of policy from the economy and state to the family and the health service.[3]

In the 1965 Bundestag elections the NPD polled 664,193 votes (2.0 per cent), and this had risen to 1,422,010 by the election in 1969. At 4.3 per cent, however, the party still failed to get into the Bundestag. At *Land* level the NPD had reached over 7 per cent in Hesse and Bavaria (1966), Lower Saxony and Bremen (1967) and Baden-Württemberg (1968), where its share rose to 9.8 per cent. From the early 1970s onwards, however, support dropped again.

By 1989 the NPD had only 1,000 members, and the Deutsche Volksunion (DVU), a party as extreme as the NPD, had 4,500. At the same time a new party, the Republikaner, began to develop rapidly in the late 1980s. The reason for this was the increasingly large numbers of people seeking asylum in West Germany. Since so many Germans had been given asylum abroad during the nazi period, the Federal Republic had adopted a liberal policy towards asylum-seekers as a symbol of gratitude for help given to Germans during their time of need. Yet from the mid-1980s onwards – and in common with a number of West European countries – those who were fleeing political persecution in their home countries were joined by large numbers of people who claimed political asylum but were really economic migrants. This caused resentment among the West Germans, and since the established parties reacted slowly, the Republikaner (REPs) filled the vacuum. Their party programme of 1987 stated that there had been very large numbers of foreigners settling in Germany during recent years and that asylum-seekers were misusing the law. Germany is densely populated and should not be regarded as an *Einwanderungsland*. It should remain German. Foreigners should be regarded as 'guests' and should not be given long-term employment contracts. They should not be allowed to take up permanent residence, bring their families with them or receive social security benefits, nor should they be allowed to vote or to join political parties. If they have come to study or be trained in the Federal Republic they should leave the country immediately they complete studies or training. Any lawbreaking should lead to deportation. Asylum-seekers can remain in Germany if they are politically persecuted in their home country, but limits should be set to the numbers allowed to stay.[4] The Republikaner reject the idea of a multicultural Germany and make foreigners the scapegoats for Germany's problems. They simplify complex political and social problems and are populist.

In 1990 the REPs gained 2.1 per cent in the Bundestag elections. In April 1992 in the Baden-Württemberg *Land* elections they achieved 10.9 per cent of the votes cast, and in Schleswig-Holstein 1.2 per cent (here the DVU polled 6.3 per cent). In the local elections in Hesse in 1993 the REPs attracted 8.3 per cent. They increased this to 9.3 per cent in Frankfurt-am-Main and 16 per cent in Wiesbaden. The Bundestag amended the section of the *Grundgesetz* that dealt with the right of asylum on 1 July 1993 and this led to a rapid decrease in the electoral support for the REPs. A survey in 1993 showed that 79 per cent of those who voted for them did so as a protest, but 19 per cent stated that they voted out of conviction.[5] Approximately two-thirds of those who voted REP were men, and working-class voters made up nearly half of the numbers. In Schleswig-Holstein 15 per cent of the voters under twenty-five chose the REPs and the DVU. In Baden-Württemberg the figure rose to more than 20 per cent.

In many respects the views and basic attitudes of those who voted for the REPs coincide with those of the supporters of the CSU and the CDU.[6] For instance, there is common ground on law-and-order issues, priority of economic growth over environmental considerations, national pride, anti-communism. Some REP voters and supporters, indeed, defected from the CDU, CSU and, to a lesser extent, from the FDP, during the 1980s as a result of disappointment at the inability of those parties to solve problems or keep promises. Others came to the REPs from the neo-nazi scene – for ideological reasons and since it seemed the party had a chance of electoral success. A further group of voters and supporters came – and still come – from those who have 'lost out' in the last ten years or so – the long-term unemployed, people dependent on social security, low-wage-earners, small-scale farmers. Interestingly, in 1993 in a survey of the Hamburg local election 88 per cent of REP supporters stated that people voted for the far-right parties as a protest.[7]

More disturbing than electoral gains by the REPs and the DVU, however, have been the actions of right-wing extremists – and the inaction of parts of the general public in the face of the abuse of foreigners and physical attacks on them.

In 1991 there were some 500 attacks on asylum-seekers and their domiciles. Of some 300 people alleged to have committed anti-foreigner crimes, 211 were less than twenty years old.

The characteristics of these people are: dislike of things or people that are 'different', conventionality, dislike of innovation, tendency to join 'strong' groups, to adhere to strongly held principles, liking for hierarchical structures. They dislike criticism and do not think deeply. They are self-opinionated, want to dominate others, are more likely to be involved in brawling, show little consideration for others. This adds up to a profile of people who are basically weak and insecure, who overcompensate for this by playing a hard, brutal role as members of gangs. In the usual manner of bullies they pick on the weakest and most vulnerable – in this case foreigners. Some are members of neo-nazi or other extreme right-wing groups, some are skinheads. Many of the acts of force used against foreigners are committed spontaneously or under the influence of drink. Some, however, are used as proof of 'courage' or 'commitment' in order to be accepted for membership of the 'group'.[8] Comments made by some of them show their attitudes: 'Der Ausländer kriegt eine Wohnung, nur der Deutsche nicht. Die kriegen alles und wir kriegen nichts' (factory worker aged fifty-two, Mannheim). Social and political shortcomings are attributed to the presence of foreigners: '... man schiebt das auf die Ausländer, weil gegen den Staat kannst du sowieso nichts machen' (twenty-year-old saleswoman); '... weil Du's da am direkten siehst ... da guckst Du mal Fernsehen, dann zeigen sie so eine Wohnung von denen und dann siehst Du, daß da halt auch ein Fernseher da drin steht und so, ich mein', ... die sind vierzehn Tage da und können sich einen Fernseher kaufen, das ist ein Ding der Unmöglichkeit, den muß der Steuerzahler gezahlt habe, sonst geht das nicht'; 'Daheim kennen sie nicht einmal WC-Spülung, und hier wollen sie Dusche ... da bildet sich bei mir der Haß.'[9]

There have been highly positive reactions to right-wing extremism and anti-foreigner activities in Germany, however. Hundreds of thousands of Germans have turned out on to the streets to demonstrate against racialism. In 1991 demonstrations were organized in Rostock and Frankfurt-am-Main, Immenstadt and Görisried in the Allgäu, Saarlouis and Trier. On 8 November 1992 more than 350,000 Berliners demonstrated against racialism, this was followed in December by a huge chain of people carrying candles in Hamburg and a large music festival against racialism in Cologne. At Christmas Germans throughout the country placed lighted candles in their windows to symbolize solidarity with foreigners and to protest against racism. Groups of Germans protected the hostels for asylum-seekers in many parts of the country, from Rostock to Hünze in the Ruhr. These individuals, and their commitment to supporting foreigners, have done much to rehabilitate Germany's good name. The Churches, too, have played – and still play – an important and active role.

Leading politicians, such as President von Weizsäcker, Kurt Biedenkopf, minister president of Saxony and Manfred Stolpe, minister president of Brandenburg, also played their part in appealing to their fellow Germans for tolerance and a rejection of racialism. After changes to the asylum law in 1993, which made it more difficult for economic migrants to find asylum in Germany, there was a defusing of tension. Furthermore, since December 1992 the REPs have been placed under security surveillance because of their anti-foreigner stance as well as their attacks on the institutions of the Federal Republic and individual politicians.

The far right remains divided and lacks a charismatic leadership figure. Nevertheless, the threat to democratic institutions is still a reality and is taken seriously by the state. Unfortunately, individual acts of force against foreigners still occur and, as in other countries, it is unlikely that these can be completely prevented.

Questions

1. What are the reasons for anti-foreigner sentiment and acts against foreigners in Germany?

2. What can the German parties, the institutions of the state, trade unions and the public do to decrease hostility towards foreigners?
3. Do you think that Germany and her political parties are more or less nationalistic, racist or anti-foreigner than is the case in other West European countries?

Notes

1. Elke Hennig, 'Rechtsradikalismus und Rechtsextremismus in der Bundesrepublik', *Wochenschau* (Schwalbach, 1994), 211.
2. Reinhard Kühnl et al., *Die NPD. Struktur, Programm und Ideologie einer neofaschistischen Partei* (West Berlin, Voltaire Verlag, 1967), 9–23.
3. 'Programm der NPD', in Hans Maier and Hermann Bott, *NPD. Struktur und Ideologie einer nationalen Rechtspartei* (Munich, Piper, 1968), 65–92.
4. See Manfred Kieserling, 'Zur Psychologie der Republikaner', in Elke Hennig, *Die Republikaner im Schatten Deutschlands* (Frankfurt-am-Main, Suhrkamp Verlag, 1991).
5. Forschungsgruppe Wahlen, *Politbarometer*, 9 (Mannheim, 1993).
6. ipos representative surveys taken in May and September 1989.
7. Forschungsgruppe Wahlen, *Politbarometer*, 9 (Mannheim, 1993).
8. Siegfried Schumann, *Politische Einstellungen und Persönlichkeit*, (Frankfurt, Berne and New York, Verlag Peter Lang, 1986), 12–15.
9. Interviews quoted in Rudolf Leiprecht, '... da baut sich ja in uns ein Haß auf ...' (Hamburg, Argument Verlag, 1990), 371, 377, 386, 425.

Bibliography

Assheuer, Thomas and Hans Sarkowicz, *Rechtsradikale in Deutschland. Die alte und die neue Rechte* (Munich, C. H. Beck, 1992).

Bundeszentrale für Politische Bildung (ed.), *Deutschland von Rechts, Wochenschau* (Schwalbach, 1994).

Farin, Klaus and Eberhard Seidel-Pielen, *Rechtsruck. Rassimus im neuen Deutschland* (Berlin, Rotbuch Verlag, 1992).

Kuhn, Rick, 'Fascism in Germany Today', *Debatte*, 1, 2 (Oxford and New York, Berg, 1993), 131–51.

Minnerup, Günter, 'Franz Schönhuber and the Re-nationalization of German Politics', *Debatte*, 1, 2 (Oxford and New York, Berg, 1993), 71–95.

Schönhuber, Franz, *Ich war dabel* (Munich, Non-Stop, 1981).

Schröder, Burkhard, *Rechte Kerle. Skinheads, Faschos, Hooligans* (Reinbek, Rowohlt, 1992).

Stöss, Richard, *Politics against Democracy: The Extreme Right in West Germany* (Oxford, Berg, 1992).

Süß, Walter, 'Right-Wing Extremism in the GDR', *Debatte*, 2 (Oxford and New York, Berg, 1993), 95–121.

Winkler, Beate (ed.), *Zukunftsangst Einwanderung* (Munich, Verlag C. H. Beck, 1992).

Concluding remarks

From 1949 to 1989 the Federal Republic, the old West Germany, showed considerable political and economic stability and success. The CDU, CSU and FDP, with their strong commitment to the market economy, produced the right conditions for economic recovery after the Second World War, and for a flourishing economy thereafter that has produced and maintained a high standard of living for the great majority of the population. These parties were also the 'right' parties for the Western Allies throughout the Cold War, for they needed an economically strong and politically reliable Federal Republic as a bulwark against the Eastern bloc and communism. The success of these parties was, in part, responsible for moving the social democrats towards acceptance of the market economy and away from Marxism and the 'class struggle'. The SPD, on the other hand, has contributed a strong 'social dimension' to the market economy, has pushed the conservative parties into accepting this dimension and has been responsible in opposition and government for stimulating reforms in many areas of life. The SPD (together with the FDP) must also be given credit for making a major contribution to *détente* and restoring workable relations with Germany's eastern neighbours in the 1970s. The major parties have always incorporated within them a spectrum of opinions, and this, coupled with the electoral system that prevents very small parties from gaining seats, has meant that the latter have withered away or become insignificant. The Greens broke this pattern, however, and acted in the 1980s as a sort of yeast that helped invigorate West German politics. They have been probably the most successful party in Western Europe as far as environmental issues are concerned.

The Basic Law has given political stability and has very wide acceptance within the population. The *Rechtsstaat*, federal system, the distribution of powers, and the judicial system have all contributed to making the Federal Republic a modern democratic state. The electoral system really does give representation to a wide spectrum of political opinion within the electorate. It has also made it possible for minorities such as the Greens, the Republikaner and the PDS to be politically integrated by having to compete for electoral support at the ballot box.

Yet however good a democratic system may be, it relies on democratic attitudes taking root in the population. Weimar failed, among other reasons, because there was not a strong democratic tradition or culture in Germany at that time. The Federal Republic has succeeded because a democratic culture has developed. This has been helped by the creation of a good system of civics education in its schools, which means that children and young people are introduced to the concepts of democracy, pluralism, the political system and the parties early in life and can, at least in theory, make sound political judgements. Political information is widely available through the *Landeszentralen für politische Bildung* and the party foundations. There is also a large amount of political and current affairs information conveyed through the media – particularly through television – in news bulletins, commentaries and fact-finding reports. German society is a politicized society in the sense that people are politically aware, they become involved at grass-roots level (for example, the millions who turned out on the streets on peace demonstrations or the large number of single-issue local campaigns), and they turn out in large numbers for elections. Over the last few years anti-foreigner sentiment and attacks on foreigners hit the headlines in Germany and abroad. The positive aspect is, however, that many hundreds of thousands of Germans went on the streets or lit candles in their windows to show solidarity with the foreigners in their midst.

The questions facing the parties in the 1998 Bundestag elections will be whether the CDU/CSU will suffer from the lack of upturn in the economy and decrease in unemployment, whether the FDP can pass the 5 per cent hurdle, and whether the SPD can break through with attractive policies and a convincing parliamentary team after being out of office for sixteen years. The question facing Bündnis 90/Greens is whether they can maintain their popular grass-roots activities and keep themselves sufficiently different from the SPD and PDS in their policies on the environment, employment, security and foreign affairs, women and equal rights. The PDS will be under attack from the other parties but is well-organized, has highly committed members and sufficient finances, so that it will probably survive, particularly since the factors that have given it support thus far are unlikely to change much in the coming year.

Without unification the West Germans would probably have continued along their well-tried political path – occasional changes of coalition government in the Bundestag, an increasing role in European integration and the CSCE, a successful economy. Unification, particularly because of its high economic costs, has changed this. Furthermore, over fifteen million people who have lived under a different system for two generations, have other experiences of politics, and different aspirations cannot be absorbed easily. Their system of government could be changed overnight but their attitudes cannot be. The West Germans, with few exceptions, have not begun to realize yet that their Federal Republic has gone and a new one is in the process of developing. (One notable exception is the leading CDU politician, Wolfgang Schäuble.)[1]

East Germans are displaying more electoral volatility than the West Germans. They have no traditional party loyalties, and most of the parties are completely new. They voted in large numbers for the Allianz für Deutschland to get them out of the no man's land between the two economic and political systems, and to get their hands on the Deutschmark and economic prosperity. There is still no middle class in East Germany that will loyally support the CDU and FDP, and the working class which has been voting strongly for conservative parties since 1990 is disappointed at the high rates of unemployment, but is still not turning to the SPD.

In a survey of East German attitudes to the Basic Law carried out in 1993, 73 per cent believed that a united Germany needed a new constitution (in a survey in 1991 only 50 per cent wanted a new constitution), while 22 per cent wanted to keep the Basic Law but introduce amendments. Only 3 per cent wanted no changes.[2]

In 1992 the word *Politikverdrossenheit* began to be used extensively in Germany to represent a growing disaffection with politicians and the older-established parties. People were losing faith in these parties and increasingly viewed them negatively. The realization that began to develop in the 1960s, that the problems confronting modern society are too big for politicians to solve and that the politicians do not adequately represent the opinions and wishes of the electorate, has grown considerably in the 1990s. There has been increasing dissatisfaction that the politicians have failed to halt rising unemployment. The image of the major parties has also suffered because of corruption scandals, the amount of money they allocate themselves from state funds to finance their elections, their intervention in many areas of life to give posts to their supporters (for example by putting them on the boards which oversee the media, commerce or organizations) and their lack of imagination and innovation.[3]

Politikverdrossenheit – in the sense of alienation from the established parties – shows itself in the increasing number of small parties (for example, there are thirty-five parties registered officially, but they are without representation in the Bundestag), in support for new parties such as the Greens, PDS and Republikaner, and in increasing volatility among the voters. A further indicator of dissatisfaction is decreasing participation in elections. Perhaps as a reaction to the years of fascism, and more recently communism, the electoral process has been strongly supported. For instance, in the 1970s more than 90 per cent of the electorate turned out for the Bundestag elections, but in 1990 the figure had dropped to 78.4 per cent (there was a slight rally by 1994 with 2 per cent more going to the polls in West Germany. In East Germany there was a 2 per cent drop in comparison with December 1990).[4] Membership of parties has also dropped since the 1970s as people devote more time to themselves, their problems and their leisure. This alienation from the established parties and career politicians is not unique to Germany, however, as election participation, party membership figures and public opinion polls in the United States, Britain and France, for example, show.

Interest in politics, in the sense of participation in local matters or in single-issue campaigns, remains strong, however. In an opinion poll carried out in West Germany in 1988 and in East Germany in 1990, 87 per cent of the West Germans who responded said they would participate in elections (74 per cent of East Germans), 81 per cent would discuss their opinions at work (84 per cent of East Germans) and 41 per cent said they would take part in *Bürgerinitiativen* (30 per cent of East Germans). Forty-five and 49 per cent, respectively, were prepared to take part in discussions in public meetings. There was little interest in working actively for a political party (18 and 11 per cent respectively) and almost no support for direct action or the use of force for political ends.[5]

A major issue confronting the parties and the state is the high level of unemployment and the possible political implications. In January 1997, according to the Bundesanstalt für Arbeit in Nuremberg, there were 4,658,300 people registered as unemployed (that is, 12.2 per cent of the work-force). This figure was made up of 3,266,000 people in West Germany and 1,392,000 in East Germany. Saxony-Anhalt had the highest rate in the East (21.2 per cent), followed by Mecklenburg (20.1 per cent), Thuringia (19.0 per cent), Brandenburg (18.5 per cent) and Saxony (17.6 per cent). The highest rate in West Germany was in Bremen (15.5 per cent), followed by Lower Saxony (12.7 per cent), North Rhine-Westphalia and Hamburg (both on 11.5 per cent).[6] According to the Bundesanstalt für Arbeit, a further 1,330,000 people were on a variety of job-creation schemes – that is, in jobs which do not offer long-term security. Up to now support for the unemployed through a strong network of social security provisions and the creation of short-term jobs has kept frustration and discontent well in check. The government is trying to reduce the burden on the state that this support entails, but it is extremely difficult in any country to take 'entitlements' away from people when they have enjoyed them for a long period. There is very likely to be a reaction against the governing parties at the next elections. Yet there is no solution to high unemployment through conventional methods. New technology is destroying jobs world-wide, the former Eastern bloc countries in central Europe provide cheaper labour than is available in Germany and have a work-force that is skilled or can be trained quickly; intense competition is building up for Germany (as well as for all the countries of the European Union and North America) among the so-called 'tiger economies' of Asia; and the full impact of globalization is still to come. How German politicians try to solve these problems will be interesting to observe, since so many countries are beset by similar problems.

Germany will continue to change rapidly in the coming years, and in that process there will be changes in the party platforms and functions. In common with other liberal democracies, the party system has its origins in the cleavages that have been inherent in industrial societies from the outset. In this, the parties have played a role as mediators between the various social groups based on class, religion and culture, and between the state and society. In the phase of post-industrialization that society is now entering, traditional cleavages are breaking down, and parties are increasingly having to compete with grass-roots political groups and activities for the representation and articulation of people's interest. The new patterns that will emerge within the German polity are still in the process of development.

In the 1950s Germany was described as an 'economic giant' and a 'political dwarf'. The developments of the last forty years, and particularly reunification, have demonstrated Germany's political maturity and her ability to play a key role in Europe.

Notes

1. 'Hauskrach zwischen Wessies und Ossis. Streitgespräach zwischen Wolfgang Schäuble und Wolfgang Thierse (SPD)', *Wochenschau, Sonderausgabe* (Frankfurt-am-Main, December 1993).
2. ident Berlin, quoted in Sozialwissenschaftliches Forschungszentrum Berlin-Brandenburg, *Sozialreport*, 1 (Berlin, 1995), 23–4.
3. Hans-Gerd Jaschke, 'Politikverdrossenheit – nur ein Schlagwort?', *Wochenschau II* (Schwalbach, December 1993), 8–9.
4. Michael Bechtel, 'Wahlen im demokratischen Staat', *Informationen zur politischen Bildung aktuell. Wahlen '94* (Bonn, 1994), 8.
5. ALLBUS, 1989, ISSP Plus 1990.
6. Quoted in *Neues Deutschland*, 7 February 1997, 1.

Comparative questions on the texts for all parties

1. Compare and contrast the ideologies of the parties.
2. What policies do the parties put forward for the 'inner reunification' of Germany?
3. Compare the environmental policies of the parties.
4. In what ways do the parties suggest that they can support women in gaining equality, and how do they view the family?
5. Compare and contrast the views of the CSU and FDP on abortion and family planning.
6. Examine the ideas of the parties on the integration of Europe. To what extent do you think that they will be implemented?
7. Outline and explain the parties' views on European security, the role of Germany in NATO and the OSCE.

Appendices

Appendix 1: The presidents of the Federal Republic of Germany

1.	Theodor Heuss, FDP	12 September 1949–16 July 1954
2.	——	17 July 1954–30 June 1959
3.	Heinrich Lübke, CDU	1 July 1959–30 June 1964
4.	——	1 July 1964–4 March 1969
5.	Gustav Heinemann, SPD	5 March 1969–14 May 1974
6.	Walter Scheel, FDP	1 July 1974–30 June 1979
7.	Karl Carstens, CDU	1 July 1979–30 June 1984
8.	Richard von Weiszäcker, CDU	1 July 1984–22 May 1989
9.	——	23 May 1989–22 May 1994
10.	Roman Herzog, CDU	23 May 1994 onwards

Appendix II: The chancellors of the Federal Republic of Germany

1. Konrad Adenauer, 20 September 1949–20 October 1953 (coalition CDU/CSU, FDP, DP)
2. Konrad Adenauer, 20 October 1953–29 October 1957 (coalition CDU/CSU, FDP, DP, BHE)
3. Konrad Adenauer, 29 October 1957–14 November 1961 (coalition CDU/CSU, DP)
4. Konrad Adenauer, 14 November 1961–16 October 1963 (coalition CDU/CSU, FDP)
5. Konrad Adenauer (restructured on 14 December 1962 to form fifth cabinet)
6. Ludwig Erhard, 16 October 1963–30 November 1965 (coalition CDU/CSU, FDP) (restructured on 26 October 1965 to form second cabinet)
7. Kurt Georg Kiesinger, 1 December 1966–20 October 1969 (Grand Coalition, CDU/CSU, SPD)
8. Willy Brandt, 21 October 1969–14 December 1974 (coalition SPD, FDP)
9. Willy Brandt, 15 December 1972–6 May 1974 (coalition SPD, FDP)
10. Helmut Schmidt, 16 May 1974–15 December 1976 (coalition SPD, FDP)
    —— 15 December 1976–5 November 1980 (coalition SPD, FDP)
11. Helmut Schmidt, 5 November 1980–1 October 1982 (coalition SPD, FDP)
12. Helmut Kohl, 1 October 1982–January 1987 (coalition CDU/CSU, FDP)
13. Helmut Kohl, 25 January 1987–2 December 1990 (coalition CDU/CSU, FDP)
14. Helmut Kohl, 3 December 1990–22 May 1994 (coalition CDU/CSU, FDP)
15. Helmut Kohl, 23 May 1994– (coalition CDU/CSU, FDP)

Appendix III: Results of Volkskammer elections, 18 March 1990

	Votes	%	Seats	%
Eligible voters	12426443			
Votes cast	11604418	93.38		
Spoilt returns	63263			
Valid returns	11541155	99.45	400	
CDU	4710598	40.82	163	40.75
Demokratischer Aufbruch	106146	0.92	4	1.00
DSU	727730	6.31	25	6.25
Total for Allianz für Deutschland	5544474	48.04	192	48.00
Bund Freier Demokraten	608935	5.38	21	5.25
SPD	2525534	21.88	88	22.00
Grüne/Frauen	226932	1.97	8	2.0
Bündnis 90	336074	2.91	12	3.00
PDS	1892381	16.40	66	16.50
Demokratische Bauernpartei	251226	2.18	9	2.25
National-Demokratische Partei	44292	0.38	2	0.50
Demokratischer Frauenverband	38192	0.33	1	0.25
Vereinigte Linke	20342	0.18	1	0.25
Others	52773	0.46		

Source: *Zeitschrift für Parlamentsfragen,* 1/90, Bonn, 8.

Appendix IV: Results of first all-German Bundestag elections, December 1990[1]

	West	East	Total	Seats
CDU/CSU	44.1	43.4	43.8	319
SPD	35.9	23.6	33.5	239
FDP	10.6	13.4	11.0	79
Die Grünen	4.7	0.1	3.9	0
Bündnis 90/Die Grünen	—	5.9	1.2	8
PDS	0.3	9.9	2.4	17
Republikaner	2.3	1.3	2.1	0
Other parties	2.1	2.5	2.1	0
Total	100%	100%	100%	662

[1]Quoted in J. Russell Dalton (ed.), *The New Germany Votes* (Providence and Oxford, Berg, 1993), 24.

Appendix V: Results of Bundestag elections, October 1994

	%	Seats	West %	East %
CDU	34.2	244	36.6	39.9
CSU	7.5	50	9.5	—
SPD	36.4	252	39.7	31.8
FDP	6.9	47	3.4	3.0
Bündnis 90/Die Grünen	7.3	49	7.1	3.8
PDS	4.4	30	0.4	20.5
Others	3.6	0	3.2	1.1

Appendix VI: Composition of the Bundestag, 1996

(Background Paper: *Parliament and Government*, Embassy of the
Federal Republic of Germany, London, February 1996)

	Seats
CDU	244
CSU	50
SPD	252
Bündnis 90/Die Grünen	49
FDP	47
PDS	30
Total number of members of Parliament	672

Prior to unification the number of seats was 519, but this was
increased to 656 to accommodate members from the former East
Germany. Similarly the number of constituencies was increased from
256 to 328. In the 1994 election there were sixteen additional seats
(*Überhangmandate*), making a total of 672 seats.

The governing coalition of CDU/CSU and FDP has forty-one seats
and a majority of ten. Of eighteen members of the cabinet, eleven
belong to the CDU (including Chancellor Kohl), four are from the
CSU (covering finance, health, posts and telecommunications and
economic co-operation and development), and the remaining three
represent the FDP (with responsibilities for foreign policy, justice
and economics).

Of the members, 5.76 per cent are women. They form the majority of the Bündnis 90/Die Grünen members, but most women
members are to be found in the SPD, where there are 85 women to
167 men.

Of the members, 224 register themselves as Protestant, 212 as

Catholic and 236 either are non-denominational or provide no details.

Over 500 members are married and have between two and six children.

The Bundesrat

Since unification the Federal Republic is made up of sixteen *Länder*. The population of the *Länder* and the number of seats each *Land* has in the Bundesrat are shown below.

	Seats	Population in millions
Baden-Württemberg	6	10.29
Bavaria (Bayern)	6	11.95
Berlin	4	3.47
Brandenburg*	4	2.53
Bremen	3	0.68
Hamburg	3	1.70
Hesse (Hessen)	5	6.00
Mecklenburg-West Pomerania (Mecklenburg-Westpommern)*	3	1.83
Lower Saxony (Niedersachsen)	6	7.74
North Rhine-Westphalia (Nordrhein-Westfalen)	6	17.83
Rhineland-Palatinate (Rheinland-Pfalz)	4	3.96
Saarland	3	1.08
Saxony (Sachsen) *	4	4.57
Saxony-Analt (Sachsen-Anhalt) *	4	2.75
Schleswig-Holstein	4	2.71
Thuringia (Thüringen) *	4	2.51
Total number of seats	69	

* denotes the new East German *Länder*.

Party representation in the Bundesrat and control of the *Länder*:

Seats held by SPD-controlled *Länder* (Brandenburg, Lower Saxony, Saarland, Schleswig-Holstein): 17.

Seats held by SPD and Bündnis 90/Die Grünen in coalition (Hesse, North Rhine-Westphalia, Saxony Anhalt): 15.

Seats from the SPD/FDP coalition in the Rhineland-Palatinate: 4.

Seats from the SPD coalition of SPD-CDU in Bremen: 4.

Thus forty-two seats in the Bundesrat are held by the SPD and its coalition partners.

The remaining twenty-seven seats are made up of ten held by the CDU in Saxony and the CSU in Bavaria and seventeen from the CDU in coalition with the SPD in Baden-Württemberg, Berlin, Mecklenburg-West, Pomerania and Thuringia.

Index